Mimi Kennedy

Taken to the Stage

The Education of an Actress

"While attending parochial school in upstate New York, Kennedy formed a lofty goal: to join her beloved saints in heaven by way of Broadway. As she explains in her good-humored, vivacious, combined growing up-catholic/showbiz memoir, she embraced the theater because it was spiritually safe, a place where she could act out earthly temptations without endangering her soul. …grace and joy—qualities in abundance in this spirited reminiscence. —PUBLISHER'S WEEKLY

"…candid, self-effacing story of an American girl of the Baby Boom generation who just happened to want to be an actress, and there is much here beyond the theater that anyone of that generation can appreciate. This is an especially well-written, funny, and insightful work…
—LIBRARY JOURNAL

SK
A Smith and Kraus Book

A Smith and Kraus Book
Published by Smith and Kraus, Inc.
One Main Street, PO Box 127, Lyme, NH 03768

Copyright ©1996 by Smith and Kraus, Inc.

All rights reserved
Manufactured in the United States of America
Cover and Text Design by Julia Hill
Cover Art by Irene Kelly
First Edition: August 1996
10 9 8 7 6 5 4 3 2 1

Library of Congress Cataloging-In-Publication Data
Kennedy, Mimi.
Taken to the stage : the education of an actress / Mimi Kennedy. —1st ed.
p. cm. — (Career development series)
ISBN 1-57525-024-1
1. Kennedy, Mimi. 2. Actors—United States—Biography. 3. Acting. I. Title. II. Series.
PN2287.K653A3 1996
792'.028'092—dc20 96-22833
[B] CIP

Dedication

To my Dear Ones,
and all who find it
and find it helpful.

•

Thanks

To Larry, for his love of me, my stories, and our language; to Molly and Cisco, for believing; to Nancy and Gerry, whose voices I could hear; to the nuns who get short shrift in this book, but whose faithfulness inspired me— particularly Sisters Petrus (Mary Sullivan) and Pius (Pat Keough); to Susie, Danny, and Jimmy, for the love that binds us; to Mildred and Al Boylan, for the memories they shared; to Jimmy and Nancy Mangan, Jac and Larry Kennedy, BJ Kelly and Sue Washburn; to Harry Shearer, whose weekly radio broadcast "Le Show" taught me the power of raising one's voice and inspired me to raise mine; to Cathleen Julian, who listened; to Jenny Delaney, fellow- mother and agent in tough times; to Marisa Smith, for the invitation to write; to Eric Kraus, for the Dickensian chapters, and to St. Anthony, quite a word- smith in his own right.

◦

Contents

Illustrations

Part One

HEAVEN

1948–1961

"This is the one who wants to be an actress, Ruth. Ruth, my
daughter Mimi. Mimi, this is your Cousin Ruth."

Daniel G. Kennedy, 1956

"Q: Why did God make you?

A: God made me to show forth His goodness and to be happy
with Him in heaven."

The Baltimore Catechism, *1954 Edition*

"You mustn't prompt the grown-ups, darlin'. Sometimes they're
actin' in those pauses!"

Harriet Warren, 1960

"Mimi, you funny little sunny little Mimi."

Lorenz Hart, 1932

"It was the way people responded to me that made me become
an actress."

Tammy Grimes, 1961

1.

Cousin Ruth

ousin Ruth entered our home with a force so powerful it caused air dis-
placement in the living room where I sat. I was eight years old and surrounded by relatives, all of whom had gathered to greet our family star, actress Ruth Warrick. When the door closed to contain her, the chair beneath me
shook.

Most of my adult relations who lived within a day's drive of Rochester had as-
sembled and braced for this event. It was our one chance to clasp Cousin Ruth to
the family bosom, and we wanted to make sure that by day's end she'd feel completely and inextricably wedged. She was "Cousin" by marriage only, to a relative
of my father's whose family tie was distant to the point of inscrutability. This made
our connection to Ruth fragile, we knew, not just because the man to whom we
owed it was obscure, but because we owed it to him at all, through marriage.
Marriage was as good-as-blood-for-glue in most of our Irish Catholic clan, but actors, we knew, tended to regard it differently. They married repeatedly and for
pleasure, more as recreation than sacrament. We sensed that if we wanted our
claim on Ruth to last, we'd have to stage this memorable welcome, then hold on
like terriers in a death grip.

Ruth had accepted my father's invitation to meet her husband's extended upstate family probably because Daddy had a past that elevated him above the level
of boring relation for even the most sophisticated of persons. He'd interned at *The
New Yorker* magazine in his youth, a protégé of Alexander Woolcott's. Woolcott
had admired Daddy's editing and writing in the humor and literary magazines of
Hamilton College, their mutual alma mater; this won Daddy the internship, a
summer seat at the Algonquin Round Table, and invitations to Woolcott's cottage
at Lake Bomoseen, Vermont, where Daddy had played croquet with Harpo Marx.
Surely this history is what lured Ruth to our suburban living room that day; the
rest of us could not have been objects of much fascination. Yet we were relations,
drawn like moths to the flame of Ruth's celebrity. She must have known this would
make us an attentive and adoring audience, and the appeal of such audiences for
actors can never be underestimated. They are our antidepressant of choice.

The tock! of Ruth's heels and jingling of her jewelry set up a clatter in the foyer
that roused us in the living room to our feet, as if commanded by the din. The

noises intoxicated me. They announced that, at midday, Cousin Ruth was dressed to the nines.

When she and Daddy stepped onto the hall rug, it muted everything but the bracelet jingling, which accompanied the pair's advancing murmurs like sleigh bells. No one in the living room spoke. We were as intent on her progress toward us as farmers tracking a tornado.

Suddenly, Ruth's voice rang out like a bell. "Put them anywhere, Gerry, that's fine." Ever afterward, Daddy would refer to Ruth's "pear-shaped tones" with fond nostalgia. A lifetime of Rochester accents had made him a sucker for beautiful voices, and Ruth had one. At Smith College, where I received training in Standard American English, I recognized it as the probable source of Ruth's aural fruit. In her heyday, such training was given to stage actors and Hollywood movie stars. My own bid for beautiful diction failed, but I didn't mind. By the time I went professional, actors wore their regional accents as badges of authenticity. Robert DeNiro made New Yawkese sexy. The cast of "Saturday Night Live" turned flat a's into a television comedy norm. On my own TV series debut, "Three Girls Three," I spoke so freely in my native tongue that one critic drubbed my voice as "so nasal as to be unintelligible."

Cousin Ruth, to my eight-year-old Rochester ears, sounded alarmingly and thrillingly phony.

When I saw them at last, Daddy was bending and bowing around Ruth, dispatching her outergear—purse, gloves, and coat—to the proper places. He handled each item with the nervous piety of an altar boy, and it slowed him down. He seemed to be struggling through an invisible force-field radiated by her magnificent physical presence. Ramrod straight on towering spike heels, Ruth was topped by hair that, even in the shadows of the hall, lived up to the family legend. It blazed orange-red, a color seen in nature, not on heads, but autumn hillsides. Nor was it seen in Rochester hair salons, because clients and colorists lacked nerve. In years to come I'd try to colorize Ruth's hair with my imagination, on our black-and-white TV screen, but I'd never conjure the hue I saw that day. In life, Ruth was positively flame-tipped, like a match.

Her accessories shed, she stepped toward us and stopped, waiting for my father's formal introduction. This brought her, as if by instinct, to rest in that portion of our home which most closely resembled the actor's natural habitat: a proscenium arch. Framed by the living-room entryway lintel, her face became visible to me for the first time, and I was dismayed to see it looked frozen in shock.

What had we done to alarm her, I worried, and so soon?! Were we so awfully rag-tag?!

Daddy surfaced beside her, took a deep breath, and announced with conclusive satisfaction, "Everyone—this is your Cousin Ruth!"

The adults broke rank and surrounded her, obscuring my view. As it became clear each of us would require some personal chitchat before relinquishing Ruth to the next guest, a line formed and I was shoved to the back. Ordinarily, my adult relatives were a generous bunch who could be counted on to promote the interests of a child above their own, but this gathering had not been deemed an event for small fry. Only my sister, her awestruck friend, my brother, and I were there, and then only because it was our turf. I sensed the adults had forgotten us and become children themselves in the presence of this most fascinating of grown-ups: a Celebrity.

It was my father who presented Ruth to me eventually, bringing her forward, with her elbow cupped in his gentlemanly palm.

"And this is the one who wants to be an actress, Ruth," he said jovially. "Ruth, my daughter Mimi. Mimi, this is your Cousin Ruth."

Up close, I saw her startled look had nothing to do with emotion, but was the effect of her penciled eyebrows, which arched in twin peaks above her emerald eyes like mountains in a child's drawing. I put my paper-cut, torn-nail hand in her be-jeweled, manicured one and blushed. Even at a young age, I'd learned public declarations of my life's ambition drew mixed responses from adults, few of them satisfactory. Supportive replies seemed patronizing, and discouraging ones annoyed me. Worst of all was the amusement with which they all seemed tinged. It made me feel silly and childish. Daddy had revealed my intentions to Ruth, I knew, to gauge her professional reaction; I wanted it too. I was hoping for her blessing, some word or look to carry into my future the way Dorothy carried Glinda the Good's shining kiss on her forehead all the way to Oz.

Ruth offered no such token. "Aaaaaaah," she said. And stiffened.

I have since experienced that same stiffening when faced with young people declaring their intentions to act professionally. I want to give my blessing, but first comes the pain—memory of my own pain; the pain of friends who tried and failed to achieve the dream; the pain of lost identity and lack of purpose that often accompanies its achievement. There is also the pain of knowing what a mercilessly gladiatorial business acting is. We actors learn to prize one another's gifts in the mutually supportive atmosphere of acting classes and production, then find ourselves competing in contests only one can win. Young hopefuls may even find themselves rivaling idols and mentors—if not for roles, than for an agent, or publicity, or a network time slot. The pains of a professional actor's life are varied but inevitable. That's what made Ruth Warrick go rigid, and what has steeled me since.

No actor is dissuaded from a true calling by anyone's discouragement, and Ruth's coldness did not dissuade me. Instead, it provoked an inner burst of autonomy that was rare for me as a child. Fine, I thought. I'll do it myself. I don't care what you think. And with that came hope, as if I realized for the first time that I'd have to be a gladiator, and that I had the right stuff.

"Well!" Ruth turned to my father. "How do *you* feel about that, Gerry?" They laughed together; it relaxed her and she turned back to me booming, "Good for you! I wish you luck!" with hearty dismissal.

Her perfume, her hair, her curvy body in its emerald-green cocktail sheath attracted me far more than her lack of faith could repel me. Nothing mattered except that I loved her unconditionally and wanted to be her.

After she'd met everybody, Ruth stood with an unimpeded view of the room, and her eyes swept it, coming to rest on something that made them light up. Opening her arms to it, she cried:

"A piano!"

My family knew a cue when we heard one, and we said our lines: "Oh, Ruth, play! Please play something!"

She obliged without fuss, sashaying to that corner of the room, which was our family's domestic equivalent of Siberia. Only my sister and I ever went there, for torturous practice sessions that killed all other life in the room. We played angrily, dutifully, obeying our music-teacher nun who'd said it was God we disappointed when we didn't practice, not her. Once, a huge chunk of plaster fell from the ceiling while Susie played, landing near enough to frighten her badly. Though much mirth was expended on my father's remark at dinner—"Every ceiling's a critic!"—the incident seemed more ominous than funny to us children, and it had further demonized that corner of the room.

Now, here was Ruth, seeking it! *Preferring* it! Striding directly beneath the place where the ceiling was patched, she banished the angry poltergeist. Siberian ice caps groaned and melted in the radiant heat of her flaming coiffure. Wiggling her emerald fanny onto the piano bench, Ruth spread her ringed fingers over the keys to tipple an arpeggio, and the family settled like geese. I sat on the floor near the edge of the disaster zone so I could keep her in full view. She struck a thunderous chord that launched her into "Oh What a Beautiful Morning."

I knew and loved the song from our "Oklahoma" cast album, and at first didn't recognize Ruth's version. She began with the less-familiar verse, but even when she rolled into the title line, it was with such an alarming vibrato I glanced furtively around the room to see if anyone else thought as I did that the woman was hopelessly out of tune. The adults' faces were rapt. Ruth rolled up, down, and all around the notes as if steady tones were just too impossibly boring to maintain. I told myself that I didn't appreciate the genius of Ethel Merman either, which proved I lacked an ear for musical talent. Turning back to Ruth, I gave myself up to the thrill of hearing a professional performance right in my own home, on my piano, being played by someone who was actually enjoying it. Ruth's unabashed pleasure in herself was revolutionary to me; I'd been schooled by nuns in the virtues of modesty and humility, which discouraged self-display. Yet here was Ruth, indulging fearlessly, up close—and at such a volume!

When she finished, we burst into wild applause, and she stood, smiling, to bow. She'd broken the ice in every way; Siberia was warmed, and a frozen block of awkward relatives had melted into the reflecting pool we'd all wanted to be. Daddy led Ruth to the conversation-pit side of the room, where she was seated in the chair of honor. Drinks were served.

My aunts peppered Ruth with questions stored up, I now realize, from years of reading movie magazines at the hairdresser's. My uncles listened, laughing uproariously at remarks seemingly addressed particularly to them. The air was charged with electricity, the kind I normally had to scuff across the rug and touch somebody to spark. Now, nobody touched, and sparks flew anyway. Our living room—that familiar collection of tables, chairs, ashtrays, lamps, mantelpiece, French doors, and covered radiators—became an after-hours bar, a big city hotel room, an exotic nightclub. Men's and women's voices rose to repeated crescendos and dissolved in helpless laughter. I knew I'd been forgotten again, but the thought didn't displease me. For the first time in my life, I was in the unconcealed presence of Eros.

Earlier than anyone had expected, Ruth announced she'd have to leave. She said it in a tone of regret, as if she wanted to stay, but the moment of departure had come and further delay was impossible. Daddy went to the hall for her things. She rose, and we did too. Highballs went down on tabletops without being aimed at coasters; condensation dripped down the glasses' sides to form rings on my mother's wood finishes that nobody noticed. Police had raided the place. We'd all been startled from the pleasantest of dreams. Changed, changed utterly.

Bracelets jingling, Cousin Ruth retreated to the hall to be draped with her things. She called good-bye, tocked loudly through the foyer, and went out the front door. I could hear her heels ticking down the sidewalk, all the way to the car. Daddy was driving her back to her hotel. The doors of our Chevrolet opened and slammed heavily shut. Once. Twice. The engine revved, and she was gone.

Uncle Jimmy, never one to be daunted by a tough act to follow, said, "Quiet, isn't she?" and the room erupted.

Tongues loosened and drinks were freshened. Our family had never needed outsiders to goose its libido, but Ruth's celebrity was one of the most powerful stimulants I'd ever seen. I went upstairs to ponder this and dream.

We blamed the divorce, when it came, on our distant cousin, who was rumored to be an alcoholic. Ruth told her side of the story to Daddy. Some of it trickled down to me. If our cousin told his version to anyone, I never heard it. The man who'd barely been mentioned before the split now faded completely. Ruth remained "Cousin" in title and in our hearts.

The family's Christmas cards stopped, and I missed them. I kept the one that showed Ruth, Daddy's cousin—a handsome black-Irishman with slicked-back hair—and three good-looking children, seated in front of a stocking-draped fireplace. They all wore striped blazers and straw boaters and were captured in poses of rapturous gaiety; Ruth had one trousered leg extended in a showgirl's kick. Everyone was laughing. They looked like they were having the time of their lives. And why not? I'd always thought enviously. Their mother was a famous actress. When the marriage ended, I wondered if such nurture-by-hilarity had ended too. The thought that it had made me terribly sad.

My first year in New York as a struggling actress, I phoned Cousin Ruth, desperate for professional contact and support. She'd graciously insisted I visit her on the set of "All My Children," where she'd become a star. We lunched in her dressing room, and afterward she'd marched me into her producer's office saying, "Give this girl a job!"

It worked; the producer passed my name to "To Tell The Truth," a TV game show on which I appeared as a lying decoy for my very first time on national television.

After that, Ruth and I stayed in touch for a few years, but she began spending more and more time in California, and our contact ceased. Since coming to Los Angeles myself, I've thought of her often, especially in regard to something my father once said she'd told him: Orson Welles cast her in *Citizen Kane* because he'd wanted his wife to be a lady, and Ruth quoted Welles as telling her, "You're the only real lady in Hollywood." I came to understand that she'd achieved her most popular professional success in New York daytime television drama partly because Hollywood, then and now, has so little use for real ladies.

While writing this book, I called Uncle Jimmy to check some facts about his mother, Frances Landy. It was she, I'd eventually learned, who was our family's first professional actor. After answering my questions, Jimmy said: "Funny you should call today because, speaking of acting, Cousin Ruth came to town last night."

I was stunned. No one in our family had seen her in years. I felt as if I'd conjured her by my writing.

"Yeah…the paper said it was the first time she'd been here since the 1950s. I was trying to remember—isn't that when we all met her?"

I told him it was, and that I'd just been writing about that day.

"Well, she's touring with *Citizen Kane* now, as one of its last living cast members. Mindy went down to see her at the Eastman Theater, where they showed the film." Mindy is Jimmy's youngest daughter. "Said she looks gorgeous. Ruth's got to be, what, in her late seventies now? And Mindy says she's still got that red hair."

A blaze of orange-red flared and died in my mind's eye.

"Mindy got in the autograph line, and when she got up to Ruth, she introduced herself as family, but our name didn't ring a bell, so Ruth asked Mindy to mention the names of some other people in our family. When Mindy got to Gerry, right away Ruth brightened up and said, 'Oh, yes Gerry Kennedy! *I remember him!*' "

My father, of *The New Yorker* and the Round Table—I'd always known he'd been the draw.

"Then she felt like talking, I guess, because she invited Mindy to pull up a chair and they had a nice little chat while Ruth finished signing autographs."

Uncle Jimmy's tone changed. "In the paper it said she was staying with relatives out in Fairport. But I can't think of who that could be. Can you?"

I couldn't.

"We don't have anybody out in Fairport that I know of," he puzzled. "Not anyone who could've known her, anyway."

"It must be some other cousins," I said gently. "From one of the other marriages."

"You're right," he said, sighing a little. "That must be it. I think you're probably right."

We'd lost her. It didn't hurt as much as it once would have. Now we had a professional actress in the family whose blood tie couldn't be severed: me.

2.

Taken to the Stage

There have been three professional actors in our family since its ancestral arrival on U.S. shores in the middle of the nineteenth century, and all three have been women. This is not because the men lack talent. My brother Jimmy is one of the finest actors I know, with a shelf full of community theater acting trophies, which are more awards than I've got. My father was a brilliant toastmaster, public speaker, courtroom lawyer, and raconteur, but he abstained from acting, even in amateur theatricals. There was, in our family, an ancestral distrust of actors and acting. This was one reason men didn't take to the stage.

The other was that men, in our family, were aimed at professions. Medicine, teaching, and law were professions. Religion was a vocation, which was better than a profession, but God had to call you to it. Business was considered a worthy life's work for the descendants of an immigrant patriarch who'd made his fortune manufacturing valves, but the business had to be dignified, or at least lucrative. This further eliminated that business we call "show" from the family short list of suitable male occupations.

We women were not encumbered—or, alas, launched—with the same expectations. Though, to my family's credit, it lavished as much money and concern on females' education as on males', what women were to do with bachelor's degrees wasn't as strictly prescribed. Even my father's feminist dreams for his daughters— that we would infiltrate traditionally male occupations and win promotion by dint of superior brainpower and a secret weapon—secretarial skills!—that few men stooped to acquire—were hampered by the tacit assumption that for women, marriage changed everything.

Men's careers were unaffected by marital status, except to be improved by increased maturity, stability, and financial responsibility. But for women, marriage meant a whole new career—homemaking—and the professional jig was up. For women in my Irish Catholic family, whose birth-control method was limited to the one seductively named "rhythm," such careers were all-encompassing and decades-long. Women could exercise languishing parts of themselves in volunteer work, which once made America go 'round at bargain rates, but in my family few women attempted paid work after they were married. In those days, one professional salary per household was enough. Though many of my older female relatives worked and had careers, only those who'd remained single maintained career *trajectories.*

Looking back, it seems to me that the women of our family were so well-suited—by looks, temperament, intelligence, and education—to take to the stage that it's testimony to the low esteem in which such careers were held that more of us didn't.

"Taken to the stage," my father told me, was the family euphemism for an acting career. He said he'd heard it from his mother when he was a child. "And I never heard it uttered," he'd gone on to say, "in anything but a tragic tone, as if somebody had died."

Somebody *did* die. A cousin of Grandfather Kennedy's, known as Beautiful Helen, had been chosen by a college humor magazine as its "Woman of the Year." Her perfect flapper face had graced its cover, which led to interest from New York agents and producers. Helen went to the big city, where she'd signed a movie contract, but done very little acting that anyone knew of, before she fell to her death from a Manhattan hotel window under questionable circumstances.

Grandma's tone might also have reflected her feelings about her own sister, Frances, having taken to the stage. The Landy girls, and brother Charlie, had grown up middle-class and Irish-Italian in Elmira, New York. That an acting career, for a girl from such circumstances, would have been considered shameful is puzzling to me now. Perhaps Grandma was envious; Fran, I heard from Uncle Jimmy, had studied her craft in London. Snobbery may have been involved; my grandmother improved her own social circumstances, inarguably, by marrying the portly but charismatic heir of the Kennedy Valve Company. But after she'd been widowed, with four small children, she remarried the man I knew as grandfather, a retired state Supreme Court justice and former Republican district attorney known by the delightful oxymoron "Judge Love." Because Grandma loved politics and the party machinery that elected her husband repeatedly to the bench, I doubt she was a snob. It must have been Catholic puritanism, more than anything else, that made Grandma frown on taking to the stage. Her immigrant version of the faith distrusted whatever smacked of too much vanity, pleasure, and self-display.

When Daddy told me Aunt Fran had toured early in the century with some of the era's leading stage actors, including Otis Skinner and John Drew, I barely understood what I was hearing. The news that Fran had been an actress stunned me, and I had to completely revise my view of the little dumpling of a woman who sat demurely, Sundays at Grandma's house, in a particular straight-backed chair. So exclusively did I see Fran in that chair that she is one with it in my memory: both were plumply upholstered and supported by delicate legs.

I began to study Fran, those Sundays, armed with this new information. There were clues to her past, I saw, now that I knew how to read them. Her dresses featured tightly ruched bodices that showed off a waistline still trim for a woman her age, and their portrait necklines displayed her penchant for costume jewelry like the jumbo pearl choker that was her trademark. Her hair was meticulously coifed, whether in the coil of gleaming gray she wore in the fifties, or the snow-white finger waves rising vertically from her brow in the sixties, when I knew her secret. Her diction, which I'd always noticed bore not a trace of the upstate flaws that afflicted most of my family, now seemed to have—yes!—pear-shaped tones!

One Sunday my father saw me hovering near Fran's chair, and called out, "Fran, I was telling Mimi that you toured with people like John Drew. Why don't you tell her something about it?"

Aunt Fran looked startled, as she often did. Her black-rimmed glasses magnified already large eyes to give her the appearance, at times, of an adorable bug being asphyxiated by pearls. "Oh dear me!" she exclaimed with a little laugh. She turned to me, her whole upper body going too, because of her training in posture. "What would you like to know, dear?" she asked, dimpling sweetly.

Daddy called out, "About the time John Drew wouldn't let you offstage."

"Oh, goodness me!" Fran exclaimed, giving a self-effacing chuckle that quivered her corseted bosom. "Oh, that was positively dreadful." She shook her head, then inquired of me, "Do you know who John Drew was, dear?"

"An actor," I replied, and she smiled. I knew I'd hear her story, having proven myself sufficiently intelligent to appreciate it.

Daddy prompted again from across the room—"He was drunk, wasn't he Fran?" and she turned to him, looking slightly alarmed.

"Oh, I never said he was drunk!" she reproved. Then, relaxing somewhat, she admitted, "Or he may have had a drink or two, I don't remember. He used to walk from town to town, you know, Gerry, instead of taking the train. I tell you, he used to wave good-bye to all of us on the platform, and we wouldn't see him again until the next night at the hotel. The walking braced him, he said. He always got to the hotel on time, and he never missed a performance, so I couldn't really say if he drank on those walks or not. Oh, I suppose he could have, but then he mightn't have always shown up on time, and he always did, I'll tell you that."

Fran was protecting her dead fellow actor's reputation, as any lady ought to do. She was also putting Daddy on notice that if she were to tell her story, she'd tell it her way. "But he was naughty, my dear, ohh, t'isn't any doubt about that!" She said this to me, lest the specter of Drew's sobriety rob the story of any potential sting. The actor's roguish character having been firmly established despite presumed abstemiousness, Fran commenced:

"Well, one night"—a glance at Daddy suspended his services as interlocutor—"I was near the end of my scene with Mr. Drew. It wasn't a long one—I played the maid, you know, coming in and out throughout the plot—and as I went to make my exit I saw him blocking the door. Well, I couldn't understand why, but when I tried to get past him, he blocked me again, and I realized he wasn't going to let me leave! Well, I was absolutely petrified, because it seemed he'd just *decided* to it that I wasn't to get offstage. He asked me, "Do you have to leave?" and I told him I did. He said, "Well, why don't you use the other door?" Well, I didn't know *what* to say then, because, of course, I *couldn't* use the other door, *that* door had lots of people behind it, in a room, which I couldn't know anything about without absolutely ruining the whole plot—! So I told him I *couldn't* use the other door, and he asked me *why*! Well, by that time, you can imagine, I was practically paralyzed. I didn't know a thing I was saying, but I came up with something —oh, 'Cook needs me in the kitchen,' I suppose, or something like that. It seemed to satisfy him, because he finally let me by. I thought I'd been out there for an eternity! When I got off, the stagehand said, "Miss Landy, you look like you've seen a ghost!' and got me a chair because he thought I was going to faint. Well, I must have looked as frightened as I felt, because someone told Miss Barrymore, and John Drew got quite a scolding for it. Yes he did. I was told she said, 'I heard you frightened the little maid half to death! How could you do that to our poor, dear Frances?' She must've given him quite a dressing-down, because he came to me afterwards and apologized. He said he'd done it just to see if I could stay in character, because that was an important thing for every member of the company to know. Well, I can assure you, it taught me the importance of that, yes it did! I'll say! I never forgot that lesson! And he never did it again."

She laughed delightedly. I sat, amazed, trying to picture my great-aunt, in bloom, an Irish-Italian girl—poor, dear Frances!—with enough brunette charm to land the part of "the little maid" in a grand theatrical family's tour. I imagined looking into the rosy, greasepainted face of one of the era's leading men, seeing the twinkle in his eyes, and feeling the terror that came from knowing it wasn't just the footlights' reflection but his delight in toying with me, while the hydra-headed audience breathed at my back, that put it there. Though surely, even in her terror, Fran would never have given the audience her back, and Drew, even in his mischief, wouldn't have been cad enough to upstage her.

Acting lessons are often absorbed in panic-inducing conditions. Some acting teachers go to great lengths to simulate them in the paradoxical safety of their classes. I suppose it's possible that John Drew was seized with the mentor impulse, onstage, to teach a junior member of the company elements of her craft smack dab in the middle of her performance, but I think the boredom of a long run, between bracing intercity walks, had much more to do with it. I suspect the actor toyed with poor, dear Frances for pleasure. And I think the little maid, in all her fright, was secretly pleased.

My cousin Betsy, Aunt Fran's granddaughter, told me Aunt Fran had spoken of me a few weeks before she died on the eve of her ninety-second birthday. By that time I was a successful actress myself. I'd become accustomed to thinking of myself as a memorable person and lacked the grace to be surprised that my great-aunt had thought of me in her last days, though I hadn't seen or spoken to her in years.

What did she say? I'd wanted to know. Betsy replied, "Well, it was weird. She said that of all of us children, you were the only one who could ever be lessoned."

The dying have a knack for choosing words with dreamy precision that turn their simplest utterances into Zen koans, which the survivors are left to ponder for years. Betsy and I agreed, after some perplexed discussion about the choice and syntax of the verb, that Fran's meaning was "lessoned" as in "taught." We presumed she'd remembered me as a uniquely educable child because I'd absorbed her stories at her silk-sheathed knee. Perhaps she considered my acting career a result, in part, of my having been so "lessoned." She would have been right.

But the other meaning—"lessened"—will not go away. Over the years, it's become an important part of Aunt Fran's message. In life, she loved turning down the volume on high spirits and people. It was she who quieted the rowdy cousin-packs that roamed through Grandma's house searching for candy. She'd urged us to more civil displays. It was she who pursed her lips in mock disapproval and staged little intakes of breath whenever someone stepped over a genteel line—but she'd also clearly loved outlandish behavior. Her son, Jimmy, the loudest and craziest of my uncles, was the apple of her eye. She seemed to relish his antics as much as, in her story, she'd relished John Drew's. You could only take people down a peg if they were hanging on high enough pegs to begin with.

I have always felt bigger than life. I think most actors do. Nature, nurture, or both has given us what we feel is our permanent sense of oversize, as if real life cannot possibly satisfy our gargantuan appetites and expectations. In children, this feeling is understandable; humans are born undifferentiated and egocentric. We think we're the whole world until we bump up against other people and things. Then we learn the limits of our own particular selves. Actors come late to these limits. Our first response to the Other is usually, "*I* can be *that!*" and our gigantism endures. But it ends, painfully, as it must, with the mature realization that we have been grossly underestimating the size of "real life," which is infinitely immense. Then, we suffer. Our sense of size diminishes, and often our sense of worth.

Actors hate diminishment. "Lessening" of any kind is anathema to us. Yet we've chosen work that ensures more regular diminishment than would have ambushed us in almost any other field. We have a phrase to rob lessening of its sting: "There are no small parts, only small actors. "We say it, but don't really believe it, when we must take a lesser part than the lead. Most of us started out in the lead in our schools and hometowns, which is what gave us the nerve to go professional. I have found in Aunt Fran's koan a blessing: if I am able to be "lessened," it is a gift. Actors must be able to expand and contract repeatedly, in order not to break but to endure.

I think Aunt Fran knew diminishment; she seemed "lessened" in old age, greeting family primarily on her sister's turf, not her own. She had never remarried, she lived alone. She no doubt felt "lessened" as a young woman, when marriage and motherhood curtailed her autonomous adventures and ended, for a while, her public attention, until she acted again on the amateur stage. When I knew her, Fran seemed to have accepted the limitations of her life with enthusiasm and grace. As I try to do the same, squishing passionate autonomy and fierce ambition into place along the chain of marriages and reproduction that brought me here, I think of her. In our family, the claims of blood are irreducible. I think Aunt Fran was as pleased to see me coming along the lineage as I was to discover in her an actress who'd gone before. I'm proud she saw in me the ability to be "lessoned" and "lessened." She must have recognized me, even when I was young, as a soul mate, a fellow actress, another adventuress with an ego big enough to survive downsizing with plenty to spare.

3.

The Baltimore Catechism

I was raised to go to heaven. That was the main thing. Life was just a means to an end, and that end was death, which sent you to heaven, where you really belonged. But to get to heaven you had to die sinfree, or at least free of any sin greater than could be shriven in purgatory, which was short-term hell. Confession erased all sins on earth, but unconfessed sins on the soul at death were punished in the afterlife. Venial sins could be burned off in purgatory, but mortal sins sent you to hell. If you went to hell, your life was a failure, no matter what you'd done with it while you were alive.

This truth, and myriad others, I learned from *The Baltimore Catechism*, the American Roman Catholic child's question-and-answer guide to the universe. I memorized it in grammar school, reciting its rote wisdom into the concealed ears of nuns, who pressed my lips against their chalk-dusted veils to mute my answers from eavesdropping classmates who might be tempted to copy. Copying was a sin. In upper grades, I answered loud and proud for priests testing my doctrinal mettle, or wrote answers word-perfect on purple-and-white religion quizzes brought to the classroom so wet from the nuns' mimeograph machine that the chemical smell made me high.

I accepted the catechism's truths with terror and relief. They provided a lifelong shield against existential angst and produced lifelong guilts in varieties so peculiar that my psyche is largely impenetrable to the unindoctrinated. But by far the most radical legacy of *The Baltimore Catechism* to me was that it—more than dancing school, children's productions, natural vanity, maternal encouragement, movie magazines, or sheer adventurousness—was responsible for my acting career.

The training in memorization alone equipped me. After conquering the catechism, I never had trouble "learning all those lines," a feat apparently so daunting to the numbers of people who ask me about it that it seems to be keeping a sizable portion of them out of the acting profession. But the catechism's most forceful push to the stage came from its unmistakable depiction of life as a dangerous trap. Living was so obviously full of pitfalls by which even the most fervent soul stumbled and slid down sin's slippery slope to hell that I concluded heaven could only be won by avoiding real life as much as possible.

The stage, when I found it, was a blessed relief. It was a haven, a place where I could fake life without incurring consequences. Emotion was real onstage, passion was real, but taking action caused nothing more real to happen than the delightful effect of applause. In other words, *The Baltimore Catechism* made an acting career seem spiritually safe.

I had a lot to learn about show business.

The catechism's threatening picture of life was confirmed by priests. They lent hierarchical gravity to religion lessons; whenever a black cassock darkened our classroom door, we children would leap to our feet and greet the wearer by his honorific and last name, in sing-song unison:

"Good morning Father Whelan!" Then we'd sit when he told us to and wait for him to illuminate some shadowy corner of church doctrine.

"In ten years, at least one of you will be dead," Father Whelan intoned one day to our fifth-grade class, gliding up and down the aisles with his hand ominously outstretched above our cowlicked little heads. Robert, at the front of my row, would be dead of leukemia by age twenty, but none of us envisioned such a tragedy then. We were preoccupied with the dramatic imagery of auto wrecks: screeching tires and shattered glass.

"What would you do," he mused, "if an angel came to that door right now asking for volunteers to go to heaven? How many of you would be ready?"

I raised my hand. I was ready. Three years before, on my seventh birthday, I'd become capable of sin, according to *The Baltimore Catechism*. What a difference a day makes! Since then, my life had been an emotional roller coaster: Fall, Redemption, Fall, Redemption, alternating from Sunday to Saturday! When the Fall happened Monday, it was a terrible wait until Saturday, the only day of the week when Redemption was available at anonymous confession. Being a good child, I hadn't yet sinned grievously, but I knew the day was coming when I would. My sister and her friends were boy-crazy; I fatalistically presumed I'd be the same. Most sex sins were mortal. Even thinking about sex was a sin. As I got older, death on the wrong day would easily damn me for eternity. Living wasn't worth the risk. I wiggled my hand at Father Whelan. I'm ready, Father. Let the angel take *me!!*

The priest droned on. A few of my classmates gave me the disgusted look we reserved for goody-goodies, and I retracted my hand, realizing Father Whelan hadn't asked his question to solicit answers. He'd merely wanted to make a point: everyone was afraid to die. He'd meant to be reassuring, but he scared me. If a priest didn't want to die, what chance did ordinary grown-ups have of facing death with courage? Did all adults wind up cringing from God because they were hopelessly drenched in mortal sin? That seemed to be Father' Whelan's message, and it was an all-too-credible one, I realized. I'd just volunteered for suicide, the worst sin of all. Only the angel at the door had tempted me to it, but that was always the sinner's excuse, wasn't it? "I chose evil because I thought it was good." And then one day we're sorry, but it's too late.

I wouldn't really have committed suicide, I knew. It sent you to hell, and it hurt. I'd spend my allotted time on earth, and that would lead me to my downfall. The problem was that I already loved life not too little, but too much. And I'd probably love it even more when I was able to drive and didn't have to go to school. Growing up was full of secular temptations. If a priest was unsure of his heavenly reward, how would *I* ever manage to live purely enough to see God in the end?

The church, in its finite wisdom, provides role models for just such crises of faith. They are the persons whose likenesses grace our stained-glass windows, our statues, our holy cards, and our medals. Their stories are told to show how ordinary people can rise above the rabble, lay and clergy, to become heavenly celebrities. They are the stars of our church. They are the saints.

I loved the saints and wanted to be one. They were so *attractive* on their holy cards, beautifully posed and lit by an inner grace that would have improved even Garbo. Their costumes were magnificent: textured robes and lush capes. Many of the saints were young girls whose main attribute was virginity. It pleased me to think I effortlessly possessed a sign of spiritual superiority. At an age when I found the alternative repulsive, I had no intention of ever surrendering it.

Other elements of sanctity, however, were harder to attain. The girl saints often ran away to become hermits in caves outside their hometowns. They prayed there, fasting and mortifying their flesh. Perhaps in large medieval families, children could disappear without incurring much anxious notice, but my father said that if any of us four ran away, his joy at finding us again would not mitigate the spanking of our lives. Fasting was impossible in our home, except as required by church law, which we observed on meatless days with fish sticks and tuna hot dogs called Tunies. These foods did not mortify my flesh. I liked them. Wasting food was a sin in our home; we had to eat everything on our plates at dinner, over which my parents presided, and which could be skipped only by actively vomiting.

Zoning and property laws also discouraged modern sanctity. In my childhood neighborhood, the last tracts of undeveloped land were being excavated for a New York State Thruway feeder, our downtown expressway. I'd been chased off its dirt mountains often enough by construction workers to make praying al fresco out of the question. Being caught on my knees by some leering hardhat would have been a mortification beyond my capacity to endure. Occasionally I'd enter our neighbor Mr. Thurston's rose garden at night to sing hymns softly to myself and draw blood on my fingers with thorns, to commemorate Christ's passion, but these ecstasies were usually interrupted by Mr. Thurston's fist-waving appearances beneath his back-porch light, and his threats to call the police if he ever found me on his property again.

Mr. Thurston's dudgeon was the closest I ever got to religious persecution. Sainthood by martyrdom was impossible in Rochester in the 1950s. Catholics were a big voting bloc; the city's establishment courted, not shunned, us. Well-educated, Republican papists like my family were being admitted to country clubs.

Daily life dragged on in my childhood. I began to realize that if it continued—and there was every indication that it would—I'd have to find some way to spend my time between grammar school and heaven. I feared it was a trick of the devil's, this luring of my thoughts away from God and eternity, but there seemed to be no alternative. Eventually, I'd have to begin planning a future on earth.

The Baltimore Catechism discussed one's personal future in terms of vocations. There were three vocations, each offering a unique system of sexual management. They were, in order of merit: (1) the Religious vocation, which required celibacy and forbade sex; (2) the Married vocation, which allowed sex for procreation; and (3) the Single life, which also forbade sex and required celibacy but without the canonical perks. Nowhere in the fifties catechism was the word "career" mentioned. In the 1954 version the most identifiable reference to actual work came in the guide to class discussion at the end of the Marriage chapter. There, the qualities for a happy marriage were listed by gender, and gave a vivid picture of what was in store for those who chose sex. You play, you pay.

For girls:

> Patience, understanding, sympathy, learning to cook,
> to sew, washing dishes, making beds, taking care of children,
> cleaning the house, letting others have their own way, etc.

For boys:

> Kindness, thoughtfulness, helpfulness, learning to fix
> things in the house, keeping one's room clean, not
> throwing clothes on the floor, respect for girls, willing-
> ness to do hard work, etc.

I remember reading this list in grammar school and thinking it unfair. Girls' requirements were harder than boys'. Our specific tasks—cooking, sewing, washing dishes, cleaning the house, making beds, and taking care of children—were much harder than keeping one's room clean and not throwing clothes on the floor. Boys had only to be *willing* to do hard work while girls were actually *doing* it. On top of the drudgery was girls' odious requirement of "letting others have their own way." I knew I'd be bad at that. I was not attracted to marriage.

But I didn't want to be a nun either. Nuns seemed to dislike boys, which I didn't. In all their grossness and disgusting provocation, boys were funny and brave, and I thought my world would be the poorer without them. I cringed whenever a boy got his head banged against the blackboard by a punishing nun, or had his ears pulled until he cried. Boys tried so hard not to cry that when they did, we witnessing classmates all died a little inside. Boys' punishments didn't seem to fit their crimes; what was so awful about standing to answer in class with your hands in your pockets? I didn't understand nuns, and I didn't want to be one.

The single state seemed best to me, even in its low spiritual esteem. But if I chose it, basic questions would remain unanswered. How would I spend my time? How would I clothe and feed myself, or put a roof over my head? *The Baltimore Catechism* did not advise on these topics the way it did on other matters, with comforting proscriptions and prescriptions. Just when life got complicated, it seemed, *The Baltimore Catechism* would fail me. And what would become of me then, unguided and weak? Would I fall by the wayside, like some poor Protestant?

Oh life! How to love you, and get away clean?!

4.

The Mirror

I f *The Baltimore Catechism* had forbidden mirror-gazing, my whole life might
have been different. A warning could have been included in the chapter under
the First Commandment—"I am the Lord thy God, thou shalt not have
strange gods before me"—but to the best of my recollection, it wasn't. Nor, as a
child, did I hear the cautionary tale about Narcissus's love for his own reflection;
it was a pagan story, not worthy of St. John's curriculum. I knew nuns weren't supposed to linger before mirrors, but we laity, as far as I knew, were free to look as
much as we liked. And I did. From an early age, I spent hours in front of my mirror. That's where I did my first acting exercises.

Emoting to my reflection took varied forms. For comedy, I preferred the
Mousketeer routine that opened the cartoon vault on the Mickey Mouse Club TV
show—"Now it's time to turn the dial to the right and the left with a great big
smile." I sang this ditty with much swinging of my hair, which I'd grown halfway
down my back. The end of the number had an intriguing hand gesture and chant:
"Meeska, mooska, mouseketeer! Mouse-cartoon time now is here!" I thrust my
arms forward and back in dramatic rhythm.

Tragedy was more taxing, but fulfilling. It was indescribably wonderful to
make tears course down my cheeks, then well up in my eyes to spill afresh. I would
think about my dog dying. Years later, Stockard Channing told me her trick for
crying every take of a scene she taped for her sitcom pilot was thinking about her
dead childhood dog. I would also imagine myself on my deathbed, bidding my
mother a heartrending good-bye. I never forced tears mechanically; poking myself
in the eye would have hurt, and the whole point of crying was the orgasmic pleasure involved. I was twenty years into my professional career before I let anyone
spray menthol into my eyes. I allowed legendary makeup artist Beau Wilson to do
it because he assured me he'd done the same for Bette Davis hundreds of times.
Once I learned I could act backward, using physical sensation to trigger emotion—do we run because we're scared or are we scared because we're running?—I
abused my eyes guiltlessly, especially in the days when I had small children at home
and few emotions left over for professional use. It wasn't as much fun as the old
days, but it worked.

School fortified my mirror performances with public presentations. Being an obedient child capable of standing still, I was cast as Mary in most of my early grade-school Christmas tableaux. Mary is my baptismal name. I identified with the part and played it to the hilt, maintaining serenity even when my Josephs collapsed into snorting giggles muffled by their prayerful palms. Beneath the taunting gaze of their friends, they became not foster fathers of Jesus, but boys in dresses with towels on their heads. I longed for the day when I would have worthy partners—real *actors* on a real *stage!*

My mother was a star at our local community theater, and she enrolled me in its children's acting class. There, my talent—which was widely presumed to be her genetic legacy—blossomed. My year-end recital piece, a monologue from *I Remember Mama*, marked my first appearance on the big Community Players stage. I sat on the stoop of a house, built for the adults' current production, with my antique skirt spread around me and a prop diary in my hands; after referring to the diary for my opening lines, I lowered it to my lap and declaimed the rest gazing dreamily into the darkness beyond the footlights' glare.

I loved footlights and missed them terribly when they vanished in the sixties, with the advent of audience participation. Footlights formed my entire early approach to acting by keeping the audience as safely distant as God, a Presence felt and heard, but rarely seen. For me as a child, spotting a particular face in the house was a terrible mishap that ruined my concentration. I begged my family never to sit where I might find them, by accident, in the light-spill. The theater revolution in the sixties that brought down the "fourth wall," crumbled proscenium arches, and popularized thrust stages and theaters-in-the-round, was not just a shock for fusty critics who resented being prodded to get naked, but for actors like me, who'd felt safe in the footlights' rosy embrace.

When I was six, I was chosen to appear in a production at our local Catholic girls' high school. Its stage would host many of my later triumphs, but my first appearance there was as a tap-dancing Morning Glory in a golden jubilee concert celebrating our parish monsignor's fifty years as a priest.

I was sent to the church basement to audition during school. As a first-grader, I was the youngest child there. We were taught a verse of the song "Morning Glory" and a shuffle-hop-step, which is still the only tap dancing I can do. We performed this snippet repeatedly, and the selection process proceeded. Eventually I realized I was losing my chances to older, more proficient girls, and I became inwardly adamant to make the cut. Who knows what expression this caused to settle on my face? In the end, I was the last child chosen. I got the nod, and stepped forward serenely to join the winners' circle.

The performance—dancing in the footlights in my pink organdy dress—was wonderful. The curtain call afterward came as a surprise to me, but was all the more thrilling for that. We Morning Glories filed out to stand in front of the towering adult and teenage cast. Bathed in footlights, I felt applause wash over me in huge waves. It felt like heaven. Then the noise subsided and everything grew quiet. Someone stood up in the front row of the audience. Because I'd performed my routine and no longer had anything nerve-wracking required of me, I squinted through the glare to see what was going on.

Monsignor Sullivan, our octogenarian honoree, was addressing the crowd. I knew it was him because of his familiar, bent figure and scratchy voice. He mentioned something about a morning glory, and I suddenly felt very warm and calm. For a few eternal seconds I was intensely alone in a pool of light and heat. Then everything shattered. The house exploded in laughter. Behind me, the cast was laughing too. I looked around to see their eyes on me. I seemed to be the center of all this, but I couldn't figure out why, since I'd done nothing to make people laugh. It was an indelible mystery. Hundreds of people were focused on me, responding unanimously in a way I'd neither invited nor understood.

In the car, my father said, "Did you hear what Monsignor said?"

"No," I responded.

"When everyone laughed? He was talking about you."

So it was true. I *had* been the reason.

"He thanked everybody for the show," Daddy continued, "and said he'd loved it all, but especially that little morning glory in the front row because he'd never seen a flower with so many missing teeth."

For the first time in weeks I remembered the gap in my mouth caused by my absent two front teeth. I'd been thinking only of how beautiful I felt in my pink organdy dress and my shiny new tap shoes. We'd been taught, in our family, not to comment on anyone's personal appearance except to compliment it. This was a cultural ethic; toothpaste and deodorant commercials posed the question of whether or not your best friend should tell you bad news about your personal presentation. I couldn't help but feel Monsignor Sullivan had overstepped his bounds by calling attention to my temporary disfigurement. As pleased as I was to know I'd been the focus of all eyes, the reason wounded my dignity. This episode was an omen for my future; I was destined to be comic in much of my performing career, whether I wanted to be or not.

My first radio appearance, arranged by Cousin Inez, who worked at a local station, was another harbinger of this fate. Danny and I went to a local toy store to be interviewed for a special Christmas program. Art Linkletter was enjoying national radio and TV success at the time with "Kids Say the Darndest Things," and a local personality, Bob Keefe, was obviously hoping Rochester kids would say darned things, too. I didn't know this then. I approached the interview as if it were the news with John Cameron Swayzee.

My brother and I took up the end of the interview line. Bob finally got to us, hunkering in front of Danny and asking his name. He established that Danny was seven-year-old Danny Kennedy, son of lawyer Gerry and his charming wife Nancy, whom Bob said he knew. Radio was very social in those days. Then Bob asked Danny what he wanted for Christmas.

"Something that could blow up all of American from one tiny test tube," said Danny in his calm, high voice.

My brother was a brilliant scientist, but I considered it stupid of him to broadcast the destructive fantasy I'd heard many times in private. I knew he was a good person, but anyone who didn't might get the wrong idea. I was resentful of Bob, and all grown-ups who thought children were comic fodder for their idle amusement. I steeled myself to prevent any utterance that Bob could turn into a laugh. The rest of Danny's interview went well, except when Danny said he wanted to make other kids obey Sister by telling her some of the things they'd done. Bob took umbrage. "That would be tattling now, wouldn't it?" he reproved. Danny maintained a stubborn silence that made me proud. The next thing I knew, Bob was hunkered in front of me.

On the 33$^1/_3$ rpm recording that was our guest memento, you can hear Bob struggling to establish my identity. My voice is shy and mumbly; I was only five years old. Finally he elicits that I am Mimi Kennedy, sister of Danny and child of Nancy and Gerry.

"What would you like for Christmas, Mimi?"

I was ready for that.

"A bride doll."

"A bride doll. Wonderful. I think I saw some beautiful ones at the back of the store. Maybe you can get your Mom to go look at those later." There is a pause. I make no reply.

"And what about Mother? What does she want for Christmas?"

"A beater."

"A what?"

Loud: "A BEAT-er."

Bob starts to chuckle. "I see. Eggs not getting beaten well enough at home, are they?"

He laughs alone. I don't see what's so funny. I'd meant egg beater, but I couldn't think of the whole name.

"And what would your father like?"

Bob almost stumped me there. To this day I find men difficult to buy for. But I adored both my father and presents enough to pay close attention to the ribbon-topped, oblong foil boxes that adults always gave Daddy at our holiday parties. The contents bored me, but Daddy smiled to see them, and I considered myself quite sophisticated to know what they were. I was proud to show off my knowledge to Bob Keete, who thought children were so laughable.

"My daddy likes bottles of whiskey."

This answer was spliced out of the radio broadcast as too potentially libelous to air publicly, especially on the heels of Mom's beater. On the record, Bob moves to the next child, wheezing and sputtering, obviously in recovery from a laughing fit far worse than the beater exchange had provoked. The whiskey answer is at the end of the record, like a coda.

Inadvertent meanings, and others' reception of them, are the stuff of comedy. A sexy glance is spoiled by a Kleenex-staunched shaving cut; a resolute departure is ruined by toilet paper trailing from the shoe; a beautiful morning glory smiles and reveals the gap between her teeth; an astute child is foiled by the mysteries of adult life. If I'd consciously understood the dynamics of some of my first performing experiences, I might have accepted certain trends in my career earlier than I did. But I was too busy, as a child, trying to be loved and admired in a world I couldn't control to value laughter that was aimed at me.

I continued to perform—in dance recitals, in an adult community theater production—and by eighth grade I took it for granted that if I auditioned for a project, I'd be cast. The Community Theater mounted a rather grand musical, with children from all over the city, about life undersea. I auditioned with my friends Nancy and Kathy; we all made the chorus. Nancy and I, who'd taken years of ballet lessons, won featured roles as turtles in a little dance quartet. Kathy, who got no such featured part, saw her role in the chorus turn from sparkling-exciting to dishwater-dull. I lacked empathy, I'm afraid. I was just glad *I* wasn't stuck in the background.

During the last week of rehearsal, I got sick. After three days of my absence, Kathy took over my turtle part. Nancy called to give me the news. She assured me my place in the chorus was being held, in case I recovered for opening.

I didn't. My diagnosis was pneumonia. On opening night, not even Nancy called, and Kathy had my costume and my part. The show went on without me as if I were dead. Realizing I was completely expendable, I wept inconsolably in my mother's arms. She stayed with me most of the evening. I think her empathy with my disappointment was so great she didn't want to show her face outside the sickroom, either.

"You'll remember this, darling," she murmured, "because it's the first time the theater's ever been cruel to you. And if you're going to be an actress, it won't be the last."

A year later, I was getting dressed before my mirror when the future was revealed to me. I wasn't acting to my reflection at the time; I'd gotten too old for such things. I occasionally put together outfits from my sister's and mother's wardrobes and posed for unconscionable lengths of time, pretending to be a *Seventeen* magazine model, or someone at a glamorous party, but this day I was on my way somewhere, and barely paying attention to my reflection. Checking some detail in the mirror—my buttons or the position of my slip—I caught my own eye, which triggered a sensation that opened a crack in time. I looked in and saw that I would be an actress.

My mother's implicit oracle the night of the turtle dance notwithstanding—she did not mention an acting career for me again with such certitude, and I came to presume emotion had made her overdramatize—few in my family, myself included, really thought I would act professionally. My father's amusement with the idea when I was younger had turned to gentle discouragement now that I was a teenager. I was smart in school, and according to popular wisdom, acting didn't require brains. I was suited for more serious work. Talent did not an actress make. My mother was keenly aware that her community theater acting was not a career. Broadway or the movies—*those* were careers. The road from my bedroom to Broadway or Hollywood was unmapped and unexcavated. No expeditions had gone, and none would be encouraged.

Yet here was the news, whole and entire: I would be an actress. It seemed to arrive from without, and I responded from within, thinking, "Oh, *that's* what it will be." As if the answer to the question that had plagued me since childhood—How would I spend my time till heaven?—were the only important aspect to be settled.

I communed with this extremely pleasant revelation for a while, enjoying both it and the persistent warp in time and space. Then I put on my shoes and left the room, never to question my vocation again until it was too late for anything but Monday-morning quarterbacking.

5.

Community Theater

I was in seventh grade when Harriet Warren, the director of the Rochester community theater, asked my mother if I could audition for *Spider's Web*. The Agatha Christie murder-mystery that had a part for a twelve-year-old girl.

Mother had acted often enough at the theater to know the pleasures of the experience, heady to her as a moonlighting housewife, would have a powerful effect on a young girl. My acting ambition would be advanced, she guessed, to the point of no return, where it would one day be met by my father's ancestral antipathy. She wondered if encouraging me now was really the right thing to do.

I was already familiar with the community theater, both from acting classes and the fact that three generations of my Rochester family had used it as an outlet for passions and vanities that without it might have led to more dangerous preoccupations. Amateur theatricals were tolerated in our family precisely for their worth as a safety valve, despite the disdain for professional acting. Rochester Community Players was, and is, the second oldest community theater in the country. Aunt Fran trod its boards after marriage and motherhood retired her from professional trouping. Cousin Inez played there in the forties, supplementing her local radio singing career. Even Daddy had done a turn, before withdrawing to preserve his credibility at the bar, fearing some judge or juror who'd seen him play-act on Saturday night might doubt the unimpeachable sincerity of his rhetoric in court on Monday morning.

But Mother was our community theater star. In the fifties and sixties she did a play almost every other season, and she served brilliantly as president of its board. "Your mother is the best light comedienne in Rochester," Daddy would boast. None of us took it as a backhanded compliment. Nor was it meant to be; we Rochesterians thought of our city as a Big Pond. If Mother, Brooklyn-born and a former Manhattan model, thought differently, she was too gracious a Big Frog to say so.

She and Daddy came to Rochester after World War II, when she was two years a bride and already a mother. Happily, she'd embraced domesticity in the first house she, a lifelong apartment-dweller, had ever known, while Daddy flourished at the city's most prestigious law firm, Nixon-Hargrave. They found themselves in social demand. Daddy maintained, Mother's urban style and sophistication "took the town by storm." It had certainly flattened him, before they ever met, when a friend of Daddy's solicited his services as a blind date for an out-of-town girl who needed an escort to a local dance. Daddy declined on principle, saying, with a touch of Harvard Law School arrogance, "I don't do blind dates."

"Go to the society page of the evening paper," his caller had replied. "There's a picture."

Daddy dutifully went to the paper and opened it to find "Miss Nancy Helen Colgan of Manhattan" pictured above a blurb announcing her weeklong stay with a local family. Such Jane Austenesque society reportage was typical of the times, but Mother's photograph was not. It was one of her modeling head shots, wherein professional lighting and makeup enhanced her already striking, self-styled resemblance to Myrna Loy. "That's the girl," said Daddy's caller.

Objection overruled counselor. Since the date was no longer technically blind, Daddy accepted. He was practically drooling over the newsprint.

"Go home and think about marrying me," he told Mother on the dance floor, "because that's what you're gonna do."

She acted mostly in comedies at the Community Players. They suited her style, intelligence, and grace, but more importantly, they were directed by Harriet Warren, and Mother was Harriet's favorite actress.

Harriet ran the theater, during its midcentury heyday, with her husband George. They were a bohemian couple, of a type once common in the theater when married actors left New York to manage provincial theaters for a living while raising their families. Now we just go to Los Angeles and do television. It's possible the Warrens seemed more bohemian to me than they actually were. In those days Rochester was so conservative that a local columnist dubbed it "Smugtown, U.S.A." in his published social history of the place, and Smugtowners never forgave him.

Harriet was one of the most beautiful women I'd ever seen, with pale blue eyes in an unapologetically lined face and gray-blonde hair worn in a ponytail and bangs, as if Harriet had never heard of the unwritten local law that women of a certain age must acquire a salon hairdo. I saw her in slacks so exclusively that even when she looked stunning, in taffeta or chiffon on opening nights, the dresses seemed ready to crawl off her back, as if the closet, not her body, were their more natural habitat. Beneath her soft sweaters and men's shirts, Harriet's front seemed to sag more than other women's. When I asked my mother why, she replied with faint disapproval that couldn't quite mask her grudging admiration, "Harriet doesn't always wear a bra." This shocked me. At the time, bras were sold in store departments called "foundations" and were not optional. They deserved architectural nomenclature. They held female flesh so firmly in place that most women's breasts looked like ready-to-launch missiles. Harriet's soft pendulance was revolutionary to me—and appealingly risqué.

In hindsight, I think my impression that Harriet was a lapsed southern aristocrat may have owed more to her actor's spirit and fierce intelligence, than to an accident of breeding. But her mesmerizing Virginia drawl suggested it; "Nancy deah," she'd say to my mother, pouring soft honey all over words we Rochesterians whistled with piercing sibilance, "ah'm thinkin' of dewin' a play, but ah simply won' dew it' without you." Mother would say yes. People usually said yes to Harriet, whose blue eyes reflected a wider world than most women knew. Those who entered it were expanded.

Visible, powerful, married women were rare in my world at the time. In my Catholic neighborhood, smart, lively women functioned brilliantly and heroically in their homes, but were often too burdened to join the public discourse. Our world suffered for it, and so did the women. I remember hearing about hysterectomies, mastectomies, and deaths from cancer, the news passed in whispers at church or school. I realize now how many of those lives were succored by addictions, large or small: cigarettes and alcohol for the rebels, food and religion for the more devout. I remember how my acting ambition was greeted by some of my friends' mothers with sighs and statements like, "You're lucky to be artistic!" They seemed to think certain gifts and opportunities were beyond their reach, or even their children's. Joyce Carol Oates, a writer who knows upstate New York well, once posited that all people are artists who get turned into consumers. The giant supermarkets that bloomed in my childhood, offering women abundant choices based on color and form, made Oates's opinion visible. The power to choose and the opportunity to enjoy themselves, denied women in so many crucial areas of their lives, were lavishly available to them as consumers. Stores were the places where I saw most married women making decisions outside the home when I was young. Harriet Warren, functioning in her theater as artist, rebel, wife, and manager, dared to suggest that women could banish a few sacred cows without burning down the whole damn barn. Her two children were older than I, so I didn't know them, but my mother praised Harriet as a devoted mother. I know the family was close. In her widowhood, Harriet moved to the country to be near her grandchildren. Her marriage to George had lasted 'til death did them part. Meanwhile, more conventional unions in my parents' circle of acquaintances foundered and wrecked on some of the very rocks George and Harriet's seasonal bill of comedies and dramas tried to warn people about.

Yet they wrangled so fractiously at the theater that I, as a child, found it impossible to imagine how George and Harriet had ever fallen in love, much less how they stayed there. George was handsome but short, which may have curtailed his fondest professional hopes and made him cocky. I found this terribly attractive. He was also profane. He was the first person I ever heard say "bullshit," using the word variously as noun, adjective, and expletive. I have since learned it is an actor's fa-vorite, useful for paring odious obfuscation from both artistic work and business deals. I myself adopted it enthusiastically as a young actress; Curt Dempster, my teacher, identified most socially conditioned, middle-class behaviors as fulsome cow dung smothering the flowers of his students' true feelings. I heartily agreed and dropped my convent-school, debutante manqué bullshit to become a New York actor, proudly spontaneous and scatological. Then I arrived in Los Angeles, where people blanched when I swore. In the town where image is everything, women can act dirty, but we're expected to talk clean. After censoring my vocab-ulary for years, until I ended up sounding like Donna Reed, I find the memory of George Warren swearing in Smugtown goddamn fucking liberating.

The couple alternated directing plays to spare each other the sole burden of theater management that would have crushed either's artistic spirit. When I vis-ited, George was usually in the office and Harriet in the theater, because she di-rected Mother's plays. One day I was in the lobby, inspecting, on tiptoe, the pro-duction pictures hanging there, when George stormed out of his office and stood in the double doors that lead to the house. He didn't see me. With half-glasses at the tip of his nose and hair sprouting Brillcreemed antennae, he began fulminat-ing to Harriet:

"Harriet?!! What is this goddamn bill for gels doing on my desk? I paid these bullshit people! This is bullshit! Did you put this on my desk?"

Harriet screamed back: "That'sa *new* bill, Geowge. I had ta replace the gels you melted durin' *Cadillac* becuzh you nevah ordehed 'em. So jes pay it an' stop botherin' me! Ah don' disturb *you* while *yoah* directin', Geowge. If ah did you'd have mah *hayud!*"

George retreated. He wore blue jeans, which no other grown-up man I knew did, and they were tight. In my mind's eye, as I see him reenter his office, I con-fess my memory lingers on his compact behind, which he swung with such bandy-legged sass I think I understood, from that day on, that it was an important clue to the Warren's mysterious relationship.

There was a photo in the theater lobby of the couple starring in *The Magnificent Ambersons*. It showed Harriet in hooded white silk, George in white tie and tails. They stood before a stage crowd, hands clasped, arms upraised. Radiant in their element—costumed and observed—our own Lunt and Fontanne have stopped arguing. I think of the picture now as the portrait of the Warren's marriage, the way it looked to them from the inside, where the actor's audience never goes away.

The theater was perhaps the most democratic institution I knew in my child-hood. Only de facto segregation, which would finally explode Rochester in its 1964 race riots, prevented the players from seeming entirely inclusive, but it drew more different kinds of people than any Rochester venue I visited. As producers, the

Warrens cannily garnished stronger fare like *Come Back Little Sheba*, or plays by that pinko, Arthur Miller, with warmed-over Broadway comedies and genre chestnuts like *Spider's Web*. This, along with community theater's basic draw of presenting familiar, everyday people in unfamiliar settings—your dentist as a murderer, the postman as a romantic lead—attracted eager audiences. The theater building was a renovated church, which seemed fitting, for the Warrens were in our midst like missionaries, bringing theater to passionate converts and local devotees while adapting to our local customs. The rest of the city respected, suspected, or neglected the Warrens; but everyone knew they weren't like the natives.

Which is another reason why Mother hesitated before saying "yes" to Harriet about *Spider's Web*. I was a sheltered child in many ways, and Mother worried about exposing me to the unrepentantly secular and adult environment that was the community theater at night, in rehearsal for a major production.

She consulted my father of course, who cloaked his ancestral distrust of the theater in purely practical concerns, like the potential neglect of my homework and the disruptive driving to and fro. Mother was unperturbed by such trivia. Once she'd decided that Harriet, friend and fellow-mother, could be trusted to shield me from questionable influences at the theater, only one obstacle to her wholehearted permission remained. But it was a formidable one, springing from a prejudice deeper and more virulent than anything lurking in my father's breast about actors. Not many people knew about it, because she sensed it was irrational and she tried to keep it hid. I knew about it because I watched television with her.

My mother hated child actors.

Every time another "precocious miniature adult"—her words—appeared on our Zenith, she'd mutter, caustically, that television was being ruined by them; they couldn't act, their false sophistication was repugnant, and their childhoods were being ruined by their pushy mothers. I liked child actors; I dentified with them. When I protested, she'd try to restrain herself. But comments leaked out, and when they did, though she'd strenuously exempt me and every child she'd actually *worked* with at the community theater from her blanket disapproval, I was reminded of the truth. My mother thought child actors were lousy versions of both things they purported to be: children and actors.

I suspect now that Brooklyn was to blame. She'd grown up there during the Depression, and according to her eighth-grade diary, she'd seen two movies a week at an age when I was lucky to see six a year. She not only saw more movies than I did as a girl but probably more child actors. Broadway and radio stardom were just across the bridge, and Brooklyn mothers promoted talented offspring for fun and profit. Mother had told me often enough about her days on a girls' basketball team to reveal that she was fiercely competitive. I suspect she may have been jealous of kids whose parents sponsored them in the activity that interested her even more than sports: show business.

It's wild conjecture, but geography colludes, and her depth of feeling begs a deep-rooted explanation. "My mother was the most selfless person I've ever known!" she once sighed to me, with such a curious mixture of resentment and regret that I pondered the subtext for years. She'd obviously regretted that her mother missed many pleasures by being so self-sacrificing, and she perhaps resented the high standard that had been set for her to follow. But could it be that she also resented Nana for lacking the killer instinct necessary to be a stage mother? With a ruthless parent, Nancy Colgan coulda been a contender.

"Sing out, Louise!" was her most bitter self-mockery, sing-songed in flattest Flatbush whenever she feared her advice about my acting veered beyond the naturally maternal and into the realm of stage motherhood. She was positively phobic about it.

Ambition is stronger than phobia, I discovered the day I boarded a plane without fear because it was taking me to Hollywood for a screen test. Thwarted ambition packs a particular punch, and it's possible Mother's repressed dreams of glory were what swamped all rational objections and provoked her "yes" to Harriet. In one merciful stroke, she soothed her own childhood frustrations and prevented them from being passed down to me.

My auditioning carried a condition, one that had garnered my father's consent: the role, if I won it, would be alternated between me and another actress. The demands of a production schedule would then fall more lightly on both little actresses and their families.

This idea appalled me. Not only would I have to share my glory, but if my parents had their way, I'd have to share it with Genevieve McCauley, the girl across the street. Our parents were better friends than Genevieve and I. She was a year younger, which made me consider her my hopeless inferior. We already carpooled to acting and ballet class; I knew convenience had hatched the plan, and I resented that my parents had blithely risked my fate by tying it to an immature child's. I knew *I* could win the role at an audition—but could Genevieve?

By the night the McCauleys came across the street to discuss the plan over a nightcap, I was praying to see it adopted. Genevieve could memorize lines and follow blocking, two crucial elements of a community theater performance. She would be a safe choice. I'd carry her in on my coattails at the audition, and afterward, the mere adequacy of her performance would only highlight the splendidness of mine. Her parents had to let her audition!

I stretched out on my bedroom floor to scry my fate in the adults' conversational swells and troughs below me. When the talk dissolved to laughter, propelling my father to the kitchen for a final round of drinks, I knew I'd won my chance. Those weren't the sounds of people preparing to cruelly disappoint their children! I leapt into bed when I heard my mother approach the foot of the stairs and composed myself in pretend sleep as she ascended.

"Are you awake?" she whispered from the doorway, so clearly expecting me to be that my fakery felt disloyal. But I'd committed to it; I had to stir and moan before sitting up, a performance which, I saw by her face in the hall light, my mother attended with more patience than credulity.

"You can audition!" she exulted in a whisper. "The answer is yes!"

She came to the bed, and I fell into her arms. Her happiness increased mine exponentially, but in our hug, too, there passed a curious caution. The extent of this joy is best kept to ourselves, it seemed to say. Being taken to the stage is a fate unseemly when it appears too devoutly to be wished by women happy at hearth and home.

Such fate was my ruling passion. I knew eventually I'd have to go professional.

o

At the audition, even the child who looked like Patty McCormack in *The Bad Seed* didn't frighten me, because Harriet greeted me like a favorite. I climbed the rehearsal steps to the stage with the confidence born of talent and a sudden, happy intuition that nepotism counted in the theater. I was right; that day I won the part. Other days, in other theaters, Garfields and Arnazes would show up to trump me.

Genevieve was cast, too, and we embarked on rehearsal schedules so delicately arranged by Harriet that our paths seldom crossed. I forgot about alternating until opening week, when a cast photo featuring Genevieve, not me, appeared in the paper.

I was devastated. Mother tried to soothe me by saying the publicity was an effect of Harriet's decision to split the assignments of opening night and press preview, about which Mother had tried to warn me by opining that Harriet's decision paid a secret compliment to me. I didn't understand it, and it couldn't make up for not having my picture in the paper. All performances were the same, but publicity was special. It made you famous.

Oh, blissful ignorance, to be so democratic about performances and audiences! Eventually, actors learn all the differences; we become experts at who's in the house. Is there a reviewer? Will the producer be in the room? Is the show network or syndication? Slated for foreign or domestic release? Shakespearean actors were advised not to play to the king, and a preferential option for the proletariat is still an actor's wisest approach. High salary quotes, good ratings, box office receipts, dressing room deals in our contracts, and the blandishments of well-meaning people who really don't understand what we do, or what we require to do it well, are cold comfort once we've lost the sheer joy of showing off to whomever's watching.

Disillusioned actors who fail to rediscover this joy begin to die, often going on real-life emotional rampages in their death throes. Lucrative careers may be conducted by the actor's empty shell, but the actor's artistic spirit has departed for sustenance elsewhere. It's pleasure and play that drive us. People think it's egotism, but our ego is so cruelly battered by a career that no actor could sustain one on the rewards to pride alone. Play and pleasure are balm to our wounded egos; without them, we die.

At age twelve, I found pleasure and play galore in *Spider's Web.* Waiting to rehearse was almost as good as rehearsing; I'd do my homework in the Green Room and listen to the adults talk. Being in their company elevated the experience beyond any acting I'd ever done. This was show business. And high art as well, because Agatha Christie's dialogue demanded a British accent. *Spider's Web* sounded ludicrous in upstate New York-ese.

My inner-ear model for the Queen's English, as spoken by the Queen, was Peter Lawford, whose inflections I'd absorbed during my devotion to his weekly TV series, "The Thin Man." For those who can't summon the audio Lawford, Robin Leach is a decades-later example of what I sounded like as Pippa. Leach is Australian, but Lawford, despite his Hollywood resume, was English. Lest we forget, there is Joe Kennedy, Sr.'s reaction to daughter Pat's engagement to remind us: "It's bad enough my daughter's marrying an actor, but does it have to be a British actor?" The Boston clan may have disagreed with my forebears about politics, but on actors they were in accord.

We had a real Englishwoman in the cast, Beryl Crown, whose ovaled vowels and clipped consonants provided a ballast. By opening night *Spider's Web* sounded at least as credible as one of those Hollywood bible movies in which American film stars spouted ersatz British to blend in with a classically-trained international cast.

Memorization came easily to me, so my work as Pippa, besides developing my dialect, lay in planning how to say each of my lines. I concentrated on *how* because I didn't always know *why.* Most child actors struggle with an information deficit. Adult character motivation is inscrutable to them. I think the plot of *Spider's Web* included sleeping around, from which both Pippa and I, the preteen playing her, were sheltered. Consequently, I "aaah'd" onstage every night to a murder solution that completely evaded me. Similarly, I've watched child costars rattle off a dozen different linereadings to a running TV camera. An editor will choose the one that conveys the impression of a child wise beyond its years. As Pippa, all I knew was that I discovered the dead body, and my play-mother became increasingly distant. These two upsets guided me to my emotional peak: a suicide threat, which I made to my mother. I don't remember why, but I remember how: I walked downstage, wrists extended, fists clenched, veins up, and bleated "Oi shall slit moi wrists end keel moiself!" in Peter Lawfordese. I think it was Harriet who suggested this blocking, after I'd upstaged myself one too many times playing the moment passionately to my mother. Once I faced the footlights, I was in heaven; I probably recall the line because it's branded on my brain by their glare. All nearby memory cells were overexposed and burnt out.

I like to think I was good as Pippa, but two extant publicity photos worry me. I can only hope they're not truly representative of the kinetic performance; I've never been good at posing for stills. The first shows me with my stage mother, Gisela Fritzching. I stand hand to mouth as she looks on in horror. I was supposed to be gasping in fright, but in fact I appear to be either yawning or snacking, which makes Gisela's look inexplicable unless she knows I'm about to eat poison. The second photo shows me and Genevieve, our grim little faces illumined by a candle whose holder we both grip. I remember the photographer had to spend some time arranging our hands symmetrically, once it became clear neither little actress was willing to relinquish control of the prop.

Alternating was a valuable early lesson to me that, no matter how huge an actor's inner vacuum, none of us can suck up all of the glory all of the time. Sooner or later, especially in successful careers that generate more offers than one actor can accept, an alternate must be found. Harrison Ford, meet Kevin Costner. Ally Sheedy, Demi Moore. Meryl, Glenn. Mimi—Ms. Allison LaPlaca, whose fine work has garnered me much praise from people on the street. Alternates often rise above their originals, but even when they don't, they teach actors to share.

My mother seemed to think my performance was good. She entered the women's dressing room, site of so many postcurtain triumphs of her own, and beamed at me, who'd taken her position.

"You really *listen* onstage!" she crowed. "You're alive *every minute,* even when you're not speaking! That's the mark of a real actor!"

Alive? Listening? I couldn't help feeling damned with faint praise—one could hardly avoid living or listening anywhere, much less onstage, where life was a hundred times more vivid than in reality! I worried that I'd become the object of Green Room Perjury. Mother had taught us all about it, how to devise discrete compliments to spare an actor's feelings. If the play were a dud or a performance lacking, such truths must *never* be told backstage. Praise for "listening" and "being alive" seemed just like the sort of equivocations Mother endorsed. But her face was unequivocal. I saw I'd impressed her. Her pallid observations were technical talk, by which she was doing me the honor of addressing me actor-to-actor. Forget about fan gush from me, she implied on her own turf. From now on, we're colleagues.

Her opinion, that staying alive onstage "even when you're not speaking" is the mark of a real actor, has proven profoundly true in my professional observation. "Real actors" have a sense of constant audience that makes us feel we are the center of attention regardless of where stage focus resides. This egotism gives us skin thick enough to withstand "all the rejection" that nonactors continually ask us how we endure. The sense of constant audience persists even in camera-work, when the camera is not on us. Still we feel the unseen eye. I've been told by crew members that they consider it the mark of a "real actor" to give the same performance off-camera as on. The sense of constant audience is not extinguished in "real actors" even when we realize no one ever attended us as assiduously as we'd hoped—even our own mothers.

The great comedian, actor, and performance artist Andy Kaufmann once said in an interview, "I don't care if the audience doesn't laugh, as long as I know the Divine Observer's smiling." I was profoundly moved by his name for this sense of constant audience; Divine Observation is often all actors have, especially in auditions, where our work can be miserably attended by observers who are not yet divine, despite their life-giving power over our lives and careers.

Another reason I listened tenaciously onstage, at age twelve, was that I knew everybody's lines. I tracked them carefully to ensure that I never lost my turn to speak, even if the adults veered perilously off text.

Child actors, their minds uncluttered by daily anxieties that plague grown-ups, easily memorize whole scenes, whole plays to which they're exposed in rehearsal. My comprehensive knowledge of our script made me think I could be of assistance to actors who struggled through "off-book" rehearsals. I hated to see them call "Line!" to the house, mired in agitation and defeat. Seeking to spare them, I took to hissing, cross-stage, opening words to lines so slow in coming I was sure they'd been forgotten. I was rewarded, not with the grateful smiles I'd anticipated, but pained looks and curt nods.

Harriet took me urgently aside.

"You musn't prompt the grown-ups, darlin'! Sometahms they'eh *actin'* in those pauzhes!"

Acting in the pauses? What an interesting idea!

Harriet spoke to me so rarely in private that her gentle reproof was all I needed to shut me up. In the pauses, a garden of behaviors bloomed that previously I'd quashed. I watched, amazed, as breasts heaved, trembling hands lit and extinguished cigarettes, glances were met and quickly avoided. Half the play was in the pauses! I was so glad Harriet had alerted me! Her constant refrain—"*PICK UP YOAH CUES!!!*"—gathered urgency as opening night approached, suggesting she had limited tolerance for the practice, but I was charmed and resolved to try it myself when I was older and more experienced.

o

The *Spider's Web* cast party was held in a home that announced, the moment I entered, that the Irish-Catholic, Republican norms by which I lived were mere cultural preferences, which the good theater folk of Smugtown did not universally embrace.

There were wall hangings.

In homes I knew, fabrics were employed as drapery, upholstery, carpet, or bedding, as if my people feared idle textiles, like idle hands, were the devil's workshop.

These exotic, ropy things seemed somehow suspect. They were matched by other signs of hedonistic excess: a long-looped shag carpet caught women's high heels and encouraged their owners to shuck their shoes and stand talking to companions while absently rubbing one stockinged foot against another. The living room was sunken, approached by three descending shag-carpeted stairs. Around its circumference ran a circular couch where people had flung themselves expansively or were huddled intimately with one another, wiggling unshod toes into the cushion-cracks. At the center of the room stood a fireplace with a flue shaped like the Tin Man's hat; the funnel rose into the ceiling and disappeared. I sat on the flagstone apron of this monument, next to some trays of hors d'oeuvres that weren't the Triscuits-and-cheddar, or even party-rye-and-Swiss, that I was used to. These were rolled and folded things, skewered on toothpicks and simmering in sauces. I tasted, and they were good. Adults approached me occasionally to compliment my performance. When they turned away for more lively conversation with their peers, I didn't mind. Theater people were as fascinating to watch offstage as they were on. I watched. More people took to the couch, lounging there until it took on the appearance of a public bed from which the party buzz rose like helium. I saw nothing overtly naughty, like the make-out scene Charles Nowicki's sister had staged with her hoody boyfriend while they'd been supposedly chaperoning our seventh-grade dance party, but after I'd eaten my fill of Swedish meatballs and shrimp rumaki, my mother led me away.

○

Robert Anderson, the famous playwright, premiered a new work of his, in the sixties, at the Rochester Community Players. Some organization in New York matched community theaters with established dramatists to give the playwrights a safe venue for works-in-progress and community theaters a taste of glory. Anderson got Rochester and Rochester got *The Days Between*, a brave, dark drama about marriage and failed dreams. Harriet directed, with my mother in the female lead.

Like most comediennes, Mother considered drama the actors' Holy Grail. She was thrilled to be doing one under the aegis of its living, famous author, and she was wonderful in the role. Even Robert Anderson said so, declaring he'd have trouble afterward imagining anyone else as the wife. His own, Theresa Wright, eventually played it in New York.

But many of Mother's fans came to *The Days Between* expecting comedy, never having bothered to read the reviews. Night after night, inappropriate laughs marred the early scenes, after which a palpable silence settled over pockets of the house, as if people felt hoodwinked into having attended something depressing and psychological. At the time most adults I knew considered Freudian psychology a wasteful indulgence of big city neurotics and navel-gazing movie stars. Having lived through the Depression and a war, they didn't see the point of wallowing in unpleasantness. They especially resented having to pay for the privilege.

Mother apologized to Robert Anderson, for the laughter and the silences. She need not have, he told her; the same thing would have happened in New York. Audiences laughed to avoid pain, he said. He *wanted* laughs in his dramas—he even wrote for some. Those that came in the wrong places were his fault, not hers, he assured her, and he was in Rochester precisely to find out where they were before the New York critics did. Greatly relieved that neither her unsuitability to the drama nor the excessive boorishness of her adopted town was to blame for the play's spotty reception, Mother was emboldened to confess to Robert Anderson that, in truth, comedies usually fared better than dramas at the Community Players box office.

So too in New York, the seasoned playwright agreed wearily; it was another reason why his play about a wife's abortion to keep her husband's dream of literary glory from drowning in domesticity was premiering on Meigs Street instead of Broadway.

In the warm glow of their mutual regret, Robert Anderson asked my mother, "What sort of comedies do your friends like?"

"Oh, lighter fare," she'd told him. "Something they can enjoy without too much thought after a few martinis on a Saturday night."

Shortly after that conversation, Mother and the playwright were standing in the theater lobby when George and Harriet began one of their famous altercations. George screamed to Harriet, and Harriet screamed back from the powder room, where she was scouring the sink for the evening's performance:

"Geowge, yew know ah can't heah you when the watuh's runnin'!"

Mr. Anderson's *You Know I Can't Hear You When the Water's Running* opened a few seasons later on Broadway with enough success to keep him out of the hinterlands for a while. Two of its characters were named George and Harriet. Its working title had been *Plays for a Saturday Night,* and it featured the first full-frontal male nudity in Broadway history when a naked man stepped onstage, dripping wet from the shower, to deliver the show's title line. Now *that's* something an audience can enjoy without too much thought. Especially after a few martinis on a Saturday night.

So it wasn't just my imagination. Our community theater was the stuff of legend.

6.

Tammy Grimes

Our whole family loved Broadway musicals. Like many suburban men of his time, my father was a closet conductor. He had a baton squirreled away in the piano bench, and he'd take it out on weekends to brandish to the hi-fi at volume ten, coaxing his will out of other men's orchestras.

He hated strings; classical music was "sawing" to him. Swing was his forte. He spent hours working imaginary dance gigs with Glenn Miller and Benny Goodman, eyes closed, losing himself in memories of college, law school, and his Manhattan courtship of my mother. But it was Broadway overtures that could make him cry.

He told me once, with tears in his eyes, that there was nothing in the world like the opening of a Gershwin musical. He'd been to a few, in his day, and his descriptions of the glittering crowd, the hush when the house lights dimmed, the excitement when the conductor tapped his baton in the dark—"Just imagine, you knew you were about to hear a *whole new score* by Gershwin!"—were so vivid I recall the images as if they were imprinted by my own experience. He rued that I might never know such a thrill in the theater, because smaller orchestras, lesser composers, and recorded music had robbed Broadway of the power to deliver it.

He took us to Broadway anyway. As each of us children fell in love with some particular cast album, he'd arrange for that child to accompany him on a business trip to New York and we'd go to see the show. Even my nine-year-old brother's sidewalk critique of *Oliver*—"It wasn't as good as the record"—confirming, as it did, my father's worst fears, didn't prevent Daddy from doing what he believed was his paternal duty.

It was to his credit that we had so many Broadway albums, played them often, and found them potent. We listened with the same absorption today's children reserve for their favorite videos, and our imaginations produced accompanying spectacles unlimited by budget, union requirements, or the properties of matter. Our selections ranged from early Gershwin shows to period oddities like "The Nervous Set (The Beatnik Musical!)," many of which Daddy had bought to plunder. He and Mother, the Comden and Green of their suburban set, were often asked to write shows for their clubs and organizations. They'd provide book and lyrics and rob some unwitting composer of his score. The hilarity that drifted up from our living room, late nights when they pursued this avocation, was further testimony, for me, to Broadway's powers of fun, magic—and sex.

My brother Danny, at age three, worshipped the album jacket of "Gentlemen Prefer Blondes" as a totemic object. He fell in love with Carol Channing's singing voice, thinking it belonged to the cartoon flapper on the record cover. My mother, failing to grasp the particularity of this attachment, wrote Miss Channing for an autographed photo. When it arrived she showed it to Danny, thinking he'd be thrilled; he wasn't. Understanding that the "little girl from Little Rock" wasn't his cute cartoon flapper, but the grown-up lady in the picture, was all too much for a child in the Oedipal stage; it ended the affair.

I achieved rapture in the Broadway theater. For the actress-to-be, destiny smiled the day I saw Tammy Grimes in *The Unsinkable Molly Brown.*

I'd learned all of Tammy's numbers and was performing them for anyone who dared share the living room with me and the hi-fi by the time Daddy bought the tickets and arranged our trip. Once the date was definite, I made preparations of my own. I wrote to Tammy Grimes and told her I was coming.

Anyone who's ever gotten a reply to a fan letter knows the thrill of finding it glittering like treasure in the flotsam and jetsam of one's ordinary daily mail. I knew what was inside the manila envelope with the New York postmark before I opened it and did so with trembling fingers, pulling out the glossy photo to discover there was something more: a typewritten letter inviting me to meet Tammy Grimes backstage after the show. It was signed in the same looping hand that graced the bottom of her picture.

I was delirious. Any reply would have been heady, but a *personal invitation* from Tammy Grimes to meet her backstage—! I was intoxicated for weeks.

Consequently I don't remember the time leading up to the trip, or anything of the trip itself, until the first moment I set foot in a Broadway theater. There, in the lobby of the Winter Garden, memory wakes up, as if I, like Rip Van Winkle, had previously been dreaming some long, dull, upstate New York dream.

"Winter Garden" is a beautiful name, conjuring trellises of scarlet roses dripping with white snow; walls, statuary, and greens mantled in ermine shot through with diamonds. The theater lived up to its name. The wall of gold-bordered, mirrored doors in the lobby dazzled me, reflecting our buzzing matinee crowd to infinity. Inside the house, where the buzz was muted to an intense thrum, red velvet walls bloomed with gold filigree everywhere I looked. The sight made me drunk; Rochester's Eastman Theater, where I saw *The Nutcracker* ballet at Christmastime, was famous, with its enormous crystal chandelier, but it was dour compared to this. The Eastman's interior was blue. The Winter Garden's was red.

When the overture began, I noticed, with a tinge of disappointment, that it seemed faster than the record. I wanted to savor the tunes that whizzed by. Later, when I performed in *Grease* on Broadway, I discovered my childhood perception was probably accurate; matinee overtures are often played fast, because daytime audiences, according to popular wisdom, skew older and younger than evening crowds and therefore need help staying attentive and awake. This rationale always seemed spurious to me. It was cast and musicians, I noticed, who often needed goosing at the matinees, and speed rarely helped. If anything, it encouraged actors to "phone it in"—our universal term for a lackluster performance. I suspected the twelve year olds in the house always recognized the hurry for what it was: a shoddy substitute for real vitality. I hoped those seeing a Broadway musical for the first time weren't too disappointed.

My momentary disillusion at *Molly Brown* vanished the moment the curtain rose, bringing the set I'd glimpsed in black-and-white on the album cover to colorful, heart-stopping life! Actor-singer-dancers playing Molly Brown's hillbilly brothers yowled at us over the footlights with unimaginable energy! Tammy entered almost immediately, diving and skidding across the men's outstretched arms!

An ovation burst from the house like a cannonade. I jumped; there's no entrance applause on the record. Daddy leaned over to whisper it was customary to applaud the star's first appearance, and I joined in, thrilled to participate in theater tradition, and welcome Tammy with all my heart! She gave the house a little look of surprise; if her shock was less genuine than mine, it was a charming deception, and the audience was hers.

She sang "The Ballad of Molly Brown"—"I'm gonna learn to read and write/I'm gonna see what there is ta see!" with all the ambition I felt crowing in my own soul. But "Stars Shining on My Own Brass Bed" was my favorite, when Tammy nestled in the arms of the impressively rectangular Harve Presnell and sang with the most touching little catch in her throat! If her line near the end of one scene, read from the inside of the ring Johnny gave her—"Always remember two things: I love you, and the name of the bank!"—seemed a bit overacted, whooped across the footlights instead of spoken to her fellow actors, she justified her choice by bringing down the house.

In *Grease*, I was often chided for leaning too hard on laugh lines, especially at matinees. Maybe I'd indelibly imprinted Tammy's lesson; maybe I've always had an instinct to pander. But I thought then, and do now, that it's better to err in the audience's direction by giving too much rather than too little. Less is More, but Not Enough never charms me.

After the curtain fell, I walked up the program-strewn aisle with my father, feeling the real world slowly return. But it was not to be for long. Outside, Daddy guided me expertly through the crowd to the stage door.

The stage door! It was right on the street! How could this be? I wondered. It was so accessible! I marveled at the people hurrying by, oblivious to the proximate magic beyond this deceptively ordinary portal. If I lived here, I thought, how I'd linger and haunt!

A fan I attracted during *Grease* used to wait for me outside the stage door, giving me roses and little gifts when I emerged. I was always touched, remembering my awe outside the Winter Garden. If fan-worship has become a problem in our culture, and it has, perhaps it's a symptom of how hungry we are for proof of what we correctly intuit: that life is magnificent, beautiful, and extraordinary. Celebrities create the illusion that they are magnificent, beautiful, and extraordinary, and fans are attracted to them to feel the same in their presence. Children should be introduced to the magnificent, beautiful, and extraordinary in their own daily lives, around people they love; then perhaps they will be less willing to surrender their own magnificence to self-appointed others. We will always have celebrities; royalty is an ancient idea, and projection a delight of the mind. But people can better learn from their illusions if they are more aware of, and less overwhelmed by, the process of creating them. For that, we need teachers, like Tammy Grimes was to me.

I learned that day, and later in New York, that the seeming accessibility of the stage door was an illusion. Like most doors in show business, it was well-guarded; but my father and I were writ in the book of St. Peter of the Winter Garden, an elderly gent of a type found at stage doors wherever union jurisdiction still holds sway. He directed us up a flight of stairs, saying we'd find Miss Grimes's dressing room at the top. We did; there was a shiny gray door bearing the legend "Miss Grimes," and, above it, a painted a gold star.

At that point my father explained he would see me inside, then wait in the hall while I visited with Tammy alone; after all, he pointed out, it was to me she'd sent her invitation. I was much too nervous to know whether this plan was entirely amenable to me, but it was too late to change it. Daddy had knocked on the door, and it was opening.

Despite my frequent adorations of Tammy's photo, I hadn't the faintest idea what she would really look like offstage. I gasped in the pale face of the woman who greeted us and was preparing to give her my total obeisance, when she said quickly:

"I'm Dorothy."

I blushed. She smiled. My father stepped into the conversational breach.

"My name's Gerry Kennedy," he declared, "and this is my daughter, Mimi, who has an appointment to see Miss Grimes after the show."

"Of course," Dorothy agreed. "We've been expecting her."

Expecting me! She opened the door wide, and Daddy and I entered the tiny room. There was a couch and coffee table tucked beside the door, and a costume rack opposite, laden with capes and coats Tammy had worn in the show. Thrilled, I stared at these, expecting them to breathe, while I heard Daddy tell Dorothy he'd wait outside.

Dorothy smiled complicitly. I knew the adults were conspiring to preserve my dignity, and I was grateful, but it only reminded me of how little dignity I possessed on my own, which made me feel suddenly young and awkward. When my father left me alone with Dorothy, I felt very young indeed. I'd already mistaken her for the great star. How else would I blunder? I longed for Tammy to appear and end my uncertainty, but I didn't want our meeting ever to end, so I had to be content that it hadn't begun.

Dorothy invited me to sit on the couch. The space between it and the coffee table was very narrow, but I managed to navigate it and sit without bumping my shins, or doing anything else childish and embarrassing. It was difficult, with my pounding heart swaying my body at every step.

Dorothy went to an inner door, which I knew must lead to Tammy's dressing room. I was dying to look, but averted my gaze lest I appear rude. "Will you be all right?" she asked.

"Yes, thank you," I murmured. How could I not be all right, I wanted to say, with the prospect of what was in store?

She opened the door. I glimpsed heaven. Tammy's dressing room was white-hot, ablaze with makeup bulbs. Telegrams were pasted to glittering mirrors that reflected flower bouquets in glorious profusion. Everything sparkled and shone.

A headless figure passed the doorway, obscuring my view. It was a tower of white petticoats, and Tammy's inimitably gravelly voice issued from within:

"Dorothy, can you help me out of here?"

I caught a strong whiff of flowers as the door closed.

Trembling, I waited, carefully arranging myself on the couch in preparation for her entrance. Moving to the edge of my seat—I'd been taught ladies only used the first third of their chairs—I crossed my ankles and tucked them at a graceful angle beneath me. Smoothing my skirt over my knees, I draped it to each side, forming a half-circle. I held this position until it became unbearable. Then I shifted. Still she didn't come. Eventually I rearranged myself several times, hoping movement would bring her the way adults thought lighting a cigarette would inevitably bring the bus.

Suddenly the door opened, and I stood up. When I saw her, I saw how impossible it was to mistake Tammy Grimes for anyone else. She was a Star, by destiny and design.

"Hello," she cooed, "I'm Tammy."

Dorothy, I realized, must have told her about my confusion at the door. The thought that my stupidity prompted this absurd self-introduction from my idol grieved me so much that I blushed, and blood pounded in my ears, deafening me momentarily until I heard Tammy Grimes's voice saying my name.

"And you," she said, "must be Mimi."

"Mimi." Everything settled. In Tammy Grimes's voice, "Mimi" sounded like a remarkable person to be. I was she. For the first time that I could remember in my twelve-year-old life, I acknowledged my name, and self, with pride. I reached for Tammy's extended hand.

Her hand, and everything about her, was surprisingly petite! She wore a coral kimono, and—oh flame-tipped actresses!—her hair was red. So it had been on-stage, but now it was quite tamed from Molly Brown's various dos. In hindsight, I realize the show required a series of wigs, and some of the time Tammy had kept me waiting had probably been spent trying to revive her wilted locks into something presentable to a young fan with glorified expectations.

"Please, sit down," she said. I did. She sat right beside me. Our knees were touching. I became even more remarkable, sitting next to Tammy Grimes as if we were old friends.

"I'm so glad you could come. We'll have ourselves a nice little visit."

As if coming had been some sort of inconvenience for me!

"I hope you enjoyed the show," she said. "Did you?"

Of course I did! I realized I had to speak, and when I did, I gushed. Or think that I gushed. Now that I've had experience meeting young girls who've just seen me perform, I know that to Tammy, every word I uttered might have seemed to be my last.

"You wrote a marvelous letter," she said, trying to draw me out. "Did you know how good a letter you'd written?"

I shook my head and smiled, pleased.

"Well, it was. One of the best letters I've ever gotten. You're a very good writer, I should think."

This was more than I wanted to hear on the subject. I suddenly realized that if Tammy Grimes couldn't see me as an actress, I would have to go home and die.

"But you wrote that you want to be an actress."

Relief! "Yes."

"And you said you had some questions to ask me."

Evidently I'd said so in my letter; at that moment, I couldn't think of one.

"Well, I don't know if I can answer them all, but you may ask." She waited. "Why don't you tell me about your acting. Can you?"

That unlocked me, and my story poured out. My mother was an actress at the community theater, I told her, where I took acting classes. I'd also been in some of its productions. I acted at my school too—I was becoming voluble when Dorothy entered with a tea tray. Tammy stood to help her set it down, apologizing for the interruption.

"I'm sorry," she purred, "I've had Dorothy bring tea because I must take it after every show to soothe my throat. I told her to set a cup for you, but I don't know if American girls take tea. English girls do, of course, but I'm not sure about here. Shall I pour you some?"

I was determined to be rare and British and take tea, which had never attracted me in the least. As Dorothy retreated, I said yes, thrilled to be sharing in the actress's after-show ritual. Pouring, Tammy called out:

"Dorothy? You know those cookies someone brought us last night—I think there are some left by those plates. Do you see them? If you do, would you put some on plate and bring them out? There's a dear!"

She turned to me. "I'll bet you'll have cookies for sure. That's the best thing about tea, isn't it? Cookies!"

I froze, knowing there was no way I could manage to eat a cookie at this time. Not only wasn't I hungry and doubted I'd ever be hungry again, but the thought of eating—the crumbs clinging to my lips, the shards falling down the front of my dress to ambush me later when I stood up, the unsightly mastication—no. It was out of the question.

Still, I nodded that cookies were the best thing about tea, fervently hoping that Dorothy would fine none. The prospect of chewing sped up the interview.

I'd known, when I'd planned this conversation in my head, that my family's prejudice against professional acting was so strong I'd have to emerge from meeting Tammy with support for my ambition and ammunition against their objections. "Tammy did thus-and-so," I would tell them, "and so will I, following in her footsteps." With this in mind, I posed what I considered to be the imminently crucial question:

"How old were you when you decided to become an actress?"

Tammy thought for a while. "I don't know," she said slowly, "that *I* ever *decided*, as such."

This was an inauspicious beginning. We had to decide things in our family, especially something as important as what you were going to be when you grew up.

"It was just something I always did, from a very early age. You know—people were always watching me and saying things like, 'Oh, look, Tammy's gotten under the table' or 'Look at the funny face Tammy's making.' And they seemed to think I was amusing, so I just kept doing these things, and after a while I got used to it, so that when I got older, I suppose it just seemed a natural thing, to me and to everyone else, that I should go onstage. Yes…. So I think it wasn't a matter so much of me deciding as it was rather a decision that was made for me. It was the way people responded to me that made me become an actress."

Dumbstruck, I recognized everything Tammy Grimes was talking about! I too had been the unwitting object of others' amusement when I was young. I too had continued entertaining them, because I enjoyed the attention. For me, too, it seemed natural that I should go onstage. I wanted to shout for joy—by Tammy Grimes's measure, I was *already* an actress!

Dorothy entered with a plate of cookies, which Tammy ignored completely. I realized cookies were really only the best thing about tea for children; if I didn't eat one, Dorothy's labor, and Tammy's thoughtfulness, would be in vain. I picked up a cookie and bit.

"Well, you still have time to decide, " Tammy concluded. "How old are you?"

I stashed sugary cud in my cheek to reply, "Twelve." Tammy gasped.

"Twelve??!!"

Her shock may have been slightly disingenuous, like her surprise about her entrance applause, but I was wildly flattered anyway, enough to swallow and ask, "How old did you think I was?"

"I thought at least sixteen! And might have believed thirteen...but never twelve! My goodness, you are a mature young lady. Your parents must be very proud."

I'd gone into that dressing room a little girl, but I'd be coming back a star.

Dorothy stuck her head in to announce the time, and Tammy thanked her. After asking Dorothy for a paper towel to wrap the cookies in, she stood up. Our time was over.

She explained that she had to rest her voice before the evening show, doctor's orders, and asked if someone had brought me. When I said my father, who was waiting outside the room, she told me to bring him in; I rose and opened the door. I can still see him, silhouetted by a window at the end of the hall. He turned with a hearty energy that makes me feel, in hindsight, that he'd just gotten there, and that he'd spent most of his time listening, at the slightest distance.

When he came in the room, Tammy extended her hand and introduced herself again, again absurdly unnecessary, but all the more gracious, I saw, watching the two adults. Daddy was excited, despite his history of croquet with Harpo Marx and sitting at the Round Table. When she sang my praises to him, he beamed; I saw he was not immune to her flattery, and somehow this delighted me. Dorothy entered with a paper napkin, gave it to Tammy, smiled at my father, and withdrew. "You didn't get to eat these here," Tammy said, wrapping the cookies, "so you must take them back to your hotel for a treat."

I took the napkin, and my father thanked her. He opened the door. When I turned for a last look, Tammy was still smiling at me.

"It was a great pleasure to meet you, Mimi," she said. "And good luck in whatever you choose. But if you choose the theater, just remember that it needs good writers, too."

Outside, my father hailed a cab. He must have asked me about the conversation, and I must have told him as much as I could, but the fact is, it has taken me more than twenty-five years to recollect and fully appreciate my meeting with Tammy Grimes. It has only become clear in the writing of it.

I never ate the cookies. I desperately wanted to keep one, and thought it might be possible with a coating of shellac, but no one in my house knew how to shellac, and Daddy didn't want perishables in our luggage. I carefully placed the cookies in the hotel wastebasket, and packed the napkin. But it was too generic to withstand years as a keepsake, and one day, when it had become more soiled than significant, it, too, was thrown out.

●

My mother named me "Mary" in fulfillment of a promise she'd made to the Virgin that she'd name her third child Mary if I turned out to be a girl. My father nicknamed me "Mimi" for a reason so deeply buried in his subconscious that it threatened, like the sunken Titanic, never to be exhumed. The world eventually glimpsed the doomed ship in photos, and I glimpsed the origin of my nickname one night, when I was twenty-eight years old, at the Westbury Music Fair.

I've always known myself as "Mimi." Only one strict great-aunt, certain nuns who abhorred my pagan diminutive, and my mother when scolding, called me "Mary." I preferred my nickname. It was fun and unique. No one else had it, yet everyone did, because they called themselves "me." "Me-me" was twice the normal person. My name made me big to myself, but cute and lovable to adults —the best of both worlds.

There was a song called "Mimi" that people often sang when we met. "Mimi," they'd warble in an accent, "you fohnny leetle sohnny leetle Mimi, am I zee guy?" I learned eventually that Maurice Chevalier, the dapper French chanteur, had popularized the song in two movies. I asked my father, when I was about ten, if the song had been his inspiration for my name.

"No, no," he said, looking hurt that I'd think him so cornily derivative. Then, sheepish, he admitted: "Although it was between 'Mimi' and 'Amy' because of that Ray Bolger song."

We had the Ray Bolger record—"Once in love with Amy, always in love with Amy." I liked it so much I was briefly sorry Amy hadn't won out. To inspire undying love and have the same name as a character in *Little Women* to boot, seemed much better than being "Funny little good for nothing Mimi." But the verdict was in: Chevalier had nothing to do with me.

"I think," Daddy had concluded that conversation, squinting heavenward as if that's where memory had fled, "I just chose Mimi because I liked the name."

And that's where the matter rested, for eighteen years. When I became an actress, my father wasn't pleased. Occasionally, even after I'd begun my career in New York, he'd tried to dissuade me.

"Even if you reach the top of your profession," he sighed to me once over dinner in a Manhattan tavern, "where will you be?" I cited Jane Fonda, an actress who used her position to affect politics, but he, being a Republican lawyer, was unimpressed. I forgave his misgivings, and attributed them to his unresolved feelings about forsaking his own creative career, the editing and writing he might have done if he hadn't opted for the security of Harvard Law School.

Once he called a college performance of mine "an evening of unmitigated embarrassment." Though I knew the student script was clunky and my performance overwrought, I'd been terribly hurt, mainly by his failure to recognize his power to wound. He'd been full of encouragement when I was young, and he knew it. That's probably why he was so severely discouraging as I got older, and my commitment gathered strength.

Like many adults, my father thought early childhood's play was just that: play, which left no lasting mark beyond fond memories. But my earliest memory of him was powerfully formative; he used to sit me on the living room couch to hear "A Bushel and a Peck" from the cast album of *Guys and Dolls*. I was interested in anything that had "dolls" in the title, and the lyric which he thought would especially appeal to me—"The cows and chickens are going to the dickens!"— did. When he urged me to sing along, I proudly proved I knew the number by heart; I even squeaked in the places where the singers on the record squeaked.

He was delighted. Many nights when he got home too late to see us children before bedtime, he'd wake me up to perform the song for him in the living room. Daddy's approval is the lodestar of many an actor's performance, and I learned to shine in the number.

My mother ended most of these sessions by calling, from the top of the stairs, "Gerry!" in a stern, low voice. He would shrug, and I'd go to bed. Those moments were more loaded than I knew; it was, I think, a rough patch in their marriage. He was flying often to Washington, working for Senator Ken Keating, and bucking for his law partnership. He was also, no doubt, trying to escape a household of three young children. When he stayed downtown for dinner, he drank too much. I didn't know this then. What I knew, and imprinted, was that "A Bushel and a Peck" delighted my inaccessible parent and guaranteed his rapt attention.

As I grew up, I learned that Daddy frowned on the idea of professional acting careers; he spun office scenarios for his two daughters' futures, in which we won promotion over dull boys who owed their traditionally male positions to mere privilege. If he advised: "Wear your hair up during the week and take it down on weekends" or "Wear glasses at the office, then lose 'em for dates—you'll really wow 'em then," it was only because he didn't want us to be all work and no play. Two of his favorite fantasy careers for me were U.N. interpreter and architect.

"Mary" might have been either. It's a serious name, a grand old name—but the song that says so is a lugubrious crooner that doesn't quite tickle the synapses demanding to be aired as urgently as "Mimi" does. If I'd gone through life as Mary, I doubt I'd have been sung to as much, or indulged in as much fantasy play with people I'd barely met. It was the way people responded to her that had made her an actress, Tammy Grimes had said, and perhaps that's true for Mimi, too.

"Mary" means "bitter" in ancient Hebrew; it's the name of the Mother of God and every nun who ever taught me, by rule of their religious order. It is the name, I discovered in letters of my mother's, which I found after she died, by which I was known for the first two years of my life.

An infant's name is a key to her identity. When I lost mine, surely it caused a little death. "Mary" departed at age two, my aunts have told me. That's when Daddy changed my name, and everyone went along. Assuming a new moniker couldn't have been easy. I'd lost my boundary description just at the point when a toddler's boundaries are supposed to be secure enough to support autonomy, and the power of "No!" Surely my work to reintegrate under a new title was eased by my father's delight in it, the singing of strangers, and the sense that my new identity was a double one—me-me—that secretly included Mary, my original self. Unaddressed and sobered by want, she sank beneath conscious memory and held on.

The only other creature I knew, growing up, who bore the name Mimi was a neighbor's French poodle. The Barbie doll has reproduced, and her child is named "Baby Mimi." It is not a serious name. The twin phonemes lack ancient or sacred meaning. But to a child it meant "myself twice" and my new identity's secret twin could slip its fragile boundaries to become other "me's." I dwelled, imaginarily, inside other people at will, feeling welcomed by our shared onomato. I remember these feelings. They are, no doubt, the source of my talent for mimicry. Deconstruct that word if you will; "Mimi-cry." I think it suggests the truth, for me: performing has always relieved an inarticulate sorrow.

I was at Westbury Music Fair, the night I discovered my nickname's origin. I'd gone to see the black revival of *Guys and Dolls*, in which my friend Debbie Allen was playing the plum role of Adelaide. We'd starred together the previous spring on TV's "Three Girls Three," and I'd heard she was stopping the show nightly with "Adelaide's Lament." Happily I went to see.

I'd been to only one other production of the musical, a charming version performed by recovering teenage drug addicts at Phoenix House. They'd omitted "A Bushel and a Peck" and other numbers; I'd assumed lack of money and space prevented them from mounting the farm number in the rehab center's cafeteria. After seeing, that day, what a hard-boiled tale of urban romance Burrows had written, I wondered how a farm fit in at all in a show that already went as far afield as Cuba. I was looking forward, at Westbury Music Fair, to finding out.

Twenty-eight years of false assumptions detonated in an instant when I saw, in the playbill, that "A Bushel and a Peck" was sung in a nightclub! Of course! I thought, smiling at my literal toddler notions —farms are not Runyonesque! Then my eyes fell on another piece of program information that brought all mental processes to a reeling halt.

One of the singers of "A Bushel and a Peck" was named "Mimi." She was part of an ensemble known collectively as the "HotBox Girls."

My heart began pounding as I rifled the pages for historical information. I found it; the show had premiered on Broadway in April 1950. By the following fall, when I turned two, my father would have known about it. That's when my aunts said my name changed.

Evidently, my father had lifted the sobriquet from Burrows and Loesser, bestowed it on me at a critical stage in my development, and forgotten the source, in a stunning act of karmic kleptomania that had profound repercussions. That night at Westbury Music Fair, I forgave him. We'd both colluded happily with fate: he, by replacing my baptismal name with that of a hotbox girl, and I, by following my bliss, traveling the path of my pentimento identity right back to its place of origin: the Broadway stage.

*

My mother's relationship to musicals was perhaps the purest of our family, for she enjoyed them with the hungry admiration of one who couldn't sing.

She blamed her tunelessness on a nun choir-director who'd traumatized her in grade school. One hesitates to paint yet another religious woman with the same tired brush, but my mother told this story so often, and with such regret, that it was impossible not to believe the pain it inflicted. Over the years, I'd certainly observed the irreversibility of its effect.

The director was rehearsing the children for some school event when she began roving their midst, bending her veiled ear to each little voice. She'd stopped in front of my mother to announce in a voice loud enough for all to hear, "It's you, dear. You can't sing. From now on, just move your mouth."

My humiliated mother obeyed that nun for thirty-five years.

Then the Catholic bishops at Vatican II decided their flocks should sing in congregation, like Protestants do. This posed a terrible dilemma for my mother. Should she sing in church, parading her handicap publicly and possibly ruining mass for her fellow worshippers? Or remain silent, and seem obdurate and rebellious towards Vatican II reforms, which she really wasn't? It was not in my mother's nature to rebel, and she tried, bravely, to sing. Many Sundays I stood beside her and heard her heartbreaking growl roam the nether regions of the bass clef in a fruitless search for a suitable pitch from which to praise her God.

That's why my memory of her and *South Pacific* captures, it seems to me, some of the happiest days of her domestic life. Or maybe they were just some of the happiest of mine, because I lived them in the aura of her palpable joy.

She would place me with my toys on the living room rug, put *South Pacific* on the hi-fi, and open the windows wide to the backyard. Then she'd leave and reap-pear outside to hang up the laundry in the sunshine, where I could see and hear her as she sang "I'm as corny as Kansas in August," "I'm gonna wash that man right outta my hair," and even "Younger than Springtime" freely and for pleasure. It was the first, last, and only time I ever heard her do so in my life.

At her funeral, a bird lit on a branch outside an open window of the church. It was May, and the bird's glorious trilling came through the transept with the spring breeze. It began shortly after the service did and continued to the end.

If the good are granted any favors in eternity, especially in the first few days when they're just getting used to the idea, surely my mother was allowed to be that bird and sing, in the church where she'd never found a voice, over her own tuneless clay:

Rejoice at my liberation! What was lost has been found! In eternity, all things will be restored!

Part Two

EARTH

1962–1970

"Is this the way you always kiss?"

Anonymous Protestant boy, 1965

"To be an actress, you must be gaunt."

John Fisher, Smith Theater Professor, 1966

"Your perfect Computer Matchmate is Larry Dilg."

Operation Match, 1966

"For Irish Catholics, sex isn't just a mortal sin, it's the only mortal sin."

Kenneth Amor Connelly,
Smith English Professor, 1967

"What happened last night can never happen again."

Me, 1967

7.

Not-So-Easily-Assimilated

At seventeen, I'd begun to shed the parochial views bred by eleven years of Catholic education. Childhood acts like lobbing iceballs at Protestants outside their church, which I passed on my way to school, had ceased. These acts, like most religious terrorism, sprang from fear, specifically my fear that if Catholicism were not the One True Religion, as I'd been told, and salvation were possible outside it, as I'd not been told, then my fierce religious scruples and the suffering they'd caused me were in vain. Safer to lob the anger provoked by this thought onto Protestants with iceballs than to aim it at my own church, which could punish me with hellfire.

With maturity, the fear I'd learned in classrooms of sixty children, where threats of damnation achieved crowd control, waned. Security, nurtured by my parents in our comfortable suburban home, waxed. Images and experiences of the world outside our enclave had always been available to me in magazines that came into our home and trips the family took out. By early adolescence I'd learned that the Protestant threat wasn't spiritual, it was social. Catholics, with our mandatory compliance, sacraments, and apostolic succession, would surely be the creme de la creme in heaven. "In my Father's house there are many mansions," was a quote I'd often heard to explain God's varying rewards. The image of heaven as real estate, varying by location, location, location—proximate to God—made sense to me in Rochester. It settled the troubling question of what would happen to good non-Catholics when they died, and reflected my image of Rochester's proudly co-existing, but economically disparate, Catholic parishes. But if Catholics would enjoy the highest status in heaven, on earth we groveled beneath several Protestant sects on the American social scale.

I deduced this by participating in children's activities organized by the lofty circle into which my parents, pioneer Catholics, had ascended. They believed, like writers Evelyn Waugh and Wilfrid Sheed, that Catholics belonged in the upper classes and thereby improved them. They introduced us children to their new world, which we found less welcoming than they did, to teach us tolerance and develop our capacities for inclusion that we might prepare for adult lives in the dominant culture.

Tolerance and inclusion do not, as humanity's history of bloody religious war-fare illustrates, come naturally to the devout orthodox believer. I'd been taught that my one true religion was the core of my identity. My parents seemed to endorse this view by sending me to parochial school and approving most of what was done there to propagate it. Mingling with Protestants upset me. I saw up close that they were enviably free of worries about damnation that constantly plagued me. Their carefree lives seemed almost worth the lousy addresses awaiting them in heaven. After pitying Protestants all my life for having been born into their half-baked re-ligions, I began to envy them. This confused me.

This confusion, I learned, was endemic to my family. Our American branch had been founded by my great-grandfather Daniel on a cultural faultline between Irish immigrant and landed gentry. Leaving Ireland during the mid-nineteenth century potato famine, seventeen-year-old Dan had spent his Atlantic crossing sketching valves in the ship's hold where he was quartered. Landing in New York, he'd joined his brother and wife running a Brooklyn boarding house. But valves were his passion, and Daniel Kennedy reputedly landed a public works contract to manufacture a huge brass valve for the city of Brooklyn before having access to a means of production. He rented space in another man's foundry to do the job, then bought one of his own and made it a success.

Returning to Ireland to troll for a bride, he cut a swath through the ancestral counties, wearing a bowler hat and becoming known as "The Yankee." The Moran family, who lived on Five Church Island, had several daughters, the eldest of whom decked themselves out to lure The Yankee home for dinner after a county fair. When they succeeded, he promptly fell in love with their little sister, who'd been deemed too young for a fair, let alone marriage and emigration. Daniel re-turned to America without her, writing poetry the whole way, which, a hundred years later, my great-aunt Dora, the couple's youngest child, recited to me by heart as we sat in her Manhattan penthouse, weeping into Kleenexes.

When Elizabeth turned seventeen, she was allowed to leave home; Daniel sent her ticket for passage and they married and set up housekeeping in Brooklyn. He reportedly surprised her with the house on the Hudson, appearing one day in Brooklyn with a horse and cart, telling her to pack for their move the following morning to Coxackie, New York. She was stupefied, the story goes, but she man-aged, and the family grew in that great house on the river, living stylishly with ser-vants, automobiles, and fireworks for the foundry workers every Fourth of July.

Investments in Republican politics and prestigious educations for the children enhanced the family status, but trappings of wealth never touched the Old Sod's religion. Three generations later, the great house was a rest home; the valve factory was sold to IT&T for a sum that made two sprawling generations very comfort-able; and the faultline beneath my own nuclear family was gathering pressure. The antediluvian mass of dreaming Ireland and strict Catholicism was countered by newer, more active forces of Ivy and Junior Leagues, *The New Yorker* magazine, and the Rochester Country Club. A quake was inevitable. It came in 1963, lifting my family out of St. John the Evangelist's middle-class parish into the upper-class one of St. Thomas More, whose coolly angular modern church was built as the result of a landmark zoning decision in U.S. Supreme Court that allowed the parishioners, then worshipping in a college chapel, to establish their institutional beachhead smack dab in the middle of an exclusive WASP suburb. Ethnicity faded to gentility in this Elysium, where we moved two doors down from Xerox's founding president. His white-pillared home was an historic landmark of the under-ground railway, but in my childhood, Rochester's beacon signaling welcome for black Americans—Frederick Douglas had published his abolitionist newspaper, *The North Star* there—had been tragically dimmed by racism and poverty. I grew up in segregation, until Rochester's 1964 race riots. I wasn't even aware of the city's African-American *Catholics.*

Our upwardly mobile move had been on my parents' agenda for a long time, but my older brother Danny and I felt displaced, and never got over it. My older sister went to college, relatively unaffected by the move; my little brother Jimmy made new friends at St. Thomas More grammar school, but not in the casual way Danny and I had known in the old neighborhood. Our new street was a busy thoroughfare where cars swept by at fifty miles an hour; no one played there. The houses were farther apart; their occupants shared fewer unifying interests. Danny and I missed the Valbys, the Dooleys, and our other old neighbors, whom we felt sure despised us now as rich phonies. We no longer walked to school; we took the bus.

Prior to the Big One, there'd been little social temblors, the most significant of which, for me, were my annual summers at camp with the daughters of America's Protestant elite. At Quinibeck, in Vermont, our day began with Morning Assembly and Protestant hymns. At first this disturbed me; *The Baltimore Catechism* warned it was a venial sin to attend Protestant services. If Catholics *had* to go to a non-Catholic wedding or a funeral, we could sinlessly ape the congregation's motions so as not to embarrass our hosts, but we could not receive their communion or otherwise show any investment of faith or feeling in what were, after all, pitiably counterfeit rituals.

I sang the assembly hymns faintly, keeping an emotional distance, which was easy. Protestant music left me cold; it was so *martial,* fit for athletic competition and the conquest of nature, not for meditation and repentance. Then I encountered "This is my Father's world/I rest me in His care/ In the rustling grass I see Him pass/I hear His voice everywhere" and felt the lyric swell my heart and voice. It was beautiful, and try as I might I could find no heresy in it. I sang it with feeling and was not struck down. I could even sing hymns penned by the beast Martin Luther, who'd led millions of Catholics astray, and God remained seemingly unfazed. He showed no sign of wrath that I was praising Him with Protestants in an unconsecrated recreation hall in the Green Mountains of Vermont.

I didn't realize that there were other voices rising in that mix which must have sounded strange to their owners, if not their Creator. Not until the day I passed a cabin and overheard a whispered conversation taking place behind shuttered windows:

"She's one."

"She is?"

"Wendy is too."

"*Wen*dy? *Really?*"

Wendy was the coolest girl in camp, my team captain. "One" had to be something good; why then the tone of unmistakable disparagement? I lingered.

"Meg and Ellie are."

"I knew that."

I understood in a flash. Meg and Ellie's last name was the same as a biblical character's. The people in the Bible were Jews; the conversation had to be about who was Jewish.

I knew Jews tended to live separately from other people because I didn't know any, that I was aware of, in Rochester. But Catholics tended to live separately too. That, and the statement of a kind nun who'd taught us "Jews are Catholics' brethren of the Ancient Law" made me presume Jews and Catholics were a lot alike. We both had religions that were demanding and proud. But the savage persecution of Catholics by Communists, whom the nuns dreaded, was no match for what the Jews had suffered under Hitler. I'd learned about it at home, from the haunting pictures of concentration camp survivors published by *Life* magazine; from the heartrending *Diary of Anne Frank,* and finally from *The Rise and Fall of the Third Reich,* which I'd snuck off my parents' bookshelves. That was my education in anti-Semitism, but at camp I *heard* it for the first time in real life, among my peers. I didn't dare confront those girls; they probably whispered about Catholics, too. I walked away from that cabin disgusted with them, but glad to realize I *did* know Jews after all, and they were the coolest girls in camp. I cast my lot with Wendy, Ellie, Meg, and Anne Frank.

Quinibeck's Catholics were not hard to spot; we took the bus, as a group every Sunday, to Thetford for mass, boarding in wrinkled dresses while the rest of the girls lazed around camp in their crisp Sunday whites. Two of my fellow papists, the Boardis from New Jersey, were daughters of canned ravioli maven Chef Boy-ar-dee. They shocked me by divulging that it wasn't their father the chef on the can, but a Boardi uncle whose mustache made him more credible in the part. Such facts gleaned on Lake Fairlee's shore—the ubiquity of anti-Semitism, the lack of truth-in-advertising—massively enriched my parochial education.

Every year I came home more proficient in the ways of the ruling class, possessed of information my Catholic schoolgirl friends didn't know they didn't know:

the social superiority of Pappagallo flats to Capezios; how to get a horse to accept a bit; how to find the "sweet spot" on a tennis racket; the precise, disgusting image that went with the term "blow job." I learned these lessons well; as a young actress, I was repeatedly typed as To The Manor Born, or at least To The Massachusetts Kennedys—an issue of mistaken identity that must be addressed here. My tie to the touch-football clan is too distant to claim.

I know because my father and JFK researched it early in the fifties, when Daddy was in Washington working for his political mentor, U.S. Senator Ken Keating. Passing by Congressman Kennedy's office one day, Daddy, on a whim, decided to introduce himself to the secretary and ask if the congressman were in. He'd barely finished speaking when he heard a voice say:

"Ah you that *Republican* Kennedy from Rochestah? I've heahd about yew."

Daddy looked up to see Jack in the inner doorway, incredulous at the sight of a GOP clansman.

"Glad yew dropped by! Get in heah!" he exclaimed, waving Daddy into his office, where the two pored over a map of Ireland.

They managed to identify ancestral seats in neighboring counties, but any connection had been hopelessly riven in the New World by paterfamilial arrivals in two great rival harbors, Boston and New York, from which stemmed, in part, the loyalties to two great rival political parties. Politics really mattered, in both clans. My siblings' almost total conversion to the Democrats, and Maria Shriver's marriage to a giant bodybuilding Republican were interesting counter moves, but Those Kennedys[1] and I brushed closest when I played Pat in the television miniseries *RFK and His Times*.

Auditioning before Thanksgiving and getting the job after, I'd heard the delay was due to the Kennedy family's contractual right to exercise casting approval. This conjured an image I've long cherished, of actors' glossies being traded over the turkey carcass at Hyannisport:

"Brad Davis? Love him!"

"Veronica Cartwright? Wonderful in *The Right Stuff!*"

"Mimi Kennedy? Who's she? Not one of ours? But what a coincidence! Sure!"

Frantic ghostly whispers about my GOP roots, or my parents' prehistoric PAC "Kennedys for Keating," went unheeded. The latter organization, whose memory shamed me in the late sixties, was formed as a gesture of loyalty by my parents to Ken Keating, who was being robbed, in their loyal Republican view, of his Senatorial sinecure by Bobby's ruthless carpetbagging. My parents' failure to support Massachusetts Kennedys for Catholicism's sake outraged local papists. When "Kennedys for Keating" was announced in the evening paper, our phone rang with anonymous hate calls. "You tell your mother when I see her in church I'm going to *spit* on her!" one good Christian soul warned me.

---

[1]My family always reserved for itself the right to be known as *the* Kennedys amongst ourselves.

When *RFK and His Times* filmed in Hyannis, longtime locals pronounced my resemblance to the Kennedy sisters striking. It was an effect of costume and hairdo, I knew, but it made me wonder again about a genetic link between those Irish counties. If all human beings are twenty-fourth cousins, as I once heard, then surely all Kennedy Irish—our name means "Big Head" or "Ugly Head," depending on translation—are related in single-digit degrees. I am content with that.

My camp acculturation was fortified by social dancing school, where I learned the box step, mexican hat dance, cutting-in, wearing white gloves, and making small talk with strangers of the opposite sex. My parents considered these lessons crucial to a well-rounded education. They weren't covered in the nuns' curriculum, so beginning in fourth grade I was driven to a local private-school gym two Fridays a month to learn them and be treated like a leper by kids I didn't know, while my schoolfriends were at each other's houses reveling in the weekend's freedom.

The private-school kids knew each other. Many were related; the rest seemed to have been family friends since birth. This gave them things to mutter about while stepping on each other's toes.

My only hope at talk, the best repartee unacquainted preteens can manage—"Where do you go to school?"—was reliably squelched by my reply: "St. John the Evangelist's."

"What?" some boys would ask, inclining their well-scrubbed ears toward my lips as if to show they weren't afraid of things strange and unfamiliar.

"St. John the E-*van-ge*-list's," I'd enunciate miserably. Then even the bravest boys would fall silent. The overt religiosity of the phrase seemed to threaten the proceedings. It was about as welcome as a chador at a fashion show.

I hated the creepy damp of the boys' palms. It seeped through my white cotton gloves and the zippered backs of my party dresses. But by high school, at country club dances, the reward period kicked in. The young Protestant lions displayed a shaggy-haired, handsome self-assurance that seemed to elude their guilt-ridden Catholic counterparts. I was delighted to find myself the beneficiary of a hormonal teenage drive to seek romance outside one's lifelong circle of kith and kin. I was ready. I could not only foxtrot well but flirt while I did it. I used my acting talent to compensate for my perceived defects in pedigree and watched my dance card fill up with names of some of the choicest boys. Even the girls grew friendlier, as if they sensed a brief opportunity for exotic acquaintanceship before their worlds contracted again, with marriage and reproduction in their own select group.

The problem with acting offstage, I've often found, is that it can easily lead to sex one doesn't want to—and really shouldn't—have. Sex stymied my assimilation to the upper classes during the crucial early mating period because I couldn't do as non-Catholic girls did. Under pain of mortal sin, I could not French kiss.

My moment of decision came at a country club dance, during a band break by Carl Dengler's green-lamé-jacketed orchestra. I'd strolled onto the golf links with an attractive boy I knew would be attending an after-dance party hosted by my distant cousin-by-marriage, too cool to acknowledge my existence at these events. I wanted to go and willingly sank beneath some sheltering shrubbery to solicit an invitation.

Adept at necking sinlessly, I delivered long lingering, kisses to the boy's lips, gently sucking with closed mouth, keeping my upper arms tight against my sides. This prevented both the side-sliding copped feel and the full-frontal press. A canny boy could wrap his hands around my upper arms and touch some rounded flesh with the backs of his fingernails, which I allowed because it was so tantalizing and not officially my fault. My own hands were free, from my elbows down, to safeguard other restricted areas.

After long minutes of osculation, my fairway companion reared back to look at me through glazed, slitted eyes and grumped, "Is this the way you always kiss?" with what I thought was a rather ungentlemanly display of disgust.

"Yes," I answered soulfully, dropping my eyes and bending in for more, hoping to convey that my subtle charms were far better than the slobbering activity *he* had in mind. His lips were moving before I got to them.

"Because if it is, I don't think I can take you to that party."

He then kissed me vehemently, parting my lips with his tongue and coating my front teeth with saliva before I managed to break free. I got up, laughing as I brushed grass clippings off my dress to show there were no hard feelings. But of course, something of his was very hard, and I was too ignorant to know. My lack of knowledge about men's erections was what made the image of "blow jobs" so disgustingly senseless to me.

What I did know was that I wouldn't be going to the party. I tried to feel valiant and good, but at root, I was furious. I couldn't believe I'd been expected to forsake heaven for some spoiled preppy who thought tonguing was his droit-de-seigneur. St. Maria Goretti had plunged a dagger into the man who'd wanted her to sin, but this smug, privileged lad I sensed, would always get away clean. It was nights like this that made me a Democrat.

8.

Smith College

On the eve of college decision, which marked a young person's first autonomous choice in our family, I was a girl with her childhood priorities intact: (1) get to heaven, and (2) be an actress. But I also wanted some fun, and my attraction to the secular world lured me to consider non-Catholic colleges. Intuitively and decisively, I chose Smith.

It had the School of Social Work, which gave Smith an aura of altruism lacking at other seven sisters schools and almost made up for its not being Catholic. The autobiographies of Drs. Tom Dooley and Albert Schweitzer, which I'd read in early adolescence, had de-programmed my orthodoxy to the degree that I'd understood for the first time that selfless servants of any denomination could achieve sanctity as surely as medieval Catholic hermits. The doctors' stories combined with my other favorite autobiography, Sammy Davis, Jr.'s *Yes I Can*, to shape a new, hybrid image of my future.

"I want to be an actress *and* a social worker," I announced to my mother one evening while helping with dinner. So overjoyed was she to glimpse the first nurturing instinct in my juggernaut acting ambition that she'd dropped everything to hug me, right there in the middle of the kitchen, thus powerfully reinforcing the dual dream. That few actress-social-worker-saints had gone before me was no deterrent—Yes I Can!

Sister Mary Brian, my college guidance counselor at Our Lady of Mercy high school, was not similarly impressed by my good intentions.

"Smith?!!" she repeated incredulously, horrified, at our first college guidance session. It would be my last; after it, Sister Brian would give up on me. For the moment, her face was frozen in horror.

"Yes," I replied, trying to remain confident beneath her hawk like stare.

"You realize that at a secular school, you stand a good chance of losing your soul? I've seen it happen, Mimi. Over and over again."

My older sister had warned me Sister Brian would say this. The guidance counselor's well-known view of secular colleges was that they were spiritual death traps. Five years earlier, Susie had defended secular colleges in a student body debate at Mercy, but she'd made up for her intellectual mischief by choosing a Catholic college for herself. Sister Brian couldn't believe I wouldn't do the same.

"Why would you risk it?" she challenged, color rising in her cheeks. "Why won't you consider one of the good Catholic colleges, like Manhattanville, or Albertus Magnus?"

"My sister went to Manhattanville," I told her calmly. "I've gone to school behind her my whole life and even my parents want me to have a college of my own."

Susan's estimable wake had eliminated the only Catholic institution my parents took seriously. Magnus was not considered, in our family, an institution of comparable worth. Its brochure stressed proximity to Yale as an asset, not for the value of shared faculty or resources, but for the easy access it gave Magnus women to Yale men. The winking implication that Catholic girls could date and marry men with superior secular educations that girls were too spiritually fragile to acquire on their own repulsed me.

I am not spiritually fragile, I wanted to tell Sister Brian. It was I, in third grade, who'd started Rosary Club, gathering my friends to kneel in Kathy Conte's rock garden after school. I'd kept the meetings going as winter approached and my friends, citing their mothers' concerns for their health, begged that they stop. It was I who'd remained in the cold mud reciting decades after the others had retreated to the house for cocoa. I knew Mary favored both outdoor settings and the young, so I'd figured I'd see her outside, and before puberty, or never. The older visionaries of Medgagorie, and the middle-aged housewife in Brooklyn who reported missiles in the subway tunnels, were then unknown; to this day I find their messages less compelling than the plea for prayer and sacrifice for world peace that Our Lady of Fatima gave three Portuguese children at the dawn of World War I. I was never granted the extraordinary grace of a vision, but between pajama parties and lip-synching to R & B records in my basement, I'd sought it.

I stayed silent before Sister Brian. I didn't yet know she was a redhead—that revelation lay a few months away, when Vatican II changes to the nuns' headgear would show their hairlines—but I knew she had a temper. I didn't want my college guidance session to become one of the ranting ordeals older girls liked to brag about having survived.

One threatened. How could I convince Sister Brian that I was actually being prudent to inoculate myself against sin in small doses at a secular college? If I couldn't hang on to my soul at Smith, what chance would it have in New York City?

My mother was delighted I'd chosen Smith. Her failure to get a college degree because her family ran out of tuition during her sophomore year at the University of Rochester was the regret of her life, assuaged in middle age by her appointment to the university's board of directors. But prior to that honor, sending a daughter to Smith had been one of Mother's proudest academic boasts. My father, loyal

Hamilton College and Harvard Law School alumnus, was hardly threatened by secular higher education. For the first time in my life, I knew my parents and the nuns were firmly opposed, so for the first time in my life, I dared regard Sister Brian's attitude as provincial and a bit paranoid.

"My mother says if I go to Smith, I not only *won't* lose my soul, I just might end up converting the whole darn place!" I said cheerily. I'd heard Mother say this to one of her friends over the phone and offered it to Sister Brian to assuage her dutiful concern.

As clearly as if the message were being teletyped across her forehead, the nun's look said, "You are a bold, bold girl." She knew she'd lose a showdown with my well-respected, prominent Catholic parents. I saw her inwardly surrender. Let the proud reap the bitter harvest of sending their children to institutions that enshrine reason above faith, she seemed to be thinking. Aloud, she described application procedures. Then she dismissed me, having done her job the best she could.

She'd done it well. I left her office with self-doubt so firmly implanted that when I lost my soul at college, by Sister Brian's orthodox standards and probably in precisely the way she'd envisioned, I had only myself to blame. Which I did, painfully, for years.

Early Decision, I'd heard, increased one's chances of getting into college, so after my guidance interview, deducing that few applications sailed smoothly to Smith from Our Lady of Mercy High, I applied Early Decision. I needed extra enthusiasm to weight my application favorably against those from girls at Master School in Dobbs Ferry, or Shipley, and Agnes Erwin, on Philadelphia's Main Line. Many of my camp friends went to such schools, and I knew they graduated flocks of girls annually into arms of the seven sisters, who gathered them up with the fond expectancy of doting aunts.

My parents drove me to Northampton to afford me the advantage of a personal interview, and themselves a little Ivy League nostalgia. In the comfortable, book-filled office of a Smith admissions officer, I faced one of the first academic administrators I'd ever seen who was not cloaked in black. It was unexpectedly liberating to be judged by a woman who had jewelry, make-up, a hairdo, and visible legs. But the total absence of religious iconography in her office made the place seem oddly chilly, disconcertingly bare.

The woman made up for it by being warm and friendly.

"Tell me about yourself—why do you want to come to Smith, and what are your hopes for the future?" was the gist of her opening question.

"Well, I'm planning to become an actress," I replied, repeating my mantra with pride.

Wrong answer here, I saw immediately. The woman frowned.

"Then I must tell you…our theater department is…not one of our strengths."

"Ah," I said, unable to think of a catchy follow-up and lapsing into momentary silence.

"You should know that before you apply," she warned. Then, on a more conciliatory note, she added, "We're working on it, and there *are* some exciting new plans being made. We're breaking ground next year for a new theater arts complex, but I'm afraid it will be just getting started when you arrive and wouldn't be finished until the time you'd leave. Meanwhile things will be in a state of upheaval."

She cocked her head at a sympathetic angle, and we stared at each other, wondering how I'd rescue this conversation from its most unfortunate early turn. She'd done her job; she'd led me to stumble, in full view, over the fact that my college application had been pitifully under-researched. Frivolous candidates such as I, applying to Smith merely for prestige, had to be culled from serious students who knew the strengths they could bring the college and what the college could offer them.

Looking at the woman's blonde coiffure, I thought of my father's dream for my future: hair up during the week, down on the weekend. Glasses worn at the office, ditched for dates. You'll really wow 'em then.

"I'm also thinking of becoming a lawyer," I said evenly, and the officer relaxed. "Like my father," I added, trying to enhance my credibility, both to her and myself.

After a glance at my application—I presumed she was checking to see that my father was really a lawyer—the admissions officer chirped.

"Well, that's certainly becoming a *popular* field for woman, and a very good one, I think! And one that requires some acting—so they say!"

We both chuckled, refreshed; then I sobered to solidify my gains.

"So I need a place with strong academics, like English. And history."

I had no intention of taking history. But two things had dawned on me, fast. The first was that a weak theater department might serve me well. If it meant savvy would-be actresses didn't apply to Smith, there would be all the more parts for me in whatever productions the department did mount! Being onstage was all that mattered; the thought of it buoyed me above the hot waves of humiliation that had begun to roil, and I became more determined than ever to impress this woman as an attractive and credible Smith College candidate.

My second realization was that I'd never made an academic decision before in my life. My education, my whole upbringing, had relegated choice almost exclusively to the moral sphere. Even my high-school electives had been assigned on the college-prep track. My free will had been left to grapple with the decisions I'd been taught really mattered: whether to sin, and if so, how grievously. I'd never appreciated the vast differences that could exist between richly endowed schools, because I'd never been to one. Thinking this, I remembered the difference that *had* led me to Smith.

"I'm also considering being a social worker," I declared. "So I'm attracted by Smith's School of Social Work."

The woman's lips pursed; wrong again. How? A second time she glanced at my application and a second time she spoke with care, as if seeking the proper tone between instruction and condescension.

"Our School of Social Work—which probably is the best in the country —is a graduate school. If you're really planning on coming here then you might want to consider spending your undergraduate years somewhere else. Northampton's a nice town, but six years of it could be a bit much for any young woman."

I stared at her without comprehension.

"The college and the School of Social Work are completely separate," she stressed, with unmistakable, if genteel, exasperation.

She hates Catholics and would be happy to see me just go away, I thought. Telling myself that such paranoia was unworthy of liberal academe, I suppressed it to wrack my brain for some jewel, some final proof of my worth that might convince this woman I needed the college and it needed me. In my whirl of unpleasant emotions, the lavish photo spread of the Phys. Ed. Department in Smith's brochure rose up in my mind's eye. The acres of netted courts and grassy fields, on which bloomered girls gamboled with rackets and sticks, had seemed so excessively preppy to me I'd made fun of them, vowing inwardly to stay as far away from gym at Smith as possible.

"Some of my other interests are athletic," I said.

"Really?" Her interest was reignited. "Talk a little bit about that."

"Well, I dove competitively for a while. I studied with Betty Perkins—she's an Olympic diving coach, in Rochester. She started taking top divers in the area for training a few years ago. I was in her first class."

I didn't bother to mention my competitions had been at the Rochester Country Club, where I'd won first place, twelve-and-under, in the 1960 Family Day Swim Meet, and Camp Quinibeck, where I routinely won top honors, or shared them with Lucy Adams. Lucy turned up in my Smith freshman class, probably without having to cite her diving credentials to get in. She'd gone to an excellent private school.

Nor did I mention that I'd quit Betty Perkins's class that first winter, when gas heaters warming her snowbound plastic pool-bubble in Rochester's subzero temperatures made me sick and swelled my extremities to a puffy, immobile state. I moved on to my coup-de-grace:

"And I was also training in gymnastics for the 1962 Olympics."

The woman practically leapt across her desk.

"Really?!" she trilled. "How wonderful!"

"At the Rochester CYO," I added quickly, to show I was being up-front from the beginning. "That's the Catholic Youth Organization, which had a huge downtown gym. Doris Fuchs used to train there. She was an Olympic gold medalist in the fifties."

The woman gave me a wide-eyed nod. She was all ears; I was teacher now.

"She came back to our gym once, to work out, because she was in the area, and she watched us practicing for the regionals. She told our coach, 'I don't like the way these kids're catching up to me!'"

My interviewer chuckled, her eyes grown fond.

The fact that my friend Maureen and I had spent as much time applying white lipstick and blue nail polish as practicing back-handsprings didn't contradict the truth of my story. Nor did a fact I knew I couldn't possibly explain in this office: we Catholic girls didn't train too hard because we didn't expect there to be a 1962 Olympics. We expected the world as we knew it to end in 1960 when the Pope opened the Fatima letter containing a secret message Our Lady had given the three shepherd children in 1917. Lucy, the eldest, had written it down and given it to the Vatican. The Pope was to open it either upon her death or in 1960. As of this writing, Lucy is still alive in a Spanish Carmelite convent.

I never heard whether anyone looked at the letter in 1960. The year came and went without a peep from the Pope on the subject. In 1958, we couldn't have imagined this anti-climax; we anticipated the event with great trepidation. A joke going around at the time, that the Pope sneaked a look inside the envelope and fainted because it contained the bill for the Last Supper, masked Catholics' grim fear that the message predicted imminent atomic war between the United States and Russia, punishing the world for ignoring Mary's pleas for penance.

Two floors above the sweaty gym where Maureen and I grunted, three above the chlorine-steamed natatorium where we squealed and swam, and its locker room where we rifled the older girls' wallets to see their boyfriends' hoody high-school pictures and read the notes scrawled on the backs, were the diocesan bishop's offices. There, celibates trod carpets all day in dry, whispering silks. This was the context of my Olympic training. The games weren't televised and the athletes weren't celebrities, but I was training for them. Swear to God. Doris Fuch's coach *said* so.

In the warm glow of my surprising revelation, the admissions officer brought the interview to a close and called my parents into her office. Everyone shook hands, a student was summoned to lead us on a campus tour, and six months later I was admitted to Smith under what I've always feared were false pretenses. Whether anyone at the college ever noticed or cared that I failed to fulfill my promise as a college athlete, it was obvious from the beginning: freshman year, I fulfilled my gym requirement in my dance leotard. Subsequently I stayed off the athletic fields, as intended, except for one semester of lacrosse, which I took in a misguided attempt to bond with a goalie boyfriend. It was a mistake. It could only have been worse if the teams had required choose-ups; mercifully, positions were assigned. I spent the entire terrified time fielding balls my teammates passed to me with generous sportsmanship, exhorting, "You can do it!"

No I Can't. The only place I really wanted to play was onstage. Bonding with one group to beat another by accruing points in the exhausting repetition of some arbitrary physical event has never been my idea of fun. Wisely or not, I'd come to Smith to act.

9.

John Fisher

I arrived for freshman orientation to find Smith's Theater Department being visibly shorn up. There was a new acting professor, John Fisher, and ground had already been broken for the promised theater arts complex. Lingering departmental weaknesses did not favor me as I'd hoped. Instead, they resulted in two horrifying rules: Freshmen couldn't act in major productions because upperclassmen needed the roles to complete their major requirements, and freshmen couldn't attend acting classes. Even Acting 1 required a year's worth of academic prerequisites.

There was no way I could endure Scenery 1 and Introduction to Theater History for a year without performing. I phoned Acting 1's professor to plead that my extensive high-school and community theater credits comprised an advanced placement course that qualified me to take his class.

"Interesting argument," John Fisher said. "Come to my office and we'll discuss it further."

He gave me a time and date on which I went to Alumnae Gym, the aging brick sports temple which the Phys. Ed. Department had vacated for better-endowed digs. Climbing the warped wooden staircase beneath nineteenth century windows, I appreciated for the first time why the college had sprung for the arts complex.

John Fisher was on the phone in his cluttered office, which I could see beyond a narrow ante-room. He waved me through two open doors, and I entered his presence to sit on the detached theater seat he kept for visitors. Then I waited for him to get off the phone.

This is the norm for actor's interviews, I've found. We try to appear deaf and disinterested in the conversation being offered up for our eavesdropping, but short of plugging our ears, it's impossible not to listen for important hints about what's in store for us. John Fisher seemed playful, calm, and mischievous. His roly-poly belly had popped a button on his threadbare white shirt, above which he gestured gracefully with his free hand. Somehow that hand, his belly, his Greco-Roman cap of blond curls, his arched eyebrows, and impish grin all suggested Pan gone to seed. I learned later that the performance of his own which he cherished above all others was his turn as a prankster god in Brecht's *Good Woman of Setzuan*. He'd obviously been playing to type.

When John fisher hung up, he leaned back in his swivel chair to take a good look at me. Sparkling dust motes snowed on our heads, falling through the light from a window still screened against vanished basketballs, as John Fisher and I sat sizing each other up. Literally: the first thing we noticed about each other was weight.

This is the norm, too, for actors' interviews, I've discovered after twenty-five years in show business. We actors do best in this situation when we appear trim and fit. Interviewers, who have fewer physical requirements for their jobs, may pack as much avoirdupois as they dare. John Fisher looked to me to be carrying about two hundred and fifty pounds.

"Miss Kennedy, I presume," he opened with a courtly nod.

"Mr. Fisher, I know," I returned sportingly. You, or Bacchus.

"You're the one who wants to be in my acting class even though she's just a Freshman," he continued, holding my gaze as he leaned forward and picked up a pen on his desk.

"Yes."

"I've received a few other such requests," he said, turning the pen in his long fingers. I searched his face for an indication of whether this meant bad news for me, or good, but found none.

"So you want to be an actress?" he asked, while regarding his pen.

"That's right," I replied, hoping brevity would supply the soul of wit.

"Lots of young women want to be actresses. That doesn't mean they can be. Or that they necessarily should be." His eyes left the pen and met mine.

"I know."

I tried not to sound stung but I hated that crap. I'd heard enough of it to let it roll off my back. John Fisher noted that I hadn't flinched, and his eyebrows went up.

"Are you a good actress?"

"Yes." I would not protest too much.

"Very well," John Fisher replied, dropping the pen and leaning back in his swivel. "*You* tell *me.*"

He suddenly spread his arms wide, like a kid offering another kid a free shot. "*Why* should I let you take my acting class?"

I was momentarily dumbstruck by his wingspread, which was enormous. He glanced at the heavens as if they contained an infinite number of right answers, then lifted his hands high in the air and clasped them above his head, entwining his fingers. With a collapse of elbows, he brought the whole configuration down behind his neck to nestle his head in his palms, leaning backwards. It was an extravagant gesture that caused such a prodigious shift of weight that the swivel chair lurched backwards with a loud groan. I was sure I was about to see Mr. Fisher upended into his rear bookcases.

Instead the chair rocked perilously at its new angle and John Fisher rode it as if it were a hammock in the Caribbean and he a vacationer awaiting a pina colada.

"Because I'm a good actress?" I said. My upward inflection ruined the intended effect, which was a bold show of pride. Midway through, I'd thought of the nuns and clutched.

John Fisher merely lifted an eyebrow.

"Cheeky!" he mock-reproved. "That's good. I admire cheek." Then he admonished:

"To be an actress you must be thin."

Those who can't, teach! I thought unkindly. This, from Bacchus overflowing! But I sucked in my stomach and crossed my legs—my thinnest feature—before answering, "I know."

The previous summer I'd read a Walker Percy novel in which the protagonist fell in love with a woman's ample rear end on the subway. Its owner had turned out to be a Smith graduate; Percy strongly implied that big behinds were a defining Smith characteristic. I wasn't planning to grow one, but just in case, I was pleased to know I'd be going to a school where large fannies were—pardon me—assets. This was just the sort of stereotypical crap, I would come to learn, that repulsed John Fisher about the Ivy League and eventually drove him out of it when he learned all too much of it had turned out to be true.

"You can't just do stage work any more," he warned me. "Today's actresses must work in television and film. The camera adds ten pounds, you know."

This adage is only slightly less ancient than "Don't believe everything you read," and only because the camera postdates the printing press. It was, and is, widely believed. I arrived in Hollywood a decade later to find it largely obsolete; where there's a will, there's a way to make those ten pounds disappear. For my TV debut in "Three Girls Three," Bob Mackie designed a bone-corseted, floor-length chiffon gown so heavy with bugle beads it essentially functioned as a full-length body girdle. Beneath it, Charles Jourdan pumps added four inches to my height, and flattering camera angles did the rest to make me appear lithe and long. After the shows aired, people often met me in person with helpless exclamations that I seemed so much *shorter*—they managed not to say "fatter"—in real life than on television! Not until I tumbled down the career-ladder to a rung where nobody was paid enough to give a damn about my beauty image did I suffer the damage an unbiased camera can do: extra pounds, angular planes, and ghoulish shadows.

On that September afternoon in the hazy autumn light, neither John Fisher nor I imagined a faux-glamour TV variety series in my future. We thought of soap operas, "Twilight Zones," or perhaps, if I really made it, a John Cassavetes movie. Then John Fisher launched his memorable epigram:

"To be an actress, you must be gaunt."

He clownishly sucked in his cheeks and widened his eyes. Across time and space, Catherine Deneuve answered him, "At some point, a woman must decide between her fanny and her face." But she said it in French, and not just then.

The words "anorexia nervosa" hadn't yet entered the pop lexicon. But the bovine feelings that led girls to starve themselves were already loosed upon the land in the images of Twiggy and Penelope Tree, whose fragile model-bodies—not for nothing did the British call them "birds"—were our pitiless fashion ideal. I would never achieve it. The prepubescent athletics that gained me entrance to Smith had denied me "gaunt" forever. Boys liked my muscular definition, because it emphasized legs and bosom, but I preferred gaunt, and I hadn't known it since age seven, when my mother worried aloud to a doctor about my "birdlike" eating habits, and he'd peddled a tonsillectomy as the cure.

That tonsillectomies were a better cure for the occupancy rate of children's hospital wards, and doctors' bankbooks did not occur to Mother, who was, like most women of her time, in thrall to the medical profession. Duly convinced that my tonsils and adenoids were offending lumps of tissue that interfered with good eating, she scheduled their surgical excision.

I awoke from surgery in the middle of the night, my throat burning and my nostrils still full of the ether-soaked-cloth smell that had smothered me into unconsciousness. Sirens wailed in the dark distance; in the shadows nearby someone whispered that the child coming into the next bed had been hit by a bus. There was a flurry of activity. Curtains swished, metal clanked, and I heard low, agonized moans. My terror was complete; even the pink case of Ginny dolls I got the next day didn't eclipse it. I went home, ate obediently, and was never gaunt again.

One more word on actors and weight before John Fisher lurches upright to roll his belly into his desk and deliver the final judgment:

Robert DeNiro established a daunting precedent, in *Raging Bull*, that weight was just another arrow in the disciplined actor's role-preparation quiver. Meryl Streep used it bravely but moderately in *Bridges of Madison County* as a farm woman too busy for vanity, but her glowing self in photographs from the premiere suggest that her seasoned wisdom told her Hollywood's publicity machine is best faced in fighting form. Kathleen Turner once said in an interview that *her* intentional weight gain for a film not only failed to garner admiration and nominations, it seriously derailed her career. She cautioned women against it in the strongest possible terms. The frequent mention of spas, diets, and personal trainers in actress's publicity interviews seem to suggest that female role preparation goes arduously in the other direction. Goldie Hawn's fat suit in *Death Becomes Her* delighted critics precisely because the fat was fake and beneath it was Goldie, lithe and lovely, health undamaged by the risks associated with massive weight fluctuation. An actress friend once confided that her studio executive husband's suggestion of a certain actress for a role at a casting session had been quashed by another participant's response: "Someone saw her at my dry cleaner's recently, looking fat." The woman's name was dropped from consideration.

In my humble research and experience, heft is a career hurdle in many ways. Talented, big friends of mine were typed as character actors early in their careers when most of the available work was for juveniles and ingenues. Actors like Rosie O'Donnell, Kathy Bates, Brian Dennehy, and the titan Roseanne Barr have proven that physically big actors can win big roles, but it takes bravery and luck. It must disconcert big women when actresses who rise to the top proclaiming "Big Is Beautiful!" go on diets the minute they get there, as if all along they've coveted thinness as the ultimate perk of big-time celebrity.

If the demand for fitness were driven by health concerns, it might be more palatable. But a smoking, drinking, lipo-suctioning, face-tucking, partying, over-medicated celebrity lifestyle has never had health as a goal unless it delivers the beauty goods. The fact that it does protects actors from ourselves. Anorexia and obesity both kill, first the career, then the body. Actors who learn early how to nurture themselves well, and do so naturally, are the lucky ones. They tend to be all too rare. I wasn't one.

"If you're a good actress," John Fisher concluded, "you can prove it to me. Can we agree on that?" He cocked an eyebrow.

"Yes."

"All right. Actresses audition. Right?"

"Right."

"So you'll audition for me. If you're as good as you say you are, you'll show me in your first scene and I'll accept you in the class. Come the first week. I'll give you an assignment. After you bring it in, I'll make my final decision. How's that? Does that sound fair?"

It sounded wonderfully fair. In parochial schools, rules hadn't been bent for me very often because they'd issued from a Higher Authority, who couldn't easily be consulted on the matter of exceptions. If one believed, as the nuns did, in human concupiscence, it was dangerous to give children the benefit of the doubt. Left to their own devices, humans helplessly chose evil over good. Trust only tempted children to sin.

Here was John Fisher believing I was good because I'd told him so. His assumption that I would live up to my own expectations terrified me. This is what it will be like, I thought, to have teachers who aren't nuns. Almost as scary as having them. I rose and shook Mr. Fisher's long, tapering hand.

"Very fair," I said. "Thank you."

10.

Wow

Fisher's class, Acting 1, was held in the Music Department's Sage Hall—more evidence of an impoverished Theater Department. The building's facade mimicked that of a miniature Greek temple, and its classrooms were buillt for chamber music. The one I entered featured small tiers of lecture seats rising above a little proscenium stage. I sat in one of the middle rows and looked around. Two other girls seemed younger than the obvious upperclassmen. One of them, I recognized with a shock, was Merrie Spaeth.

Merrie Spaeth was a movie star. She and another young actress named Tippie Walker had co-starred with Peter Sellers in *The World of Henry Orient*, a movie my best friend Nancy and I had seen repeatedly in eighth grade. We'd spent hours pretending to *be* Tippie and Merrie, doing everything they'd done in the movie that was within our power to imitate. Seeing my former fantasy self, a real-life professional actress, in my first college acting class was extremely daunting. The credits with which I'd faked my way in did not include a major motion picture. For the first time I feared I was over my head.

I remembered having read that the movie's director, George Roy Hill, wanted someone utterly natural for Merrie's part, so he'd cast her after getting her name from a society wedding list. This explained Merrie's presence at our society college, but it didn't assuage my intimidation.

Julie Nixon, another prominent figure in my childhood fantasy life, had turned up in my Psychology class. When I was eight, I'd written her letters offering my loyal Republican self as a pen-pal while she traveled the arduous road—or so I imagined—of her father's vice-presidential campaign. That she had probably never seen the letters grieved me at eight; at eighteen, when I saw her in Psychology class, I was grateful. I sat down next to her on purpose that first day, and when the class introduced themselves, and Nixon and Kennedy were revealed sitting side by side, everyone tittered. Julie and I had forged a fragile bond. We liked each other. The fledgling acquaintanceship was a casualty of the Vietnam War, which I opposed passionately, eventually attending SDS meetings and demonstrations within shouting distance of Julie and David Eisenhower's honeymoon apartment in Northampton, where they tried to finish their studies and begin married life with fury erupting all around them.

But I didn't have to debate Julie, or run against her, in Psychology. Acting class would be different; skill levels would be on display.

The other Freshman in Acting I was a beautiful spritelike girl named Ellen Parks. She was the first to audition, with a scene from *Hedda Gabler*, and she was brilliant. When Ellen pulled that gun on Torvald, her feet were so firmly planted on-stage that her tiny dancer's thighs, pulled taut, looked as massive as a Henry Moore sculpture's. Her voice shook in the unnaturally low register she'd adopted to convey authority, but it didn't matter. Ellen transformed herself into a titan by sheer artistic imagination and physical will. Fisher took her into the class, and she became a favorite.

Merrie auditioned next, with a Shakespeare monologue. I don't remember which one. I didn't hear it. Merrie wandered onstage so casually it took most of us a moment to realize she'd begun. She drifted downstage, all the while addressing an imaginary companion as casually as if they were traversing the quad discussing homework. I found her pronounced disregard for the audience almost admirable; my obsession with my reception was one of my worst faults. My version of the speech, I knew, would have included lots of dramatic yelling—this was the classics, after all, the Bard!—preferably downstage with imaginary footlights illuminating my exquis-itely expressive face.

We knew the scene was over when Merrie's mouth stopped moving. She looked directly at Mr. Fisher and so did the rest of the class. He remained impassive. Without removing his cheek from the hand on which it rested, he said:

"Fascinating. I'm interested in why you didn't think it was necessary for us to hear."

Cool and unruffled, Merrie replied:

"That would have been overacting. George Roy Hill hated it. He always said most actors overact and that the camera always knew a lie, so we were never to do anything that didn't feel real to us. I consider it very important to speak in my nor-mal voice when I act. I *hate* shouting. I won't *do* it."

John Fisher, too wise a man to oppose experientially gained self-knowledge with mere words, discoursed in general on the different requirements for film and stage acting—which would become my lifelong study—then said to Merrie:

"Next I'm going to assign you a contemporary monologue, all right? Realism, absolute realism. You'll do nothing that isn't real, as you wish. But you are to find every shred of reality that's in the piece for you. *Every shred.* Then bring it in to me. And I want it *full.* If you're going to whisper, you'd jolly well better be *full.*"

Merrie was in. Sophomore year, she dropped her theater courses and plotted a major in American Studies, which took her to law school and a career in interna-tional law. That's what she told me one afternoon on 79th Street in Manhattan, where we bumped into each other by chance, two New York career gals. After we'd swapped quick catch-up stories, she graciously invited me to join her weekly bridge group, which she said contained some very interesting men who were international lawyers. At the time, I was in acting class and holding down a job; I used these ex-cuses to demur, but the real truth was bridge bored me, and the one lawyer to whom

I'd already been introduced by a Smith friend had said, on our first date, "If you want to sleep with me, fine, but I'm sick of sleeping with girls who aren't thinking about getting married, so if you don't think you could marry me, let's not bother sleeping together." I wanted a little more romance than that. I still receive Christmas cards from Merrie, who has three gorgeous children. Her husband used to wear cowboy boots and a Stetson hat with his three-piece suits in the family picture, which gave me the happy impression that Merrie's life was not devoid of the showbiz spirit. That impression was correct. She is currently a reporter for National Public Radio's economic news show, *Marketplace*.

My audition assignment from Mr. Fisher was a role in Maxim Gorky's *The Lower Depths*. A theater illiterate, I knew mostly the plays I'd seen or performed: *Peter Pan, Junior Miss, Little Women, Spider's Web*. I'd seen and read *The Tidings Brought to Mary* in French class, and I knew my mother's community theater comedies and some plays by George Bernard Shaw, whose stage directions captivated me. That was about it. I was impressed by Gorky's Russian realism and delighted to find out my part was that of a woman dying of tuberculosis. It appealed to my melodramatic tendencies.

For the next week, whenever my roommate was out, I stripped my bed, took a sheet to the dorm bathroom and sprinkled it with cold water until it was good and clammy, then returned to my bedroom. Closing the door, I'd strip to my slip and wrap the damp sheet around me, imagining blood, urine, and sputum against my skin. Then I'd lie down on my bare mattress and rehearse in whispers, punctuated by self-induced coughing spasms. In this way I worked up a fever of death-dealing, poverty-stinking, lung-gutting tuberculosis to present to John Fisher without the slightest doubt on my part that I was no terrified acting student, but Gorky's dying whore.

On my day of reckoning, I carted my sheet to Sage Hall, wet it in the restroom during the class break that preceded my scene, and lay down on the stage modules I'd arranged as my cot while the room was empty. People began drifting back, and when Mr. Fisher entered, he told me to begin when I was ready. I waited for an expectant calm to collect. Then I began in a halting voice.

I interrupted my words with little coughs, then a whole spasm, before allowing poignant flashes of the woman's former self to shine through as I gathered vocal power. At the end, illness overtook me, and I succumbed, falling back, clutching my filthy sheet and hacking until I could hack no more. The little theater fell silent. Half-believing myself that I was dead, I stayed supine until Mr. Fisher said, "Wow."

He'd never said "Wow" before. Everyone knew it was high praise.

"I go to the theater to see dying *acted* onstage, not to watch somebody actually *die*."

The class tittered. I sat up. The wall clock clicked and class was over.

"Very impressive, Miss Kennedy. Congratulations. *That* is realism," he told the group. Then he returned to me. "All right. Now I know you can be real. Next time I want to see something completely formal. Not real. Read Lorca— *The House of Bernarda Alba.* We'll choose something from there."

Lorca Who? I didn't know. But I knew I'd find out. At last I had a teacher.

I stood up to the sounds of people gathering their books and bags with the soft plop-plopping sounds that mark the beginnings and endings of things in academia.

"I'm not sure I want reality in the theater," John Fisher mused above the muffled din. "I think I go to the theater for something else."

He brought his hands together as if in prayer. "I don't want you to be real. I want you to—"

His hands burst open, Kabuki-like.

"—Astonish me!"

◦

One man's astonishment is another man's bullshit, I learned while acting in a summer troupe at Dartmouth College five years later. Smith had accepted men into its M.F.A. program beginning my sophomore year, so the Dartmouth troupe consisted of both men and women who'd been Fisher students. Everyone but me had also studied with Curt Dempster, a New York actor/director who'd been artist-in-residence at Smith while I was on my junior-year-abroad in London. Returning to Smith, I'd heard his name and his teachings invoked with such reverence that I'd become very sorry to have missed him. Our Dartmouth group called itself the New Theater Ensemble, presaging Curt's Ensemble Studio Theater, which was founded later in New York with many of the same people.

Curt traveled to New Hampshire to see his protégés perform Oliver Hailey's *Who's Happy Now*, the opening production, in which I played Jerry Zaks' mother. All the characters aged over a period of thirty years. Curt critiqued my performance privately to the director, Charlie Karchmer. It was only much later that Charlie relayed Curt's exact words:

"Why does that actress do so much bullshit?"

He gave Charlie exercises to help focus my performance, and I became absorbed in the process they set in motion. By the final production, *Journey of the Fifth Horse,* I built my tiny part entirely on what I'd learned: emotional preparation, an objective, and an activity.

The role, which consisted largely of exclamations like "My hat! My hat!," was of a type I used to dread, not just for the unkind brevity, but for the insistent punctuation. Line-readers look at exclamation points and think of all the different ways to exclaim, which drives us crazy. I preferred long, lush speeches for character revelation. My main scene found me strolling in the park with Jerry Zaks, my husband. We sit on a bench. My hat gets crushed. I exclaim.

But this time, my emotional preparation had me fully engaged. I'd chosen to concentrate on pride, shutting my eyes backstage to vividly conjure an episode in my life when I'd been excessively proud. There were billions to choose from; I don't remember which I used. This fed my objective, which was to bring all eyes to my hat and keep them there. My activity was to display the hat to its best advantage by maintaining proper carriage, holding my head at a flattering angle, and repairing the hat when it got crushed. Like Merrie before me, I did nothing that wasn't real. Jerry had a suggestion—"Think of the hat as our baby"—which was magically effective for focusing my concentration. The world has since learned that Jerry is full of magically effective suggestions; he's one of the leading directors in our contemporary theater.

Curt's exercises freed me from the tyranny of visualizing words in print. "My hat! My hat!" became an organic keen by which I rediscovered the truth I'd known as a child crying rapturously in front of my mirror; there is liberating pleasure in expending real emotions on patently unreal situations.

John Fisher came to see *Journey of the Fifth Horse*. He too critiqued my performance out of my presence, to my friends. I must have been dallying with some boyfriend, as was my wont in those wild days of postgraduate freedom.

"Mimi's done the most curious thing," were his words, as reported by a friend. "She's eliminated everything from her performance but the comic elements. I don't know how she did it, but she pulled it off, and I found it absolutely fascinating."

Once again I was reminded that people found me funniest when I was concentrating on being serious.

◦

John Fisher left Smith that summer. Rumor had it that his divorce sunk his prospects at the college, but that explanation seemed dubious, because a prominent tenured professor had not only divorced his wife, but had done so to marry a student, in a much more conservative era. I suspect John Fisher's fundamental unsuitability to Ivy climes was what sabotaged him in the end. When we last spoke, he told me he was teaching at an all-black college in Georgia and could see the wide, blue Atlantic from his window as he talked on the phone. "I'm happy," he'd said, in a tone of wonderment. "I can say that, at last, I'm really *happy*." If tears can be heard in someone's eyes, I heard them in his. He died not long afterwards, of natural causes.

I've always been glad he glimpsed the quality that eventually led to my professional acting success—that of being utterly but mysteriously comic. I was proud to have fascinated him in the theater. It wasn't quite astonishment, but it came close.

11.

Operation Match

One day during freshmen orientation at Smith, I went to get my mail and found the mailboxes in our dorm hallway flocked with white. Tubes protruded from every cubby like the tailfeathers of nested doves. I unrolled mine to find a multiple-choice questionnaire reminiscent of the college board SAT's.

Its letterhead was "Operation Match." The "O" was formed by intersecting medical symbols for Man and Woman; the questions were about dating preferences. Anyone sending a completed questionnaire and ten dollars back to Operation Match's reassuring P.O. Box in genius country, Cambridge, Massachusetts, would receive the name of a Perfect Computer Matchmate, within four to six weeks.

What fun, I thought. Some mad scientist at Harvard or MIT has programmed a campus UNIVAC for fun and profit.

I'd never seen a computer, personally, in 1966. On TV and in the movies they were room-sized machines that launched spaceships and bombs, which made them seem ill-equipped, technologically and metaphorically, to launch anything as delicate as a human relationship. Somehow computer dating had always seemed to me an element of The Future, that postmillennial time when humanity, in unisex jumpsuits and bubble-enclosed cities, would probably need help with natural selection. But did we now?

Yes, Operation Match seemed to whisper; The Future has arrived, dressed in the humble garb of a questionnaire. The Future always comes disguised, I thought; otherwise we'd never let it in.

Other girls came to get their mail, unrolled their tubes, and read dubiously. We began to ask each other: Do you believe this? Can we trust it? Should we give it a try? My senior Big Sister, whose job it was to acclimate newcomers to dorm life, came in, attracted by our perplexed murmurs. She took them as a troubling sign she wasn't doing her job.

"What're those?" she chirped.

"Computer dating forms," I replied. Jaynie's jaw went slack in disbelief, but after fetching her tube and skimming it, her smile reblossomed.

"Listen! I came down to say I'm making brownies for you all, but this is even better! Why don't you bring these forms to my room and fill them out together while we eat?! It'll be a party!"

Jaynie was engaged to be married and didn't need desperate dating measures, but her enthusiasm for Operation Match was contagious. Whether it sprang from dread of eating a pan of brownies by herself or hope that Cambridge would produce the sort of brilliant love-matches within a prescreened elite that she as a debutante was culturally conditioned to promote, she made her invitation sound irresistible. Several of us dispersed for lead pencils to reconvene on her floor and mull our multiple choices while fueling our fantasies with chocolate.

I would prefer a Matchmate who is:
1. Very Attractive
2. Attractive
3. Fairly Attractive
4. Fairly Unattractive
5. Unattractive

Very Attractive, I thought reflexively. This was Computer Dating. If one could not shoot the moon here, then where? If not now, when? In real life, I would not have permitted myself to be so shallow. The only physical flaw that qualified a boy for my immediate social rejection was halitosis.

I was about to mark 1 when I paused, realizing my answer would be matched with boys' self-descriptions. Self-anointed 1's might prove flawed by narcissism, or worse, self-delusion. By marking number 2, "Attractive," I might access a better pool of men, those with both inner and outer beauty. The test was, I saw, trickier than it looked at first glance. I marked 1. Sue me. I was paying ten dollars for the privilege.

I consider myself:
1. Very Attractive
2. Attractive
3. Fairly Attractive
4. Fairly Unattractive
5. Unattractive

In the early nineties, a sex survey taken in the United States surprised pollsters by revealing that the question people were most reluctant to answer was not about sex. They happily spilled their guts about sex. They didn't want to say how much money they made.

In the sixties, "How attractive are you?" was, for baby boomers, such a question. We hadn't been raised with today's emphasis on self-esteem. A large number of us who'd made it to college had been brushed, scrubbed, polished, carefully dressed, and wired for braces on the way, all of which left the impression that it took a lot of work to make us look presentable. We could only hope we did. Few of us were sure. Those personal ads published in respectable journals today were then the province of perverts in the back pages of fetish magazines. Even now I find their confident self-portraits suspicious. If "SWM" is so "Very Attractive, Fun-Loving, Intelligent," why must he rely on print advertising for companionship?

I wanted to be honest in evaluating my looks, but beauty is in the eye of the beholder. How accurate could a subjective opinion be? I'd heard myself described as attractive. On good days that's how I felt. In real life, modesty and scrupulous honesty would have enhanced attractiveness and caused me to say I was "Fairly Attractive." But character meant nothing to a computer. As a 3, I'd simply fall beneath the statistical reach of male 1's seeking female 1's and land perilously close to the female candidate pool of 4's and 5's, categories, which I found heartrending. Any girl marking them honestly could fall prey to fraternity pig parties and other collegiate cruelties. The thought made me shudder. I marked 2.

After physical scrutiny, the rest of the questions were easy.

On a date, I would prefer to:
1. Go to dinner and a movie
2. Go dancing
3. Go to a museum
4. Go somewhere quiet to talk
5. Listen to records in my room

Go dancing; but what boy would make dancing his first choice? Few I'd ever known; I selected dinner and a movie. Listening to records was great, but I feared marking it as my first choice might attract slugs.

I'd give anything to see that questionnaire and my answers today. I don't remember the rest. I finished it and stuffed a ten-dollar check written on my brand-new college-girl bank account in Operation Match's return envelope. I dropped it in the outgoing mail tray at the "bells" desk downstairs. Mr. Sandman, Bring Me A Dream.

In four weeks, I received a reply:

Your Perfect Computer Matchmate is:
LARRY DILG
of Amherst College.

There were starry little asterisks circling this announcement. I stared at it. Dilg? How did you pronounce that? There seemed to be a vowel missing. The computer had probably misspelled the name. Computers often did that, as anyone who'd trafficked with one complained. They multiplied typographical errors, which without human oversight, became the gospel truth. I couldn't be sure this was my Perfect Matchmate's name, and if it were, I couldn't pronounce it.

The news "Amherst College" was the real disappointment. Amherst was right down the road; Smith girls who dated there had to be back in their dorms by curfew because both college's administrations presumed the only reason for staying overnight so near one's own bed would be to have sex in someone else's, which the colleges, in loco parentis, couldn't condone.

I'd anticipated overnight stays in exotic locales like Boston, Hanover, and New Haven as one of the most exciting perks of my college education. I didn't want to give them up for a Perfect Matchmate, who, if he were really Perfect, would be the last man I'd ever date. How ironic, I thought, that science would deliver me the guy nature produces every time: The Boy Next Door.

Below the starred announcement were five names listed under the heading: "The following matches were also compatible, but not as compatible as your Matchmate." Most of them were linked with colleges farther away. I tucked the list in a bureau drawer and waited for one of the nominees to call.

Down the road, Larry Dilg—"soft g, even though there's no e," I've learned to instruct brightly since the name became mine—was also disappointed. He'd gotten only one name, while his friends scored supplemental lists like mine. Larry felt gypped. Especially when he looked up Mimi Kennedy in the Smith freshman directory, a book of high-school graduation photos which is kept at Amherst dorms and fraternities the way *Players' Guide* and *Academy Players' Directory,* rosters of actors' photos, are kept at show business offices, and for the same reasons—to enlighten, inspire, and entertain.

He swears it wasn't my failure to be attractive that kept him from calling. I believe this, not only because it makes the marriage go better, but because my hairdo in the picture was meant to conceal more than it revealed. You couldn't tell what I looked like exactly. The Jane Asher–Cynthia Lennon hair-curtain was sported by half the girls in the book and was meant to make the wearer look fashionably hip. Whether she was really Julie Christie's twin or just another gawky teenage Beatlemaniac was a revelation reserved for the personal encounter, where imperfect features could be softened by the grace of an animate soul. Larry liked my looks, even though he'd asked for Very Attractive, wanting a 1 and marking himself 2. In this we'd matched, as in so many other answers that I'd somehow left all other female respondents in the statistical dust, even as also-rans. What turned Larry off was the name of my school, though Smith wasn't his objection. It was Our Lady of Mercy High that worried him. Larry had looked forward to getting laid as one of the most exciting perks of *his* college education.

He was a sophomore and still a virgin. Time was passing him by. He correctly assumed that a Catholic Matchmate would not be Perfect as a guide to those mysteries into which he sought prompt initiation.

He didn't call me, and I didn't call him. That's how I missed my husband on the first pass.

Two of my compatibles did call.

The first took a bus to Northampton; as I walked downhill to the Trailways station to meet him, I saw a figure lurching toward me in what appeared to be a billowing, full-length cape. At closer range I saw it was an antique raccoon coat, the coolest collegiate fashion accessory of the season, and the boy inside it as beautiful as an archangel. I knew he was my compatible; beyond Very Attractive, he was Breathtakingly Gorgeous. We introduced ourselves and walked back to the dorm, drawing glances. For the first time in my life, I knew how it felt to have a Trophy Date.

We settled in the Gillette House living room and talked. Or rather, he did; I didn't get a word in edgewise. But I was content to look and listen; he sat like a berobed king, never shedding his coat, telling tales of his world travels and upbringing in Japan. He repeatedly brushed a strand of shoulder-length blonde hair out of his lake-green eyes with his long, artistic fingers. College had disappointed him, he said, because his fellow students were narrow-minded and xenophobic. He'd applied to Operation Match in the hope that somehow, somewhere in this barren Ivy landscape there existed someone like him.

Provincial Republicanism and Catholic orthodoxy oozed from my every pore as I thought how resoundingly I was not she. How had the computer matched me with this ethereal, airborne boy? I wondered, and sensed him thinking the same. After a while we stood and walked back to the bus station under a little cloud of mutual regret. I mourned that the wings I imagined hidden beneath his coat might soon become vestigial in his low-ceilinged new life, with its perceived oppressions. He seemed regretful that I wouldn't fly away with him. But I needed someone more grounded. We said goodbye, and I never saw him again.

My second compatible was wonderfully grounded. Built low, like a wrestler, he liked being on the ground too, or at least supine, preferably with me beneath him. I discovered this when we began our weekend on his campus with going somewhere quiet and talking, his preferred date activity. The fact that "somewhere" was his bed, in his room, didn't alarm me. He was a fascinating conversationalist, and I was getting a word in edgewise, which is also how we sat on the bed, our legs stretched innocently across it, our backs against the wall. When I felt him pressing on my shoulder, I presumed it was accidental and made subtle adjustments, but he stayed with me. Soon I was propping him up as if he were a broken bookcase.

Never one to mention physical awkwardness with boys, I continued squirming until, during one last giggling feint, he grabbed my wrist and took me down. When we were horizontal, eye-to-eye, he smiled and said, "Gotcha!"

I laughed and suggested we go out to some parties. He asked why I was so uncomfortable. I said I was Catholic and didn't believe in having sex before marriage. It was his turn to laugh: he was Catholic too, he said, but didn't I believe in individual freedom? He'd obviously been educated at secular private schools.

The wrestler remained amiable, and we set off for an endless round of fraternity parties. We drank too much and stumbled back to the women's boarding house where he'd booked me a room. I remember him standing on the lawn and opening his arms to it, proclaiming, "There it is!" I entered, found my room somehow, and passed out on the virginal bed while he returned to his dorm cot. We slept off our drunks separately. That was the college alternative to sex in the fall of 1966.

Just as I'd suspected, computers didn't seem to have the fine-tuning to handle what matchmaking required. Maybe science nerds lacked the sociological savvy to give certain answers greater statistical weight. I'd have thought the combination of "Catholic" and "Religion is very important to me" would have screened out wrestling dates. I could get those on my own. I began to date on my own recognizance and threw out the list from Operation Match.

12.

It

My high-school training in male-female relations was guided by tips-for-teens manuals that insisted girls could discourage a boy's sexual advances by drawing out his interests on other subjects. "Get him to talk about himself!" advised teen experts from Dear Abby to Pat Boone to Daniel Lord, S.J.

In case the boy wouldn't talk about himself, and things got heavy, Father Lord's pamphlets codified, with Jesuitical precision, make-out sins according to the degree of "venereal pleasure" they induced. The greater the pleasure—naturally—the greater the sin. The term "venereal pleasure" mystified me, except for associating pleasure with disease, which was surely Father Lord's clever intention.

College boys seemed to consider the make-them-talk-about-themselves approach a recipe for a cocktease. Their interests, I discovered, were overwhelmingly sexual; drawing them out wasn't a problem. The problem was keeping them in. I didn't want to be that most coy and frustrating of female creatures, but I wanted something too, and it wasn't sex. It was "Walking in the rain/And wishing on the stars up above/And being so in love."

My senior year in high school I took the "Marriage and Family Life" course required for all graduating Mercians. Our instructor was a shy young priest who couldn't say "intercourse" without blushing. It was his first year at our all-girls' school as chaplain; previously he'd served as a parish priest. Anecdotes from his pastoral experience made up most of his lectures.

"Girls, I'll tell you how beautiful that first kiss can be. I knew a man who told me how *glad* he was he'd saved that first kiss until he and his wife were engaged. On the day they brought the whole family together to announce that they wanted to get married, the man asked the girl's father, in front of everyone, for permission to kiss his fiancee for the very first time. 'Father,' he said to me, 'I walked across that room and put my lips on hers, and I tell you, it was just like taking Holy Communion.'"

The Old World romance of this story was lost on us jaded seniors. We found it hard to believe such embarrassing nerds existed. Another couple, however, seemed even more blighted.

"This man and woman were very much in love. Unfortunately the mother did not prepare the daughter very well for marriage, which the husband found out on their honeymoon because every time he went to touch her, his wife recoiled. He didn't know what to do, but she was so terrified, he didn't want to force himself on her. So he tried to enjoy other aspects of their trip, and when he got home he took his brother aside privately and asked if *his* wife could maybe go to the new bride and explain to her about conjugal relations, and that this was all the husband wanted. The sister-in-law talked to the bride, who was *so* relieved to find out that what her husband had wanted was perfectly normal! Eventually she learned to accept him in their conjugal relations. I can't think of a better example, girls, of the gentleness and patience of true love!"

I wouldn't have believed these stories if I didn't know Father Busciglia was incapable of lying. But even in my dire lack of sexual sophistication, I suspected the stories, for the women involved didn't have the neat happy endings we heard in class. The human mind was too devious. Women with such strict upbringings might never really *enjoy* sex; the phrase "conjugal relations" alone defied it. It sounded like heavy lifting.

Most of my education in sexual psychology came from books. But one day, when my father caught me reading *The Sterile Cuckoo,* about a college student love affair, he offered me a glimpse of his own views on the subject.

"I don't think you're old enough to be reading that," he opined, frowning.

I assured him I was. I couldn't believe his concern—I'd be off to college soon. The novel, set at Daddy's alma mater, had some racy stuff, like the couple shooting b-b guns naked off the fraternity house roof, but it was hardly shocking. I knew people had affairs. *I'd* never have one, of course. But I knew people *did.*

"I don't see how," Daddy insisted, "since it's about how sex is different for a man than it is for a woman. You see, sex involves a woman's whole self, because she invests her emotions, but men can have it as just a physical thing. I don't see how can you see that yet."

"I don't think that's necessarily what the book's about," I replied. "I think the man shows lots of emotion." I was near the end, when the narrator finally feels guilty about using, and dumping, the girl. She has a nervous breakdown. That's what you get for having premarital sex, I thought. She was too fragile, and it was too bad she didn't know any better. That's how I read the book.

"All right," Daddy grumped, and walked away, leaving me shocked by his casual admission that all men, and he'd made no effort to exclude himself, were unfeeling cads. No girl wants to believe her father is a bad guy. I hoped his opinion was primitive and inaccurate, colored by the generational views he held on so many other topics about, which we'd begun to find ourselves in opposition. But I was glad he'd offered it. It was the sum total of my home education on the subject before I went to college.

My education in sexual biology, like most of my peers', took place on the street. It began the day Larry Hayes snuck up behind me on his bike as I walked home in fourth grade and sniggered, "Wanna hear a joke?"

I did not, and sneered to indicate the fact. I heard the joke anyway, as I'd known I probably would.

"Eddie Fisher said to Elizabeth Taylor, 'I have a car.' And Elizabeth Taylor said, 'Well, I have a garage.' So Eddie Fisher to her, 'Mind if I park my car in your garage?'"

He pedaled away snorting, delighted to have mystified Miss Smartypants. I mulled over the stupid elements of his story. Eddie Fisher and Elizabeth Taylor were so notorious at the time it was easy to believe they had something wrong with even their cars and garages. And it was easy to imagine that boys, who reveled in disgusting information, would know it but I wouldn't. Still, why would Eddie Fisher have to ask Liz Taylor if he could use her garage? He was still married to Debbie Reynolds; didn't he park in their garage?

Because, came the cognitive flash, "car" and "garage" don't mean those things. They stand for Liz and Eddie's bodies.

Which meant somehow a man could "park" inside a woman.

At age nine, this was news to me. The notion of being so invaded, and Larry Hayes' obvious glee in it, was completely revolting. I clung to the faint hope that what Liz and Eddie did was a perversion of Hollywood movie stars unknown and unpracticed by decent people in upstate New York.

The hope was dashed by my friend Carol Dooley, who was a year older than me and whose mother had just had a seventh baby. Carol was suddenly, irrepressibly eager to talk about "it" when we roller-skated after school. I knew, from her tone, that the indefinite pronoun must refer to the same thing Larry Hayes had attributed to Eddie and Liz.

"'It is how women have babies," Carol confirmed, her breath steamy in the autumn chill. "And I know how it happens. The man goes to the bathroom inside the woman."

This conjured an image for me of a man and woman, naked, face-to-face above a toilet bowl. They straddled it, grappling, while he—how?—peed—where?— inside her. It was too horrible. God could never have planned such filth for human beings, I decided, and skated away to dismiss the image.

Some days later Carol added that a woman bled as part of "it." I told her I didn't want to hear any more of this information. She crossed-her-heart-and-hoped-to-die it had come straight from her mother. I assumed either Carol was getting things wrong—understandable with such an upsetting topic—or exaggerating. With six sisters and brothers, Carol often did that, I'd noticed, to get attention.

But when I accompanied Carol into her parents' bedroom to see the new baby in her bassinet, I couldn't take my eyes off the big double bed. It was messy, even with the spread pulled up, and there was an intimate smell in the room, not just of baby diapers, but of something else.

My parents slept in twin beds. On weekends, when it was the children's job to clean upstairs, we changed the sheets. Mother's covers were often barely touched, and we marveled aloud that she was such a *light* sleeper, while *Daddy*, whose sheets and blankets were strewn on the ground, was such a thrasher! None of us guessed what the Dooley's bed had made so crystal-clear to me: that two had thrashed and slept in each other's arms.

I began to suspect Mrs. Dooley of being capable of the thing Carol had described. And that furthermore, she hadn't confined "it" to the sanitation of the bathroom; she'd done it in her bed.

The Dooleys had seven children. We only had four, which made me glad Mother's fastidious nature had been offended three fewer times by the necessary act. I pitied Mrs. Dooley. I was sure she'd have been horrified to know her daughter had blabbed the sorry details of her marital life all over the neighborhood.

One day I found myself alone with her. We were in the kitchen—I consuming the crackers and peanut butter Mrs. Dooley had lovingly put out for children to snack on in passing and she at the sink doing dishes. This was, I knew, a golden opportunity to probe Mrs. Dooley about her difficult life; she was usually surrounded by the teeming horde. I couldn't address the toilet-bowl act directly, but I could skirt it.

"Isn't it hard having seven children?" I asked.

"What do you mean?" she said, looking over her shoulder with a smile that, in hindsight, melts me. She loved children so much she was absolutely delighted to be the object of their interrogation.

"Well, you know—" I suppressed the image of the couple in the bathroom "—it just seems like so much work."

"Oh. You noticed that, huh?" She laughed, and I could see why, even with her overbite and frizzy copper hair, her name always topped the guest list when my father planned his fantasy Dinner Party Honoring the Neighborhood's Most Beautiful Women.

"Isn't it?"

"Sure! It's loads of work," she said, "but it's also so much *fun*. That's why I did it. You'll see, when you have children."

"I don't think I will. I'm going to be an actress."

She nodded gravely. Then she smiled and said:

"Even actresses have children."

Carol had two pictures of her mother that she cherished. One featured Mrs. Dooley and her father, an army Colonel, on horseback. Mrs. Dooley wore jodhpurs and riding boots. Her mother had grown up rich, Carol explained, and didn't miss it a bit—"She says I'm luckier to have brothers and sisters than she was to have a horse." We both looked longingly at the horse before Carol put the picture back on her cluttered dresser-top. "And I guess she's right, because I could never, ever be happy without my baby sister," Carol declared stoutly. Her loyalty impressed me. She produced the second photo from a drawer. It showed Mrs. Dooley a little more recognizably grown-up, but in a very weird pose, barefoot, dressed in a short tunic, and lit very dramatically. "And this is from when she studied with Katherine Dunham," Carol said in that faint tone of braggadocio that made me want to challenge her. "Who's Katherine Dunham?" I sniffed. "A famous modern dancer in New York," came the reply. That shut me up: New York! Carol took tap lessons; she'd performed on the back of a flat-bed truck in public parks. She knew about the dance world. This was solid information, and it gave me new respect for Mrs. Dooley. She'd been somebody, in New York, before she'd been a housewife.

Another day I sat at their kitchen table, this time with Carol, while Mrs. Dooley was at the sink. It was Saturday; Mr. Dooley came in, from working outside, to rinse his hands at the tap. To do so he encircled his wife, pressed up against her, and sang:

"Anything you can do I can do better!"

She laughed. They began to rock together. He finished rinsing, then shook the excess water off and placed his hands on her hips.

"I can do anything better than you!" she sang back, and on the "you" she gave a bump-and-grind that shed his hands. She glanced backwards at him and they laughed again. As he walked toward the dining room, she threw him a dishtowel that landed on his shoulder. Without stopping, he removed it, wiped his hands, and placed it neatly folded on the edge of the counter before disappearing through the pantry, whistling.

It was the sexiest scene I'd ever witnessed.

I saw that Mrs. Dooley was happy, despite her life with "it." This was a mystery I hoped I'd never understand.

I was eleven when my mother confirmed some of Carol's information. She breezed into my room one night with a studied, casual air that always betrayed that she'd given the subject at hand much anxious deliberation before entering, and lilted:

"Your sister used a word while you were at the table doing homework tonight. It reminded me of something I wanted to talk to you about, and I wondered if you knew what it meant."

I knew this was our talk about "it." The urge to laugh gripped me. I fought it, composing my face in a quivering smile that I hoped passed for pleasant surprise at seeing her.

"The word was 'ovulation.' Do you know what that means?"

I shook my head "no," and she began to explain what it meant. She handed over a pamphlet. By the time she left, I knew the meanings of "ovulation," "menstruation," "period," "Kotex," and "Moddess." She emphasized "period" in a tangent that was clearly, for her, the conversational highlight: naming.

"That's the term *I'd* like to use. You might hear some of your friends calling it 'The Curse.' Have you? Their mothers might use it. I think it's very Old World; I don't really like it."

I shook my head. I'd heard "period" from the girls and "Kotex" from the boys, who in fifth grade had begun hissing, "Hey, you dropped your Kotex!" whenever girls passed them in the aisles. I'd thought they'd meant bra, like "Playtex." It was disgusting to find out what they'd really been thinking. I hated it that boys knew stuff about girls before we did.

"I think it's too crude," Mother continued, "and not fair. Anything that leads to something as wonderful as having children doesn't deserve to be called a curse. Because it's really a blessing. Even if it does hurt a little—and that's not really much. You'll see."

Our family pursued the Right Word for things with a passion that would have impressed Flaubert, the legendary novelist whose talent with "le mot juste" was lost, I always thought, in translation. Surely Madame Bovary's "torpors" were something more instantly evocative in French. In our home, the right word unlocked the riches of a reference library, and we had one right under our own roof. My father, in the mid-fifties, had invested in an Encyclopedia Britannica. "Passing the word" was often the sum total of home education on topics my parents weren't prepared to discuss.

By the end of our talk, Mother had failed to pass the word about anything male involving reproduction. She'd left me with a Moddess napkin, a pamphlet, and the impression that women had babies by parthenogenesis. I skimmed the pamphlet immediately for news about the toilet-bowl act, but there were no hints in the cartoon illustrations of girls who looked about thirty doing things clean enough to illustrate. Then I found a diagram of the womb and ovaries, where sperm met egg in a process captioned "reproduction."

Reproduction! At last, a word with which I could do research! I went to our library shelves and pulled down the first "R" volume of the Britannica, which gleamed proudly atop the shelf of old, thin maroon volumes Mother had redeemed with Topps Value Stamps at the supermarket. I had settled on the floor with this tome open on my knees to the "Reproduction" article—which at first glance looked distressingly full of information about plants—when I heard my father say:

"What are you looking up?"

He was standing in the doorway, beaming with the self-congratulation of a man seeing returns on a very costly investment.

I'd gotten the worst spanking of my life for lying to him as a toddler, but even that bitter memory couldn't make me tell the truth to him now: that I was looking up how a man's penis goes into a woman.

"Roosevelt," I replied evenly.

"Really? Theodore? Or Franklin?"

I withdrew my hand from the thick sheaf of pages I'd flipped over it, and obliterated my place. Franklin was hated by my mother's uncles for single-handedly ruining the country with the New Deal. I knew less about Theodore.

"Franklin," I said.

"Really?"

I bowed my head to search for Roosevelt and saw the volume didn't go to "R-O." I had to get rid of Daddy; if he came any nearer I'd be sunk. I stared him down; sometimes that worked.

"Well, good!" he blustered. "Glad to see you engaged in a research task!" He disappeared.

I returned the book to the shelf and never again attempted so public a pursuit of such delicate information. My ignorance persisted.

So I had no word for the feeling that seized me so hard one day that I went to the attic, took off my clothes, and began rolling around naked on the floor just to feel the rough wood scratch my skin. I was desperate to feel where *I* ended and the world began. My bones knocked against the wood and my skin picked up grit as I turned over and over, catching a glimpse, every revolution, of the view out our half-moon window near the floor. It was familiar, yet strange, because I saw everything from above, at a distance. The tops of our maple trees and the red brick sidewalk beneath made me ache, as if I were dead and I'd already lost them. I wanted to fly out the window and embrace them, or fly over the neighborhood and embrace *it*—or something—*something!*—that was beyond my power of imagining. My spirit stretched and strained, but it couldn't escape my body. It couldn't even rise to the surface of my skin for satisfaction by bumping and scraping. My soul was trapped inside my body, which couldn't satisfy it. The two were hopelessly disconnected. Exhausted and frustrated, I got dressed and went downstairs, trying to pretend nothing out of the ordinary had happened. But of course, something had: I'd rolled around naked on purpose. It would have to be confessed.

I didn't know if my act was a mortal sin. It seemed likely, but such private depravities had never been discussed, in books, or in the classroom. Everyone would have died of embarrassment. My ignorance, I thought hopefully, might save me; one of the conditions of sinning mortally was knowing the sin was serious before you consented. I had to hope I'd live until Saturday to find out. Presenting myself at the rectory to confess out-of-control nudity was out of the question.

On Saturday I went to Father Reddington in the dark. He had little to do with the parish children and I hoped he wouldn't know me. Disguising my voice

slightly, I recited my list of the usual venial offenses—disobedience, lack of char-
ity, fighting with my brothers and sister— then dropped the bomb. Father
Reddington didn't even flinch. In fact, he seemed to think I could have done much
worse.

"Was there a boy, by chance, anywhere present, my child, when you did this
thing?"

A boy? How disgusting! Why would I *ever* —!

"No, Father!"

"Good. That's good." The priest sighed. "As you get older now, you'll find
yourself visited by these feelings more often. They're natural, but God gives us
prayer and the sacraments to help us resist them. Whatever you do, never, ever do
this thing in the presence of any boy. Not even if one asks you to. Is that clear?"

"Yes, Father."

And that was when the last piece of the puzzle clicked into place. A priest, of
all people, had provided it! I knew what sex was now. Sex was the feeling. The feeling led to sex. Women did "it," even *sought* "it," in their beds, because "it" was sex.
That was what the feeling wanted. The toilet-bowl act, I realized, must scratch our
insides. Sex had been the thing I'd longed to embrace.

"I firmly resolve with the help of Thy Grace, to sin no more and to avoid the
near occasion of sin," I intoned, hearing the Latin absolution wipe me clean. Now
that I knew the truth, I would never do such a thing again. I would ignore the feeling, just as I ignored Friday hot dogs and sleeping late on Sunday morning. Sex
was something I would simply leave out of my life.

13.

Body and Soul

I stood on the Gillette House landing overlooking our mixer. It was packed. I knew the brother of my Mercy high school classmate, being tall, would be easy to spot. But he wasn't the one I was looking for. I was waiting for the boy my tall friend had promised to bring to the Smith mixers—Jonathan Pratt.

The previous weekend, the tall friend had arranged a blind date for me on his campus. It hadn't worked out; the date and I had bored each other, and he'd gotten drunk at a room party, while I struck up a conversation with an attractive couple sitting on the floor against the wall. The boy had sweeping, long lashes and beautiful blue eyes. When the girl stopped talking animatedly, she passed out, slumping on his shoulder, and he told me their story; she was his ex-lover and an old friend. Her hand, in sleep, was flung over the boy's patch-madras Bermudas near his groin. This drove me crazy. The boy seemed barely to notice. He was too busy flirting with me.

His name was Jonathan, and in the course of the weekend he managed to corner me for a little more conversation. By Sunday I suggested to my tall friend that, when he came to Smith mixers the following weekend, he bring not my blind date, but that cute boy, Jonathan Pratt.

I spotted a tall man winding his way into the darkened Gillette living room. A curly head bobbed in his wake. My heart somersaulted. The two passed the front windows, and for a moment, streetlights backlit the curly-headed one and made him look just like —

"Bob Dylan! I'd know you anywhere!" bleated an adenoidal male voice below me, dripping with sarcasm. When I descended, I made sure to give the speaker a punitive brush. Out of my way, preppy asshole. The rebel is a better breed. For me, Bob Dylan associations have always been a powerful aphrodisiac.

Jonathan was as happy to see me as I to see him. Our magnetism was potent and immediate. We danced and drank beer, then went outside to cool our sweat in the autumn chill. We walked to Smith's quadrangle, where he said, "I like you."

His understatement charmed me. I was sure he meant more. He was looking away, into the distance, as crashing drum sounds and the throbbing guitar lines rose and fell all around us, from doors opening and closing on parties in full swing.

"I like you too," I offered.

"I like you so much, I'm not going to leave you this whole night," he finessed, with a fetching sideways glance.

"Yes you are!" I sputtered. Was he crazy? Not only would I never do such a thing, no Smith girl could stay out all night in Northampton if she wanted to; we had a curfew!

Jonathan told me much later that my vehemence had amazed him. As the melting sensation in my stomach had amazed me, for his verbal declaration of sexual intent had touched my mind, which no boy's mute gropings had ever reached. It opened at last to the desire for sweet surrender.

"It's a purely physical attraction," I told my roommate Pam, after the campus was quiet and the men had gone home. We were standing in the doorway of our room so I could smoke a cigarette during our mixer post-mortem.

"Really?" she said, shivering slightly at the prospect of sex for sex's sake.

How lordly it felt to shock, instead of being the eternally shocked!

"Yeah." I blew a stream of smoke over her pink-rollered Indiana head, feeling suddenly released from my suffocating provincial girlhood. Free at last, free at last, thank God Almighty, I'm free at last.

●

I dated a boy from Harvard just to see Cambridge, but he was a stuffy conservative and I found him insufferable. Even the grand Charles and the ivy-covered brick of my father's old stomping grounds couldn't make me forget Jonathan's blue eyes. I decided not to try to see anyone else. I began spending most weekends on Jonathan's campus.

I stayed at a Town House Motor Inn, which Jonathan paid for with social security money he got because his mother had died when he was young. We'd spend all day making out, sitting down or standing up all over his campus, then drive to the motel on his motorcycle, kiss goodnight at my room's door, and I'd enter alone, limp and damp, to lie down for a chaste night's sleep. This, and my conditioned resistance to French kissing, helped me convince myself I was not sinning mortally. But I was having venereal pleasure, that much I'd figured out. And by Daniel Lord's reckoning, I was in the red zone.

The night before Christmas break, I took my suitcase to Jonathan's campus by bus. In the morning, my tall friend would take us home in his car. Jonathan's Thruway exit was just a few stops before Rochester. We partied at Jonathan's fraternity, then wandered back to his room, which his roommate had already vacated; we climbed to Jonathan's top bunk and lay down.

Once before, we'd done this, but I'd insisted on being taken back to the motel. This night, in the scenario immortalized by the Everly Brothers in "Wake Up

Little Susie," we fell asleep and our goose was cooked. I awoke in the darkness to feel Jonathan's hand at the back of my neck, unzipping my dress.

Intense waves of pleasure shot through me. I touched his arm and made him stop, but the zipper stayed open at the neck, and I stayed awake, my whole body quivering. In a little while he tried again.

It took most of the night for that zipper to reach its nadir, and every inch imperiled my soul. With the dress entirely opened, my soul flew away. Jonathan gently pushed the sides off my shoulders while I lay still, lacking any will to protest. But as he eased it down my body, over my slip, I raised my hips to make it easier. It continued down my legs. Jonathan freed the dress from my feet and dropped it overboard. It sounded loud, hitting the ground. It had a long way to fall.

I lay awake, suffused with pleasure and shame. Occasionally I drifted into a dream, but a ravishing sense of exposure snapped me awake every time. Undressed, in my slip, I clung to Jonathan like a drowning sailor to a mast. Clinging brought kisses, and kisses more pleasure, but we didn't make love. What had happened was enough. I felt terribly alive, as big as the world itself. Before, I'd only felt so alive onstage. This was different. Onstage, I was bright, safe, defined, and free. In the dark, I was floating, invisible, imperiled, and lost. I didn't care; I was drunk with pleasure.

When gray light showed at the window, I climbed quietly off the bed to retrieve my dress. Jonathan awoke to the sound of my zipper and asked, "Why?"

"Because," I told him, returning to bury my head in his now-bare chest. I couldn't remember him taking off his shirt, and I couldn't explain my shame at being revealed in the light as I'd been in the darkness. In the darkness, he'd been cover enough, but in the light, I needed my old self, even if it were just an empty shell.

Riding home on Jonathan's lap I whispered, "What happened last night can't ever happen again."

"I know," he said.

I was afraid he didn't understand the depth of my guilt, or my resolve. "I mean it," I insisted.

"I know," he repeated. This time he sounded penitent and miserable, which inflamed me. We kissed passionately all the way to Junius Ponds.

He came to our house for dinner over vacation. He started to sit next to me at the table, but my parents cheerily directed him to the opposite chair, saying they'd reserved it for him. He stared at me through the candles all through the meal, secret messages glinting from beneath his sweeping eyelashes. He answered my parents' conversational forays with false heartiness, but initiated no topics of his own. I could tell they found him intellectually wanting, which infuriated me. Their intellectual snobbery blinded them to Jonathan's good qualities; I wanted to protect him. But talking to him afterward, I found that he didn't need protection. My parents hadn't intimidated him at all. He said he'd found them laughably uptight.

Before I went back to school, Mother appeared in my room one morning with a pile of clean laundry. Its delivery was a pathetic ruse, I thought, to corner me about Jonathan. Now that they'd seen him, my parents were worried.

"I hope you know what you're doing, Mimi," she'd ventured. "Where do you stay when you visit him, in motels? I worry about that. Even in my day, a lot of heavy petting went on in those."

"I don't let him inside the motel, Mom," I said.

She'd correctly guessed that my romance, proceeding far from home, wasn't proceeding by home rule, but I resented that she didn't think I had boundaries.

It was precisely her presumption that I *did* have boundaries that had her worried. She'd grown up Catholic, romantic, and naive, too. She knew what she hoped I as yet did not; that the exquisite, slow process of boundary-breaching was far more romantically obsessing than sexual blitzkrieg. She knew the inexorable progress towards consummation was one of life's sweetest journeys. And she wanted it to begin with an engagement ring and end on a honeymoon, neither of which she hoped was in sight for me and Jonathan.

"I just hope you're being careful, that's all," she grumbled.

"I'm being careful," I said.

In show business, there is a form of bad news called "The Hollywood No." It refers to the crashing silence after auditions during which we actors pester our agents, scan our horoscopes, and wait in daily hope to hear we got the job. Instead we hear that principle photography has begun or wrapped; that someone working on the project has met a friend of ours who says hello; that the show is on the network schedule; that previews folded in Boston. Any of which reveal the truth no tongue would tell: we weren't wanted.

My mother, who had excellent show-business instincts, left the room.

My slip was on the top of the laundry pile. It won't be so easy, I thought with a pang, to get myself clean. I picked it up to pack in my suitcase, and the satiny folds composed by my mother's sure hands slithered apart in mine.

○

By spring, Jonathan was in the motel with me, remapping boundaries.

He was *in* the room—lying, fully clothed, on the bed.

He was *on* the bed. Not *in* it. The sheets were the new metaphorical hymen.

He stayed *most* of the night. Not *all.*

Only when Jonathan left at dawn did I crack the covers for a few hours' virginal sleep.

We were naked *above* the waist. Not *below.*

His shirt had come off first, that prevacation night. Mine was shed, more intimately, much later. We spent months exploring the mutual fields of flesh we'd discovered.

On Sundays Jonathan drove me to Mass. Sometimes he'd come into church, but more often he'd drop me off and pick me up, as I'd seen men do outside Catholic churches all my life.

Sometimes I dared take communion, if only as an offering to my absent soul. I imagined it as watching me from a great distance. I needed God; if ingesting Him was a mortal sin, what difference did one more make? Somehow I hoped He'd be modern enough to accept that, in this day and age, my technical virginity was sullied proof of my good intentions. With which, I knew, the road to hell was paved.

Eventually, guilt overwhelmed me and, one Saturday, I asked Jonathan to drive me to confession.

Jonathan understood about religion. His father had been a minister, and Jonathan became one. He also understood about guilt, having borne his own since age seven, when he'd found his mother dead of carbon monoxide poisoning in the family car while his father and brother were at church. Waiting for them to get home, Jonathan had walked around the house removing liquor bottles from the places he knew his mother kept them. He thought only he'd known her secret, and hoped by removing the evidence no one would know she'd been drinking, and that would make the tragedy more bearable for his father. I thought Jonathan's driving me to confession was proof of his bravery and goodness. I didn't know what kind of priest I'd get, a modern Cure d'Ars,[1] or a hell-and-brimstone executioner who'd make me choose between God and my boyfriend. I couldn't make that choice. Sister Brian would have said I'd already made it, at God's expense.

I got off the motorcycle and entered the church alone, choosing a confessional line at random in the darkness, my fate in God's hands. As I approached the booth for my turn, the shriven penitent emerging held back the velvet curtain with a beatific smile. It heartened me. I hoped she wasn't just a goody-goody, with nothing serious to confess, as I'd once been. I spotted the kneeler in the half-light and let the curtain fall, plunging me into total darkness. The murmuring of the sinner across the booth was loud; I plugged my ears. The hum changed when the priest began intoning absolution, and I folded my hands, awaiting my turn with a pounding heart.

Their wooden screen scraped shut. Mine opened. Beyond the wire mesh I saw a gray-haired man shielding his eyes with his hand.

I began formally: "Bless me father, I confess to almighty God and to you, Father, that I have sinned." The priest shifted his weight. Next I had to say how

---

[1]St. Jean Vianney, a parish priest who became famous for his compassion and insight in the confessional

long it had been since my last confession. It had been too long to state pro forma; my distance from the church was all of a piece, and to explain it I had to pour out my heart.

"It's been over a year since my last confession, Father. I'm in college, and that's made my life so different…I've fallen in love, Father. He's a good man, but…we're doing things I've never done before. I know it's probably wrong but I'm not sure I can stop. We're not having intercourse, but…we're doing everything else. Heavy petting, and….We want to get married, Father, but we can't yet, and I can't leave him, his life has been so sad, Father. His mother committed suicide, and I never want to abandon him again….But I still love God and I don't know what to do—"

I broke off, sobbing, to bury my face in my hands. I heard the mesh screen slide back and opened my eyes to see a wad of Kleenex being proffered through the opening. Truce.

I took it and blew my nose. The priest waited, then spoke to me, kindly and gently. He gave me a nominal penance, not the pilgrimage to Rome or year of novenas I'd imagined when I'd dared hope for absolution at all. Then he said the words that stayed with me all down the long, lonely road I'd chosen:

"As long as you feel you're not doing anything against the Love of Christ, you'll be all right with God. Stay close to Our Lord. I think He must love you very much."

●

Despite the ban on freshman acting in major productions at Smith, John Fisher cast me in the one he directed, Garcia Lorca's *Yerma*. I coveted the lead, a frigid Spanish woman who can't get pregnant because she's guilty about sex and never has it "just for pleasure." But the lead was out of the question.

There were six laundresses, and Fisher used us as a Greek chorus. We sat at the back of the set throughout the play; we *were* the back of the set, in our outsize, El Greco–distorted, looming Spanish chairs, staring fixedly into space. My eyes stung; tears streamed down my face. I didn't move except when we came alive for our scene on the banks of the river, kneeling on raked ramps criss-crossing the old thrust stage at Alumnae Gym. I remember one of my lines was, "A woman looking at roses is not the same as a woman looking at a man's thighs!" I brayed it in a vulgar, throaty voice, rocking back on my heels with a guttural laugh. I was acting to beat the band; I had no emotional connection to what I was saying. Looking at Jonathan's thighs in real life made me quiet, shivery, and shy.

But it was wonderful to be onstage again, even if it meant staying on my own campus two weekends in a row.

That summer, Jonathan and I remapped our boundaries.

I worked in a War-on-Poverty program in Rochester's inner city, and Jonathan worked in his town an hour away. We couldn't be together at night, but he came to drive the inner-city kids around the parks with me in his "raggedy car," as the kids called his old Checker. We spent weekend afternoons trespassing lush upstate farmlands, lying beneath trees in our favorite apple orchard, caressing on a slab of sun-heated slate above our secret waterfall.

Before I ever saw Jonathan's penis I touched it and was shocked. It was erect, and I had no idea what I was touching. I'd felt the lump in his pants for a year, but I'd never seen a naked erection. I visualized the closest thing it seemed like; one of those hard, molded-rubber dog bones.

"Lover," I said, "...is that all you?'

He melted at this, as what man wouldn't, having his ardor greeted with such awe? "Yes," he said shyly.

"You're not...wearing anything?"

"No." He sounded puzzled. "Like what?"

I realized I was more ignorant than even he, after a year of intimacy, suspected. But it was much too late to be coy.

"A...rubber?"

"No." He seemed mystified.

By "rubber" I'd meant "dildo" but I didn't know the word "dildo" any more than I knew what a condom was.

The last time I'd glimpsed a penis in real life I'd been four, still young enough to be permitted to snuggle in either of my parent's beds as they got up and dressed. My mother's body was familiar to me; I thought her aureoles and navel made a funny, surprised face. But my father's body was not familiar; he was careful to be more modest. One day he entered from the bathroom and the towel slipped from his waist. He turned to hide himself at his bureau but before he could, I saw what he kept hidden. Between his legs was something brownish-maroon, shiny, and wet. It looked like a bloody slab of raw liver.

Horrified, I went to my older brother and asked him to show me the thing I remembered, from our toddler days of casual bathroom-sharing, as a peach-colored hose, very useful for doing what I straddled the seat above the rushing waters to do. Unless age turned all boy's hoses into grotesque bloody slabs, something had gone terribly wrong with our father's private parts, and I wanted to alert someone. Danny refused to co-operate. This reassured me in a way, suggesting that something indeed happened to all men and was probably happening to Danny, which understandably made him shy. But I was also disgusted to know what I'd seen on my father was normal. This concluded my study of live male anatomy.

In *National Geographic* magazine and *Life* magazine articles on art, I saw the male member in repose. At camp I heard the word "erection," which made me think of erector sets and led me to think penises lifted at simple ninety-degree angles for insertion. I never pictured a change in shape or size. I didn't want to picture function.

Somewhere along the line I'd gone on a date with the brother of one of my sister's country club beaus. He surprised me, and deeply overestimated my sophistication by taking me to *I Am Curious Yellow*, a scandalous Swedish movie. He told me where we were going as we drove there; I was too embarrassed to say I shouldn't see the movie because the Legion of Decency, our Catholic movie-rating system, had condemned it. Catholics were dispensed from scrupulous observance when it would cause undue embarrassment or inconvenience to their hosts, so I granted myself the dispensation and closed my eyes through most of the movie. But the panning of a newsstand caught me by surprise, and what I saw transfixed me: scores of male nudie magazines, whose cover boys sported things that looked like giant, inflatable attachments waving in front of their abdomens. Those perverted Swedes! I'd thought. Flaunting some evidently widespread perversion! But I kept looking at the first scrota I'd seen in years and thought about them all through our polite, postmovie dinner at a continental restaurant.

After I touched Jonathan, he showed me everything, and I understood. His beauty overwhelmed me. Soon I returned the favor. We still didn't make love.

Sophomore year, I took the most thrilling course of my Smith education. It was taught by Kenneth Amor Connelly on the works of James Joyce and William Butler Yeats. We surveyed Yeats' poetry, and read Joyce's *Portrait of the Artist as a Young Man* and *Ulysses*.

"For Irish Catholics," Mr. Connelly lectured, "sex isn't just a mortal sin, it's the only mortal sin." Far up in the lecture hall, I almost wept to hear him say this in a fearless, reasonable tone. I looked around me and wondered how many of the girls could appreciate the terror of mortal sin.

"Joyce believed in 'the sacramental of the ordinary,'" Mr. Connelly said. "Yeats, too, believed the physical was holy."

"They say such different things at school," the Dancer tells her instructor in one of my favorite Yeats poems, "Michael Robartes and the Dancer." I was ecstatic to discover Irish people, at last, who weren't afraid of sex! Yeats, Joyce, and Mr. Connelly were my new heroes. Reading Yeats' poetry aloud was the work Kenneth Amor Connelly was meant to do; sometimes the effect was so intense I'd have to go back to the dorm, pack, and visit Jonathan mid-week. "Even from the foot sole," Robartes tells the Dancer, "think it too." He was urging her to think with her body, because women who did so lived in "uncomposite blessedness"— body and soul united!— inspiring men to do the same. The poem seemed written to accompany my physical awakening.

It was classes like this, I supposed, that made Sister Brian warn me a girl could lose her soul at a secular college.

The final boundary collapsed sometime during my sophomore year, in a motel, just as my mother had feared. It was unplanned, but long awaited. I wept tears of joy, saying "You're in me, lover, you're in me," surprised that it was so easy, trying to make the act conscious on every level. I never wanted to be wordless again.

It may have been self-fulfilling prophecy that I, who'd been taught that body and soul were separate and opposed, would have to lose one to claim the other. It was horribly painful. But until I discovered how the two were one, and why the physical was holy, my soul would remain lost.

14.

Le Mot Juste

John Fisher noted my transformation from the single-minded creature whose devotion to acting had impressed him so my freshman year into what he perceived as a distracted, detached dilettante. I was, in his eyes, to becoming one of those Seven Sisters types he loathed: a girl born to breed for the upper classes.

"You're such a Smithie!" he groused. "There are only three of you here who might make actresses: Ellen, Sarah, and you. And I'm not so sure about you."

We all became professional actresses. But, sophomore year, only Ellen and Sarah were in *The Seagull.* It was the major production, which Madame Eugenie Leontovich came to direct as artist-in-residence. The department buzzed with excitement the week of her arrival. Auditions were set for Thursday night. I snuck out of town Wednesday to see Jonathan after a particularly inspiring Yeats-Joyce class and wasw back Thursday by dinner.

Arriving at the recently completed studio wing of the partially built theater center, I found Fisher, Leontovich, and all of my friends seated in a friendly fashion that suggested they'd been there a while conducting not a casting session, but a rehearsal. Which is exactly what it was.

John Fisher looked up, saw me, and, glowering, came to usher me out of the room.

"Where *were* you?" he seethed. "She arrived last night and was so overcome by the department's welcoming party that she started to cast the whole damn thing then and there! When I saw what was happening I tried to reach you but no one knew where you were, at that number you left at your dorm! It's all over! It's cast!"

I'd been at the motel. He'd obviously called Jonathan's fraternity and gotten some lounge lizard.

Sarah was Arkadina, and Ellen was cast as Nina. Masha, the part Fisher had mentally reserved for me, would be played by a girl whom everyone knew wouldn't have gotten the shot if I'd been around. No one was going to take it away from her.

I left the premises. Fisher called me the next day, telling me to meet him at the theater. When I got there, I saw him, Ellen, and Eugenie. They were gathered to offer me their collective proposal that I alternate the role of Nina with Ellen.

Alternating? A buzzer went off in my head. No thank you. I'd hated it when I was twelve years old and presumed it would be far worse at the conscious age of nineteen. I declined, which made Ellen burst into tears.

"I knew it! See? Oh this is just so *awful!*" she blubbered. "I *knew* she wouldn't take it. I told you! Then let her have the role herself, please? Just give it to her! I don't *want* something that feels like I've taken it from someone else! It's *terrible,* this jealousy and this competition! It isn't what acting's about! Just *take* the role—take it!" she sobbed.

Boy, I thought meanly, *you're* the one Mr. Fisher should worry about not having the stuff to become a professional actress, not me. How could anyone survive in the business, who felt so decently miserable and was so genuinely unable to enjoy her good fortune because it had come at somebody else's expense?

As I thought this, I drifted very far away, and the whole scene suddenly telescoped. Ellen sobbing, Eugenie shaking her head, Fisher glaring was all part of human ambition—what Yeats called "the struggle of a fly in marmalade." I'm above all this now, I thought.

"That's all right Ellen. You have the part," I said, thinking, I *am* Nina. I don't have to play her. "You deserve it," I assured her. "I don't want it, honestly. You'll be wonderful. Thank you anyway."

Love had made me real.

Fisher's mouth went tight, and in that moment, I saw him write me off. I walked back to the dorm believing every word I'd said, feeling mature and level-headed.

I caught the play on a Thursday night, before taking off to see Jonathan. It was magnificent. I applauded my brightly lit friends, feeling generous and brave in my anonymous darkness. Bravo, little pretenders in the spotlight! Bravo, dear little fools with your pretend lives—Chris Jones, Bill Cwikowski, Jerry Zaks, Susan Haddad, Ellen and Sarah! Ellen had been particularly wonderful. The moment when she'd leaned her cheek against Konstantin's outdoor proscenium and breathed, "A dream!" as she watched her future lover and destroyer depart, had been indelible.

She'd been so fragile! See? I lectured myself, shuffling back to the dorm. You could never have been fragile.

❂

I applied to Tufts University-in-London for their junior-year-abroad Drama program. I did it to get away from Jonathan and get back to acting, but I couldn't admit that to anyone, least of all to myself.

My acceptance letter came when I was home in Rochester for spring break. Before he sat down to dinner that night, my father came to my place and kissed me, saying, "I didn't approve of you doing this, but you went ahead anyway because you wanted it, and did it all on your own. I'm proud of you."

"Why are you going away for a year with a chain around your neck?" said one of the male students as we crossed the Atlantic on the S.S. *United States.* He meant Jonathan's fraternity pin, which I wore on a necklace. I found the remark offensive, but I didn't have a good answer.

I wrote to Jonathan daily and received chock-full, tissue-thin, blue aerogrammes daily from him. By Christmas we'd planned to meet in London. I would visit Italy first, for which my parents had sent me vacation money. But I'd be frugal; Jonathan and I would need most of the money. I rented our love-nest in advance—a bed–sitting room, with a hot plate, in Camden Gardens. It was decorated in ancient chintz and smelled of old cooked cauliflower.

I made one other preparation for Jonathan's visit: I visited a gynecologist for the first time in my life.

My roommate Connie made me do it. She heard my lover was coming to town for two weeks and that I'd never been to a gynecologist. She quickly got her American friend, who lived with her American boyfriend while he recorded his first album at the Beatles' Apple Records, to recommend a doctor.

His address was in Harley Street. I'd once read that Paul McCartney's girlfriend, Jane Asher, was above his social station because her father was a "Harley Street surgeon." In happier circumstances I would have been thrilled by the pedigree of my referral—Apple Records, Jane Asher, the Beatles!—particularly if I'd known the source's boyfriend was James Taylor. But I was too guilty about going to a doctor, as an unmarried woman, and asking for The Pill. I rang the bell at his handsome, black-lacquered door in Harley Street as if I were sneaking to a back-alley abortionist.

The doctor himself answered. He ushered me into a beautifully appointed waiting room that seemed like part of his home, everything was so utterly personal and discreet. I don't remember any office staff. He took me into an examination room where he left me alone to disrobe and don a gown.

When he came back, I told him the story I'd devised: I was a student in London, doing my junior year abroad, but my longtime boyfriend and I had decided to get married! He was coming to London for the wedding at Christmas, but since we were both students, we couldn't have a family at this time. So naturally, I needed The Pill to begin married life.

He nodded and helped me into the stirrups, which are such an unpleasant shock for every girl, her first time. He proceeded to examine me. I hadn't realized until right that moment that he would know immediately I wasn't a virgin.

"So you and your boyfriend have already had sexual activity?" he asked, with a tinge of nonjudgmental surprise.

"Yes." Yes, doctor, I'm an American slut.

He did the rest of his tasks in silence. When he was finished, he told me dress and come meet him in his office, whose open door I'd see outside. Then he left.

I entered the office to find it awash in leather, baize, brass, and mahogany, and him seated at his desk.

"About how long have you and your fiancé been having sexual relations?" he asked with kindly British detachment.

I figured I'd never see him again, so I decided to be truthful.

"Over a year."

The moment his eyebrows went up I was sorry.

"Over a year?"

I cringed.

"How often?"

"About…every weekend."

I waited for him to scream "Jezebel!" but he merely hunched forward and squinted.

"How on earth have you avoided getting pregnant up until now?"

Oh, that.

"Withdrawal," I assured him, which caused a large startle reaction.

"Withdrawal?!" he repeated, incredulous.

I despaired. What new ignorance of mine had I revealed? I'd trusted Jonathan on the subject. Withdrawal, he said, was fine. I hadn't gotten pregnant. What was wrong?

The doctor leaned back and took me in as if seeing, for the first time, the full measure of fear, naivete, and bravado before him.

"That can't be very satisfying," he said sympathetically. "For you or your young man."

I looked at him blankly, wondering, Why not? I had orgasms. I thought I'd been pretty cool to figure out ways to help guide Jonathan into making sure they happened, every time. Jonathan didn't complain about withdrawal, though he preferred finishing inside me, just before and just after my period.

"Oh no!" my mother would say, ten years later, when I described the "safe" times, during our official, if tardy, birth control conversation a week before my wedding. "You can get *pregnant* before and after! It's only safe to make love in the *middle!*" Not believing my ears, I'd corrected her. "You can get pregnant in the middle, Mom." "No!" she'd insisted in horror, repeating, "It's in the *middle* that it's *safe!*" I don't know if she had mother-of-the-bride wedding jitters or what, but the woman who'd had four perfectly spaced children using no artificial birth control that I knew of explained the rhythm method to me backward. Twice. After I was married, she also confided that she'd never had an orgasm until after she'd had a baby. This may have been because she conceived two months after the wedding, then Daddy departed for his tour in the Pacific, but in later years, she blamed it on ignorance. Her own mother, my Nana, told me during the 1970s in New York that she'd been reading so much about the female orgasm, she was beginning to wonder if she'd ever had one.

"Of course I felt *pleasure* with Bill," she'd reassured me, "but the feeling *they're* describing sounds so—oh, I don't know—so utterly *fantastic*. Like something out of this *world!*" Nana's escape from her controlling mother, who'd turned four sons into bachelors who only left home when they died, did not suggest the history of a sexual shrinking violet, but there she was, shaking her gray head and saying:

"We knew so little then, really. The first time Bill ever kissed me I slapped him in the face. Can you imagine? What was I thinking? I suppose that he was taking liberties, or some such rubbish, and I had to teach him to be more respectful. But, oh…! We were standing on opposite sides of the mantel. You remember how tall he was—all he had to do in order to kiss me was take two steps and lean over, which is what he did. And for that he was rewarded with a slap in the face! How cruel! Here he was, only trying to say he loved me in the tenderest way he knew…" Nana's face trembled with regret. My grandfather had been dead over a decade. "What shame, what ignorance. We knew so little then. I really didn't know a thing."

The Harley Street gynecologist looked at me and said, "You're in perfect reproductive health. I imagine you're extremely fertile. Someone's been watching over you, my dear. You ought to have conceived ten babies by now."

He gave me a six months' supply of the pill from his cupboard and waved my Barclay's bank checkbook away.

"Let it be my wedding present to you," he said, seeing me to the door. "I hope you and your husband have a very happy marriage and a very happy life."

I stepped out into the winter gray of Harley Street. With no mother, friend, or fiancé to greet me, I was utterly alone. I smiled goodbye at the doctor; it would have been hard to find a bleaker bride in all of London, and both of us knew it.

At least we'd done the right thing. My sad, uncertain, shifting little world was no place to bring in a baby.

●

My mother found the pills while she was helping me unpack in June. "What are these?" she asked, frozen above my suitcase with a half-empty foil packet in her hand.

"Just something," I said, taking it from her and disappearing into the bathroom. I refused to say the word, and there was no further discussion, since you couldn't talk about "something" any more than you could research "it." I knew she knew what they were. I'd seen the plastic dispenser of Ortho-Novums that had appeared on her bedside table while I was still in high school. She'd even volunteered that they were prescribed by her doctor to regulate her cycle, lest I be scandalized—that same doctor later secretly fitted me with a diaphragm, the birth control method I use to this day. God bless him.

She didn't bring the subject up again, but I imagine she went back to her room that day, sank to her knees to pray for my soul, beside her Ortho-Novums, and rose up with a huge sigh of relief.

"Larry Dilg," my friend and mentor Liz Siegel murmured across the Gillette living room one day, staring at the Amherst student newspaper. "Wasn't he your Perfect Computer Matchmate?"

She handed me the paper. It featured a murky photo of a boy onstage, seated on a stool, bent over an acoustic guitar.

"Looks cool," she commented.

Very cool. I nodded in agreement, and gave the paper back to her, experiencing a fleeting pang. Jonathan played hockey and lacrosse. I would have preferred guitar. But such thoughts were tantamount to adultery. Because I was no longer a virgin, I was as committed to Jonathan as if we were already married and living in a parsonage in New Rochelle with two kids, a dog, and a station wagon. That was our dream. He would only serve parishes near New York, and I'd commute to my acting jobs. Some day he'd make the princely sum of forty thousand a year, and we'd live happily ever after, the Bishop and the Showgirl. Not many had gone before us, but—Yes We Can!

The summer I returned from London, I acted in the Smith-Amherst repertory company, and some of the Amherst actors took me to a fraternity party one night. Larry Dilg was the band's lead singer.

I watched from the sidelines, numb. He was Very Attractive, dressed in denim, and singing "I Shall Be Released" with great passion. The Bob Dylan effect kicked in. I decided to introduce myself. Not to begin anything, but to end that silly little story Operation Match had started.

I watched him place his guitar on a stand, and when he stepped offstage, I accosted him.

"Hi," I said brightly, "I'm Mimi Kennedy. I was your Perfect Computer Matchmate freshman year!"

He surveyed me with a look both hot and cool.

"Far out," he said. And walked away.

Into the arms of a blonde, with waist-length hair, who wound her arms around his neck and delivered a long, deep kiss.

Hmmf, I thought.

And that's how I missed my husband on the second pass.

❂

Three years later I was an actress in New York, desperate for work that could win the attention of a legitimate agent when, in the actors' trade papers, *Backstage* and *Show Business,* I saw a casting notice for an Off-Off Broadway production of *The Seagull.* It was to be directed by Eugenie Leontovich.

Everything lost is restored! I thought ecstatically. I have a second chance at what is rightfully mine! I prepared the final scene, in which Nina returns to the summer house where she had been young and in love and finds Konstantin. My soul soared on the downtown bus ride. I was still young enough to play Nina. And I knew *all* of her now!

A dream!

An acolyte led me into Eugenie's presence in a large room. I gave the stage manager my resume and addressed Madame Leontovich:

"My name is Mimi Kennedy and I went to Smith. I was there, Miss Leontovich, when you directed this play. Only I wasn't in it because the day you had auditions I'd been—"

"I'm sorry, dear, but I don't remember you. Vat are you goink to read today?"

I swallowed. "The final scene where Nina comes back," I replied.

"Och! Such a defeecult one," she grumped. "Vy you chooce sumsing so deefeecult? But go ahead. Very good. You try."

I turned upstage to gather my thoughts and become Nina, coming in from the cold. When I turned, I stepped immediately into that warm, familiar room of my childhood. I was home.

My edition's stage directions indicated that Nina sobs at a certain point. Long before I got there, my face was wet with tears. From my line to Konstantin— "Every night I dream you are looking at me and don't recognize me"—I began to cry and couldn't stop.

Eventually I had to give up speaking and surrender to the great, heaving gulps of pain and loss. Eugenie looked on, mystified. It had mattered so much to me— so *much!*—that I'd missed that audition! In the war between art and love, and body and soul, I'd profoundly lost myself.

"Dot's all right dear, eet hoppens to all ov oss sometimes," Eugenie clucked. But when it became obvious I couldn't continue, she signaled her acolyte to get me out of the room.

I went, docile, led by the elbow. We were at the door when I heard Ms. Leontovich whisper to the stage manager remaining behind:

"Next."

❂

In l982, I was at my cluttered Santa Monica kitchen table enjoying a moment of solitude after breastfeeding my son, which I seemed to be doing every twenty minutes even though the books said it should only happen every three hours. While Larry did the diapering, I chose to lavish my three precious minutes on a biography in the *New York Times* of Judge Douglas Ginzburg, whom Ronald Reagan had just nominated to the Supreme Court. The nomination was in trouble because of allegations that Ginzburg had smoked pot at Harvard. I was torn between glee that it was conservative Ronald Reagan being embarrassed by the brouhaha and sympathy for Ginzburg, who seemed due to pay the penalty for what many of us had done in college without such severe consequences. And the brouhaha was big; ten years later, it would prompt presidential candidate Bill Clinton to say he "didn't inhale." The scorn heaped on his blonde brillo head was better than what joints had done to the judge.

In the middle of the article, I came upon the statement that Ginzburg had been an entrepreneur for a few months at Harvard, running a short-lived computer dating service called Operation Match.

I stared at the forgotten name, linked medical symbols rising up on my mindscreen. How briefly, I thought, the window opened and shut through which our little family's fate had flown in!

"Larry?!" I shouted. "We were matched by the pot-smoking judge!"

I saw the forgotten UNIVAC, roughly the size of an eighteen-wheeler. This time, the students shoving perforated computer cards into its maw were giggling. A supervisory figure puffed a big cheroot, then passed it around, as cards marked DO NOT BEND, FOLD, SPINDLE OR MUTILATE slipped to the floor and were trampled. At tables, other students marked more cards, sometimes referring to their stacks of questionnaires, sometimes poking willy-nilly, waiting for turns on the spliff. They puffed and puffed until the scene dissolved in smoke and vanished, leaving only maniacal laughter to echo down the time-tunnel of sixteen years. I returned to my kitchen table.

Did this explain the marital arguments that suggested Larry Dilg and I had never agreed on one thing, let alone a hundred? And those incompatible compatibles? Were we all the work of sky-high computer nerds?

Larry returned, bearing our son.

"What did you say?" he asked.

I gave him the article; he gave me Cisco. In the steadiness of my son's gaze, my panic evaporated and only returned, over the years, when I didn't get enough sleep. After my daughter was born I sent Judge Ginzburg a photo assuring him that even if he'd missed a sinecure on the Supreme Court, he'd done good work arranging these two children's fine and particular DNA configurations, when he'd been the father of Operation Match.

◦

On the weekend of my graduation from Smith, I went to my parents' hotel room to tell them I loved Jonathan and was probably going to marry him, so they'd better get used to it because there was nothing they could do to stop it. I'd said goodnight to them at the Northampton Inn, but as I was walking back to the dorm, I'd turned around, determined to confront them and get the weight off my chest.

My father answered my knock in his pajamas. He and my mother had retired and were reading; they were happy, though wary, to see me. He propped his pillow against his headboard and sat down. I perched on the covered radiator at the foot of their twin beds. In their nightclothes, my parents looked oddly touching; it was not a position of strength. Which is probably why Daddy exploded at what I'd come to say.

"I don't want to hear any more of this!" he bellowed, leaping to his bare feet. "You are *not* in love with this boy and you are *not* going to marry him! And *that's final!*"

What a red flag to wave in front of a lover! I was about to protest violently when what I heard next stopped me cold.

"This is just your first *affair* for Chrissakes! So let's not have any more foolish talk about marriage!"

His hands, which he'd been waving, fell to his sides and were swallowed by pajama sleeves. I stared at him, dumbstruck. He knew Jonathan and I were lovers. And didn't think that reason enough for me to throw myself away on an ill-suited, premature marriage. No matter what the church said. My father thought I was more valuable than that. Stunned, I left the room in what I hoped seemed a purposeful, dignified silence.

Outside, tears streamed down my face. Thank you Daddy, Thank you Daddy, Thank you Daddy, said every beat of my heart, all the way back to the dorm. For passing the word. For giving me le mot juste.

Affair. I didn't have to look it up. I knew what it meant. It meant something that could come to an end.

Part Three

NEW YORK
1970–1971

"You must have something to fall back on."

Tenet of Daniel G. Kennedy

"We are not just three girls waiting around to get married."

Liz Seigal, roommate, 1970

"Don't act. Just be yourself."

Non-Equity director, 1970

"You don't enjoy this as much as I do, do you?"

Actor, in bed, 1971

"Andy likes your face. He wants you in the play."

Andy Warhol's Stage Manager, 1971

15.

The Yellow Wood

I graduated from Smith College with a red armband around my sleeve and a daffodil in my hand; this was our class's agreed-upon protest against the Vietnam War. It capped a year of less polite actions, including refusal to consider our classmate's father, the president of the United States, as our commencement speaker. Many graduates in those years disdained cap and gown as fascist uniforms of the ivory tower, but Smith said, No gown, No graduation, and I donned the costume. I couldn't bear to deny my parents closure after they'd paid four years' tuition without getting much to celebrate in return.

My affair with Jonathan was over and both of us knew it. We just didn't know how to separate until Jonathan thought of applying to the Peace Corps.

Within days of my Rochester homecoming, two FBI agents appeared on my doorstep. In the reign of J. Edgar Hoover, this was enough to make an antiwar activist named Kennedy paranoid. But the big, blocky upstate New Yorkers looked like my uncles or the ushers in church, and they assured me their visit was part of a routine background check on Peace Corps candidate Jonathan Pratt. I trusted them and I talked.

I told the tale of star-crossed, headstrong young love, leaving out details like naked hippie picnics and psychedelic experimenting that no church usher, Irish uncle, or federal agent wanted to hear. By the time I got to describing the letter I'd written to Jonathan's dean pleading for his reinstatement to college after suspension for repeat motorcycle violations, one of the feds was dabbing his eyes with a handkerchief. It may have been a signal; the interview ended shortly after that. But I like to think the G-men were genuinely moved by my story, as I was in the telling. It was the general sense in the room that star-crossed, headstrong young love was the right of the free, and anyone who'd tried it was a patriot. Jonathan went to Africa.

And I, to Cambridge, Massachusetts, to launch the rest of my life. I went to the cradle of American intellectualism to attend Katherine Gibbs Secretarial School.

Katy Gibbs, as it's known to friends, is a women's junior college that once dispensed its business curriculum with the airs of a girls' finishing school. My father had always admired its dress code, which for years demanded hats and white gloves for students and graduates. Such haberdashery had always been a reliable indicator of the secretarial creme de la creme at my father's law firm, and he happily paid my tuition for Gibbs's summer crash course. I never told him the dress code had dwindled to pantyhose, no shorts, or that I took classes in miniskirts and a pair of red clogs.

"You must have something to fall back on," was one of my father's major tenets for adult emancipation, and he'd said it early and often to all his children by way of warning us that after college graduation, he didn't expect us to fall back on him. We were to acquire a marketable skill. So I rented the extra bedroom of some Smith acquaintances' Cambridge apartment, installed my mattress on its sunny wood floor and my powder-blue Smith Coronamatic on an upended cardboard box, and there learned to type, turning out reams of paper that read, "The fox ran down the hole."

I wrote two letters to Jonathan in Africa, saying fondly that I still loved and thought of him. They were intended to gently loose the karmic winding-sheet, but they had a terrible effect. One day I received a telegram: "GOT YOUR LETTERS MISS YOU TOO AM COMING HOME THURSDAY," and the next day, Jonathan was in my bedroom doorway at dawn. "You can't stay," I said, blinking in disbelief. He'd wanted to leave Africa anyway, he said; my letters had just given him the excuse. He left that night after a hippie feast honoring the planned visit of another roommate's childhood friend. The honoree and I talked animatedly over the brown rice, prompting Jonathan to reproach me as he shouldered his duffel and headed for the stairs, saying, "It's just so obvious what you want."

I was offended that he, of all people, would dare to censor me. He'd enjoyed my easy virtue, and now that I'd ended our four-year affair, intact virtue would be irretrievable. If I did go to Maine with the brown-rice honoree, or take off for a weekend rock festival with a pick-up from Harvard Yard, what business was it of Jonathan's? I'd lost both my virginity and the man to whom I'd lost it, which made me, in my own eyes, a spiritual outcast. If earthly men would take me in and console me, I was grateful. I had my diaphragm in my purse and I used it; in those hippie days, when HIV was unknown, I believed in the democracy of free love, the solace of physical affection, and the reassurance of conquest. They filled the empty space once occupied by the security and clarity of my childhood. In confession, a sinner had to intend not to sin again for absolution. I wouldn't confess dishonestly, so I didn't go. I didn't even know where the Catholic church was in Cambridge. But I meditated at night on Harvard's observatory lawn and found myself weeping bitterly. Sometimes I imagined a shining figure sitting a few feet away who attended me with great compassion. Stay close to the love of Christ, a good priest once told me, and this was my attempt. But my prayer wasn't one of conversion, like Magdalene's; she'd gone and sinned no more. I was echoing, unconsciously, St. Augustine of Hippo: "Give me chastity, but not yet!" In childhood I'd worried about living 'til Saturday if I suspected I'd sinned. As a twenty-one year old, I thought I'd live forever.

The brown-rice dinner was the second to last time I saw Jonathan. Two years later I went to a wedding near his seminary; I called him, and we planned to see each other for the evening. He was waiting for me in his dorm room, reading and looking deathly pale. He had lacrosse practice, he said, and I should stay there; he'd return in forty minutes. Alone, and terribly nervous, I sat on his bed and smoked a cigarette, feeling myself grow paler, too. An ash dropped, melting a dime-sized hole in my nylon-jersey hippie dress; I removed it, put on another from my suitcase, and wrote a note: "I'm sorry. I can't do this." I left the note on Jonathan's desk and the dress in his wastebasket. Those two items, I knew, would explain the finality of my departure. We never contacted each other again.

But I met his college roommate on the streets of New York, in the mid-1970s. We hadn't seen each other since those weekends when he'd tactfully spent most of his time out of his room. He insisted I come to his nearby apartment for a drink, and I went, to discuss old times and discover we'd both lost track of Jonathan. Peter was mourning that people dropped out of one another's lives so completely when the phone rang. It was Jonathan, calling to say he was getting married. There was no need to come, he assured Peter; he'd just wanted his old friend to know. Peter never mentioned that the cosmos had delivered another old friend to the room to hear her lover's happy ending.

But in Cambridge, when he'd left, Jonathan had been wrong to think I wanted any particular man. What I wanted was to get to New York.

I could have gone to real graduate school; my father's standing offer to pay for his children's further education wasn't rescinded just because of his doubts about the value of an advanced acting degree. But my mentor at Smith, John Fisher, had hated the ivy league so much I'd loyally refused to apply to Yale Drama School, the only place I really wanted to go. It was a costly and karmic act; advanced acting degrees, I found out later, do have value, primarily in the bond of students who pursue them together. But when the road diverged in the yellow wood, I was feeling smugly populist and took the one more traveled by, to New York City.

The truth was, I'd wanted out of school ever since freshman year when Merrie Spaeth told me I was the best actress in our class, and she wanted to bequeath me her acting career. We'd planned to meet in New York that first Thanksgiving, so she could introduce me to her agent and to director George Roy Hill. My horrified parents nixed the idea, instantly amending the family rule requiring bachelor's degrees with a special actors' codicil: No Professional Contacts Before Graduation. Four years later, Merrie was bound for law school, and her offer, always more remarkable for its generosity than probable efficacy, had lapsed. I'd forgiven my parents and planned to conquer New York on my own.

The Smith theater department caused a momentary hitch in my plans by submitting my name, as one of its outstanding seniors, to the London Academy of Music and Dramatic Art. LAMDA responded by giving me an audition, and the thought of returning to England, older and wiser, made me dream anew of an academic afterlife untainted by class supremacy. If RADA were England's Royal Academy, LAMDA *had* to be the People's Choice! Anyway, in Britain, all Americans were dirt.

For the audition, I prepared a monologue from my favorite Chekhov play, *Uncle Vanya*, in which my character, Sonya, mourns to the beautiful Elena that her secret love, the doctor, doesn't "see" her. Two years away from my first visit to a therapist, I did not suspect that invisibility was a risky topic for a high-stress audition. The whole point, in such situations, is to be seen, and heard, in the best possible light. Rehearsing alone, I felt lovely and notable, airing Sonya's plaint as Everywoman's, a charming, fleeting moment of self-doubt that showed my own sensitivity to good advantage. My staging was lyrical: kneel-sitting in a spreading pool of rehearsal skirt, with my elbow perched on a chair where I imagined my invisible Elena.

The audition took place in an auditorium whose location I can't recall. What I do remember is stepping onstage from the towering wings to move the all-purpose antique rehearsal chair upstage from its previous user's position and feeling terror ice my veins as I realized two terrible things. The first was that I didn't believe in Elena, having spent not one minute of rehearsal time conjuring her by any means, such as personalization or sense memory. I'd thought only of my own lyrical self. Now that I needed a sympathetic listener, I had no one but a bunch of British judges.

This epiphany washed up the second as a wave brings flotsam to the beach. I expected the judges' rejection as surely as Sonya did the doctor's. Despair engulfed me, and I recognized, too late, that it was the engine of the speech. "When a girl isn't pretty they say she has beautiful hair, beautiful eyes," Sonya says. Lacking her insight completely, I'd obviously hoped a beautiful voice and a beautiful rehearsal skirt would make the judges fall in love.

There was nothing to do but begin as rehearsed. My speech and gestures shook; the panic was irrepressible. I decided to vent. Were not these feelings Sonya's, after all? some distant part of me reasoned.

Had I rehearsed with terror, I might have gotten away with this, but terror had never occurred to me before the moment of judgment, and it was too late to tame it to the text. The rush of prose I let loose sounded so much like a garbled scream that it alarmed even me; I quickly retrenched to phony lyricism. When I verged on collapse again, I vented again, and again retrenched. The performance lurched along this way until I cried, as Sonya, "There's no hope! No hope at all!" By then it was apparent to everyone in the room that there wasn't.

"She is not yet in control of her craft," ruled the judges with devastating British understatement in their rejection letter to Smith.

The experience scared me into applying to two American graduate schools just to prove I could get in. I chose the University of Minnesota, for its connection to the Tyrone Guthrie Theater, and the University of Michigan, for vague, unfathomable reasons that I later found were shared by my friend Wendy Wasserstein, an esteemed observer of women's lives, who privately agreed with me that we might have had perfect happiness had we chosen to become librarians at the University of Michigan.

For my Minnesota audition, I selected Lady Bracknell's "handbag" run from *The Importance of Being Earnest* as my comedy piece. I'd triumphed in the role at Smith-Amherst rep and trusted familiarity to shield me from the pitfalls of the LAMDA ordeal. I did avoid ambush by surprise emotion, but I stumbled, mid-audition again, on yet another unpleasant truth: people meeting an actor for the first time don't want to imagine him or her in a role that requires a vastly different physicality from what the actor brings into the room. I was ten feet from the judges in a classroom, sitting stiffly on a chair, leaning on my prop cane, and declaiming in a fake, throaty British-dowager voice. I felt cartoonish. My success as Bracknell, I realized with embarrassment, owed much more to padding, costume, lighting, and audience distance than my actor's ego had ever suspected.

But I demonstrated damn good breath control.

I tried to remain calm, so my understated dramatic piece could redeem me. I'd chosen three minutes' of Molly Bloom's monologue from the end of *Ulysses*, lifting it whole hog from James Joyce's novel. Fionnula Flanagan's romping-on-the-bed Molly in her one-woman show, *Joyce's Women*, and Barbara Jefford, in the movie version with Milo O'Shea, were unknown to me. I'd never seen a dramatization of the character I did that day; neither did the Michigan judges. I unpinned my Bracknell bun and shook out my hair. This dramatic hair-loosening and my adoption of an Irish brogue were all of the actor's craft I brought to a reading that was otherwise very like that of my beloved Smith English professor, Kenneth Amor Connelly. Perhaps it would have won me admission to a graduate program in literature.

My actor's ego unbowed—I'd taken to blaming LAMDA for British bias against Americans doing the classics—I pressed my ear to the door, after I left, to hear the Michigan judge's reactions. Someone said, "I thought the Bracknell was terribly forced, didn't you?" There were strenuous murmurs of assent. I fled, not wanting to hear what they thought of Molly Bloom.

The University of Michigan accepted me without an audition, which is probably why. Not having to audition can do wonders for an actor's success rate. It is a coveted perk of both career pinnacles and powerful agencies, where it is used to lure actors into projects on which, if the actors had to audition, they'd pass.

Acceptance buoyed me, but it came too late. I'd already been approached by two friends from Gillette House who needed a third person to make the rent on an upper–west side Manhattan railroad flat. Did I want to join them on West One Hundredth Street, between West End Avenue and Riverside Drive, starting in September, for $117 a month?

Yes, I said yes I will. Yes.

16.

The Aqua Living Room

The first time I walked into apartment 201, 306 West One Hundredth Street, I faced a kitchen window about three feet from my nose whose vista was a brick wall maybe half a foot farther than that. It was dark and depressing, and my heart sank.

But when my roommates called hellos to my right, I peered around the open, reinforced steel door to see a view that lifted my spirits. There were my friends, silhouetted against tall windows that let in some light from One Hundredth Street. Outside, this light shone silver, due to the mighty Hudson River's reflection onto the upper–west side smog. In our living room, however, the silver light fell onto a turquoise carpet that transformed it, at a certain time every afternoon, and turned walls, ceiling, people, and bookcases the most beautiful shade of aqua blue! Liz and Sherry moved through this suffusion now like shadowy fish, to relieve me and my parents of suitcases. For a moment I thought it seemed as if I'd come to live underwater.

My parents took the three of us out to a restaurant, gorging us on expensive proteins they suspected might be our last for a while. Afterward they dropped us off and bid me blithe, discreet goodbyes, as if leaving me at summer camp instead of the wide, wide world. Liz, Sherry, and I retired to the aqua living room and discussed House Rules.

There was only one, and it involved eating.

"We're going to have a real dinner together every night," Liz declared. "With meat, a starch, and a vegetable."

"Or salad," amended Sherry.

This impressed me. In Cambridge I'd ignored regular meals, and no one had noticed or cared. The release from eating's dreary physical repetition had been exhilarating but it had also made me spacey and anorexic. I knew long-term indulgence could do damage and was grateful that Liz, a master's student in clinical psych, understood the psychology of eating well enough to institute dinner as a pillar of autonomy, even if she were primarily motivated by her parents' proximity in Forest Hills, where they were near enough to notice if she neglected good eating habits, which was a Jewish sin.

The rationale she gave me was, "We are not just three girls waiting around to get married."

Instantly I feared for the stability of our living arrangement. Doth Liz protest too much? I wondered. Then I calmed myself with the notion that Jews didn't demonize sex like the Irish; Jewish parents, thinking sex a good thing, sometimes pressure their children, with the best of intentions, into marrying early as a hedge against promiscuity. In this light, Liz's statement was a feminist manifesto, dinner a conscious political act.

"It was the thought that counted," Liz sighed recently over the phone from New Mexico, where she's now a teaching neurologist with two school-age children.

That winter, four cute guys moved into 308 West One Hundredth Street. Liz and Sherry befriended two of them; we were all invited to their apartment, where I heard, for the first time, John Brent and Del Close's landmark recording, "How to Speak Hip" and laughed harder than I had in years. The two guys began joining us for dinner, showing exquisite political sensibilities by helping buy and prepare the food as well as eating it. Soon they were breakfasting at our place too, and within a year and a half, the couples were married.

०

The first day of My Career, I walked to the newsstand at Ninety-sixth and Broadway to buy a copy of *Variety*, which I knew from my father and general lore was the show business newspaper.

I was radiating joy to be a New Yorker at last! The junkies and winos of upper Broadway greeted my soaring stride with their appreciative sucking noise: kiss! kiss! kiss! I moved through it as if through a shower of rose petals. Until I had a real audience, I thought, these streets would provide my applause!

But *Variety* had few audition notices, and I walked home sobered by the prospect of a real audience being much farther away than I'd imagined. The paper contained, amid its boring box-office and net-gross charts, only two casting calls, both for "Equity actor-singer-dancers" to replace those leaving unspecified Broadway and touring musicals.

I wasn't daunted by the "singer-dancer" requirement. Though I'd never taken a voice lesson in my life and the only pair of dance shoes I owned were ballroom pumps, I was perfectly willing to pass myself off as an actor-singer-dancer. The problem was I couldn't pass myself off as an *Equity* singer-dancer; you can't fake being in the union.

"Equity" is short for "Actors Equity Association" the professional stage actors' union. In its laudable attempt to preserve working wages for working professionals, Equity frustrates beginners by restricting open auditions for union shows to union members. An agent can submit nonunion actors for Equity jobs, and producers can audition whoever they damn well please, but the only people allowed at open Equity auditions are Equity actors. These auditions are known to the pros, with affectionate disgust, as "cattle calls" for the herds of actors who turn up to show their cards, take a number, and meet the casting director and producers for a pitifully brief instant during which an actor can only hope to convey an indelible positive impression.

Struggling nonunion actors yearn for the cattle's chance, but they're barred by the actor's catch-22: You can't audition for an Equity show without an Equity card and you can't get an Equity card without doing an Equity show.

There were two ways I knew of around this: apprenticing in an Equity company, slaving backstage and spear-carrying in enough shows to win automatic union membership, or getting an agent. The agent method was the one I'd plotted, since apprenticeships seemed doled out according to mysterious connections I didn't have; it was equal-opportunity and required talent and luck, both of which I confidently believed I possessed in equal measure. All I had to do was get in some non-Equity off-off Broadway show and make a splash. My private schedule for "making it"—getting the crucial role, the agent, then the Equity job—was two years.

When *Variety* ran the same two casting notices the second week of My Career, I began to get nervous. Was there an off-off Broadway season, and I'd arrived in New York at exactly the wrong time? If non-Equity auditions were so few and far between, I'd be lucky to get a significant *non*paying role within two years!

A girl had to eat. I fell back, as I'd equipped myself to do, into the corporate arms of Manpower, Inc. and Career Blazers, two temp agencies where I tested at ninety-plus words a minute and immediately went on their A-lists. Career Blazers sent me out first. "We specialize in the exciting field of advertising!" was their boast, but they sent me to the unexciting borough of the Bronx. The job, I was told, required typing and dictation and would last a week.

I followed the agency's subway directions to some Grand Parkway and found the address, a massive prewar building whose elevator I rode to the third floor. There I found two men, sweaty and breathless, surrounded by boxes in a dim hallway. They were hauling the boxes into a bare office I could see through an open, frosted-glass door. When I announced that I was their secretary, they leapt forward to greet me as if I were the Second Coming. With manic energy, they told me I was the crowning touch to a team about to rock the advertising world with a powerful new medium.

"Plastic records!" the shorter of the two men beamed, fishing a cardboard square out of one of the boxes and holding it up. "We're going to make a *million* in plastic records!!!"

The opalescent disc in the cardboard's center told me I'd seen these thing before. My brother and I had torn them out of magazines in our childhood, to play once or twice on our phonograph before they curled, warped, and became useless. Then, no coinage taped to phonograph arm could restore function; the needle pressed into the shallow grooves, pinning cardboard to turntable. Coins taped to the outer edges of the cardboard made the record too heavy to turn on its soft, perforated hole.

I shook my head in stupefaction, which I hoped passed for silent awe, but passivity made the manic men nervous. "I mean, if you saw one of these in a magazine," the shorter of the two pumped me, "wouldn't you play it at least *once?* Just out of curiosity? Just to see what was *on* it?"

Who was I, I chided myself, to judge these two as bottom feeders, devoting their precious lives to filling the world with ugly, unnecessary junk? What was I doing for the world? My acting wasn't necessary. My time could be better spent teaching, perhaps, in New York's desperate public schools. These people were my soul-mates. Creative types.

"Yeah! Sure, I'd listen," I said. "At least once."

"*That's* what we're telling our customers!" the short boss beamed, revived. "If you put your message on one of these, it *will be heard!* You can *depend* on people to be curious! We're going to get *every* business in America to want to advertise this way and we're going to get plastic records into *every magazine in the country!"*

They showed me to my desk, bare except for a rented IBM selectric, and I spent the week typing labels and cover letters for their demo packages. I could hear, dimly, the partner's phone conversations; their pitches never quite soared to the altitude from which I'd received it. They had to bark, whine, and wheedle. Sometimes the bosses left for lunch depressed, but they'd return two hours later having restored each other to their original, vertiginous levels of excitement. At such times, they'd chat with me, to calm themselves before resuming the calls to dimwits who failed to grasp their genius. During one such chat they discovered I was an aspiring actress and became ecstatic, taking it as a starry omen of their own imminent success. I mentally unhitched my career from theirs as soon as they left and bent to my task so they wouldn't see the doom I feared for their enterprise written all over my face. I'd grown fond of their insane optimism. Maybe they knew what they were doing, I thought. Maybe overwrought, crazy guys like this had launched all our culture's inexplicable million-dollar novelties.

At the end of the week we all shook hands, and they said they'd brag they knew me when, and I could do the same with them.

"When you see those plastic records!" the short boss winked.

I never did. But I like to think they persisted, focused on one industry, and broke through with a revised product. They convinced cosmetic companies to put perfume strips and lotion packets in every magazine in America, and we've been sniffing and sneezing ever since. They retired to estates in New Jersey purchased with proceeds of timely junk bond investments.

My second job furthered the impression of the first: that on the fringes of the exciting field of advertising, many men lead lives of manic depression. I went to assist the advertising editor of *Men's Hairstylist and Barber's Journal,* reporting to offices in midtown Manhattan that looked so old they seemed embalmed. The wood was dry and bleached; the floors were warped to rolling. The only person I recall in the environs was my boss.

I asked a barber recently if he'd ever heard of *Men's Hairstylist and Barbers' Journal.* He hadn't, and he'd been barbering since 1970. In Southern California alone, he told me, 4,000 barbershops closed between 1970 and 1971, their customers lost to unisex hair salons. This confirmed the impression I formed during my week at the journal: that the attempt to address barbers and men's hairstylists as one big happy demographic was historically doomed. A revolution was on in men's hair. Barbers, who'd once reigned supreme over the stuff in strict sexual segregation and who'd tried, unsuccessfully, to laugh their harbinger of doom, the Beatles' mop-tops, back to fruity England in the sixties, were disappearing. The seventies brought Afros, shoulder-length male hair, and the popular helmet style worn by Donny Osmond and Bill Clinton during the period. Men grew tired of begging their barbers to leave a lot more on the sides and top, and defected to salons, which subscribed to *Vogue* and *Esquire.* That's why working at *Men's Hairstylist and Barbers' Journal* felt like working in a coffin.

My boss's task was to compose copy for the magazine's ads, which were placed, he told me, by small marketers, sometimes the product's inventors, who were often barbers moonlighting to improve the tools of their trade. Descriptions and photos of their wares accompanied their typed or handwritten letters and their checks to assist the editor in his task. The first day, before he began dictating, he showed me a finished ad so I would understand the goal toward which we strove. It featured a black-and-white paste-up of a barber's chair floating forlornly on a white background, with copy praising its revolutionary adjustability. A mandala of testimonial quotes from satisfied customers, like "Tom Sampson, Barber, Skokie, Illinois," radiated from the picture. I suspected my boss of making them up.

As he wove his words, the advertising editor chain-smoked Lucky Strikes, lighting one from another and stubbing the unfiltered butts in an ashtray that was overflowing by lunch. He was obese and had hacking fits that strained the seams of his suit, whose shoulders were snowy with dandruff. The shoemaker's children always lack shoes, and the advertising editor of *Men's Hairstylist and Barbers' Journal* evidently saw no hair professional on a regular basis.

I sensed I was in the presence of a man who was slowly and deliberately killing himself. The wedding ring choking his swollen finger like a tourniquet made me sad about this; was there nothing in his life to make it worth living? I thought of a friend of mine, who had come to New York to sell short stories. He'd ended up working for an airline magazine, and I'd felt sorry for him until everyone told me how great it was he'd broken into publishing. I hoped he was better off than this. On Friday I left, thoroughly sobered, and more determined than ever to realize my dream.

17.
The Trades

I n the reception area of Springer and Associates Public Relations, I sipped the first of hundreds of complimentary beverages I've been offered since in my career, sitting in well-appointed show-business offices waiting for someone to see me.

That day I waited for John Springer, the firm's founder. He was an eminent publicist to the Super Famous, notably Elizabeth Taylor and Richard Burton at the time. He'd agreed to meet me as a favor to my mother.

She'd hostessed several of his movie-star clients as honorees at Rochester's annual Eastman House Ball, a fund-raiser for the proposed Eastman Museum of Film, one of her pet projects. Her movie fanship and enthusiasm for actors charmed Mr. Springer, probably reminding him of why he'd gone into P.R. in the first place, and her impeccable manners had charmed his clients. Springer became Mother's fan and phone friend, the sort who urged her to call him if there were ever anything he could do.

She'd cashed in her chips for me. Ostensibly, Mr. Springer was to advise me —helpful hints for the fledgling actress—but I suspected our meeting had a hidden agenda, and that he'd be calling Mother afterwards to render his candid opinion about my appearance, my approach, and my progress. Ever since I'd come home from college a devotee of LSD-experimenting Harvard psychologist Baba Ram Dass, née Richard Alpert, my mother had ceased taking my level-headedness for granted.

As I sat with my Tab, the discreet, energetic hum of Springer and Associates started to depress me. If it took all this work to keep the famous famous, how would there ever be enough time and energy to make someone new famous, like me? Even in public relations, show business seemed like a closed shop.

"Mr. Springer will see you now," announced his assistant, waving me toward the burnished-wood double doors. As I opened one, Mr. Springer's jolly greeting revived my spirits. His warm praise for my mother seemed by extension to include me, and his interest seemed genuine. We sat. He began by asking me how I supported myself. When I told him I temped as a secretary, he expressed the awed admiration that seemed universal in older show-business men when they found I could type and take dictation. This puzzled me until I finally deduced that having those skills to fall back on, as my father had insisted I do, made me safe from the cynical presumption that young actresses, to support themselves, occasionally fell on their backs.

This presumption wasn't entirely cynical. One night in a bar on the upper west side, a nurse watched me talking with two male friends. As we left, she accosted me and said in a throaty, suggestive voice:

"If you could entertain Hal Prince and Len Cariou like I just watched you entertain your two friends tonight, you could make a lot of money in this town."

Two men—not those she'd just mentioned—stood at the bar, watching and listening. I looked at them in amazement—What does a nurse know about making money in this town with Hal Prince and Len Cariou? They turned away, smiling into their drinks. Then I remembered hearing once that New Orleans brothels were the best because they offered not only beautiful women but impeccable hygiene. The nurse was unremarkable, with an auburn page-boy and no make-up, but she advertised health. I also recalled that whenever police busted Manhattan high-rise call-girl operations, building residents always averred they'd had no *idea* that their genteel neighbor was a Madam.

"Think about it," she'd said, sauntering back to the men.

John Springer asked how I was doing with auditions, and I was relieved to finally divulge to someone knowledgeable that there hadn't been any in *Variety* to which I could go.

"*Variety?*" he repeated, as if I'd told him I'd done audition-hunting in *Field and Stream.*

"Isn't that the show-business newspaper?"

"You don't want *Variety!*" he scoffed. "*They* don't have what you need. Your auditions are in the *actors'* papers, *Show Business* and *Backstage!*"

I reached for pencil and paper to write the names down but he waved my hands back to my lap. "*Show Business! Backstage!*" he reiterated almost testily, as if nothing could be more obvious.

Stage, Show, I repeated to myself, crossing my legs and smiling confidently. It was essential I get over this gaffe and impress Mr. Springer as a quick study and a sensible girl. The last thing I needed was for him to report back to my mother that I was wandering around Manhattan like some vague hippie.

"You'll find them right downstairs in the lobby!"

This was good news. Stage. I didn't have too far to remember. Show.

"Great. Thanks," I said. He nodded, dubiously. We proceeded to discuss the theater in general, about which I knew enough to re-establish myself, precariously, in Mr. Springer's esteem. When I finished my Tab, he wished me well, walked me to the door, and shook my hand. Stage. He urged me to call him if there were ever anything he could do. Show.

I said I would, but I already knew he couldn't do what I needed, which was give me a job. Or call someone else to give me a job—"She's marvelous! She's extraordinary! I'm sending her over right away!" But when I got to the lobby I saw he'd given me precisely what every publicist ought to give: the right information. Stage! Show!

The actors' trades, once I saw them, seemed so obvious! They weren't glossy, like the moneyman's *Variety*, but tabloid newsprint rags. *Show Business* had its name written in red. I bought both papers and opened one immediately to feast my eyes. There they were! Non-Equity auditions! Page after page of them! They were obviously these publications' raison-d'être.

Back home at the table in the aqua living room, I conducted the first of my weekly sessions with the trades, which were to be my delight that first year in New York and proved to be some of the happiest hours of my career, for they were rich in hope undimmed by disappointment. I made lists of errands and auditions, imagining the shining possibilities of each. I sent my picture out willy-nilly, like a rural person entering contests who mails so many entries she knows one of them *must* hit and deliver her the life of her dreams! I was using a picture I'd had taken in London two years earlier; seeing the photographers' ads in the trades, I resolved to sit for a new one as soon as I had the money. I wanted everything the papers purveyed: new glossies, classes, the Actors' Answering Service, JU6-6300.

When I finished these sessions, if I were alone and had no pressing errands, I'd sit at the piano and compose songs of passionate yearning, or sing to old records, weeping with the same satisfaction I'd once had as a child crying in front of my mirror. I was close to the source of those tears now; I felt it was a deep longing to have the world know me at last as I really was: an Actress! Here, in New York, that would happen. I was unbearably happy that my time of revelation was at hand.

18.

Putting on the Dog

One of my first auditions from the trades was for a non-Equity repertory company that was casting roles for *The Music Man*. I'd done no musicals in college; my last singing audition, for *Peter Pan* at Mercy High School, had involved singing "Tell Me Why (The Ivy Twines)" the ditty by which our director, the redoubtable Sister Mary Pius, separated talent from tin ears. Girls who didn't know the song could sing "Happy Birthday"; an important goal of Mercy's drama program was inclusion. Sister Pius tried to pack all comers onstage, but her proud perfectionism made her put the tone-deaf where they could do no harm and the talented out front, where she railed at us to "OPEN YOUR MOUTHS!!" I'd won the schools' Best Actress award for my Captain Hook, which many observers asserted had erased their memory of Cyril Ritchard's. This was in the days before Cyril Ritchard's Hook could be restored by shoving a cassette in the VCR. It's a good thing; his performance would have proved I'd copied everything he did.

I arrived at Showcase Studios prepared to sing "Bye-Bye Blackbird," alto a-cappella, to show off my chest voice and perfect pitch. I'd never seen *The Music Man* and didn't know the roles. But what musical didn't need female belters?

There was an actor in the hallway studying sheet music for "Trouble in River City." Behind a closed door, I could hear a gorgeous, operatic "Till There Was You" in progress. I immediately realized I'd miscalculated the necessary level of professionalism; just because a theater doesn't pay didn't mean it auditioned like a Catholic high school.

I approached the studying actor.

"Excuse me, but—could you refresh my memory about the score of *The Music Man?* Tell me some of the songs…?"

He was affable in the face of this odd request. Actors are usually friendly unless they're jealous, offended, or the food is bad.

"'Till There Was You' is the big song for the female lead," he said. "That's the one you'd probably be singing."

I thought probably not. The voice behind the door was soaring to the stratosphere. Shirley Jones had played Marian the librarian in the movie I'd never seen, and her trained soprano was hard for me to match on songs I knew. I didn't count "Till There Was You" as one, not realizing I knew the words from *Meet the Beatles,* and from Paul McCartney's appearance on the second Ed Sullivan show, which was taped at the dress rehearsal for the first, throughout which my friend Nancy Lomenzo and I were sobbing and screaming our heads off in the back row of the Ed Sullivan theater.

"Uh-huh," I said, urging the fellow to tell me more.

"Well...there's 'Trouble in River City', the song I'm doing," he added proudly. I knew it was a difficult number, from the rendition my parents' friend David Curtin used to give at the end of their raucous parties. I'd heard it as a child, upstairs in my bed, then seen it as a college girl; in the boozy wee hours, Curtin would summon breath control, memory, and diction to berate the crowd with the song's mock-condemnation of revelry. It not only delighted and amazed, it inspired everyone to gather their own wits for the drive home. This memory uncovered the one I needed; I had an album of movie themes that included a song I hated. But it was from *The Music Man.*

"Thank you," I said to the actor. "That's all I need."

"Till There Was You" came out, smiling, and "Trouble" entered to do well. When the door opened again the producer and director were smiling, bidding him hearty goodbyes that sounded like he'd be hearing from them soon. I swept in on those smiles, which faded when I announced that I hadn't brought sheet music, but if the pianist knew it, I would like to sing "Seventy-Six Trombones."

The producer and director just stared while the pianist went lower and lower, searching for my key. The men's faces got blanker and blanker, so I quickly halted the music's descent and approved a key. Would we be doing the verse? asked the accompanist? Or just the chorus? I hadn't known there was a verse. I said, The chorus. He gave me a martial intro and I jumped in after the suspended chord:

"Seventy-SIX trombones led the big parade!

And a hundred and TEN cornets led the band!

"Dah-dah-dah-dah-dah-DAH-dah-dah-da-da-da-dah DAH —"

Too late, I'd realized I didn't know this song, either. But I DAH'd with gusto to the first conceivable stop and ended with a flourish.

The incredulity on my auditor's faces softened to weariness, as if they, non-Equity producers, had seen all too much of incompetence. It fell to them to cull crazies from diamonds-in-the-rough, and they accepted this. Their prepared spiel was admirably tactful: There were no suitable roles for me open at this time, but if I wanted to try them again next year with something a little more prepared they'd be glad to see me, because I certainly had an "interesting energy." Thank you and goodnight.

Shortly afterwards I did a musical audition for a non-Equity project described in the trades as "an original Country-Western-Rock" musical. I prepared the hell out of Jimmy Rodgers' "Honeycomb," practicing in the sheet music's original key on our apartment piano. I even added a nasal twang that I thought made me sound a little like Skeeter Davis.

I entered that audition to smiles again and handed the young director my resume. "Smith!" he exclaimed approvingly. Everyone always liked Smith except my high school guidance counselor. I gave the pianist my music, the director nodded, the music began, then I did. "Waill, itsa darn good lahf n' it's-a, kahnda funny—"

At approximately: "A-lookin' aivrywheah, a'takin' love-uh from heah, a-love-uh from theah" the director screamed "MIMI! STOP!!"

I stopped. I liked that he'd used my name; I thought maybe it meant he'd already decided to work with me.

"Why do I feel like I'm being lied to here?" he asked.

"Lied to?" I repeated, horrified. I wasn't lying! I assumed it was so obvious I wasn't a trained singer that I didn't have to state it. I'd hoped my pitch, my style—

"Yeah. It's like—I think maybe you're puttin' on the dog for me a little bit."

Putting on the dog? I glanced down at my jeans and Frye boots; had I gone too Western? No—overdressing would be puttin' on the Ritz. The dog. Did he mean—

"That's not your real voice."

The accent? Yes he did.

"No, it's not," I said in my real voice.

He reared back his head as if delighted to have his suspicions confirmed. "I *thought* you were acting," he crowed.

I stood there bewildered.

"Don't act. Just be yourself."

Thus the Great Mandate that echoed down all the decades of my career was spoken to me for the first time, and I couldn't believe my ears. All my *life* I'd been waiting to *act* in New York, I wanted to tell this man, and now, at an *audition,* you are *forbidding* it?

In my mind's eye I saw my peers at Yale, Minnesota, and Michigan, striding across campus in leotards, stretching in movement classes, yah-yahing in voice lessons, practicing dialects and Psychological Gestures, all to perfect the techniques of disguise by which I'd always thought we actors were judged.

"Just start over, and sing the song as you would normally," smiled the director.

Normally? As myself? At twenty-two, I had no idea who that was, if not an Actress. No identity, for me, was more profound. It contained all my multiple selves. Now, at mid-life, I see that young people don't have enough autonomous experience to declare with conviction to the world, This is Me and Only This! Ordinary young people have enough trouble projecting confident, coherent self-images, but young actors are at a particular disadvantage, because they've spent much of their brief lives fantasizing being other people.

No actor can become great without discovering his or her uniqueness, but we tend to make this discovery gradually, from behind a series of masks. Once we identify what is the same behind all masks—the roots of our own emotions—we can work differently, directly from our own experience. Film actors and child actors sometimes start working this way immediately, but even for them, working directly from themselves is never quite *being* themselves. Role playing is crucial to acting out stories. Physical and emotional transformation is the actor's stock in trade.

I'd always performed the parts in school that required transformation: the old people, the men, the comic relief—the character parts. The masks. Behind them was the Actress: Me. I was stunned to find out this identity would not suffice in the professional theater. Mentally, I inventoried my other possibilities: Catholic girl, Smithie, Daddy's girl, Mommy's girl, rebel, colleen, student, secretary, hippie, sex-kitten, friend; I was stumped on how to proceed.

The director was waiting. I began "Honeycomb" again, singing it like a Mercy girl from upstate New York. He didn't cast me in his Country-Rock-Western musical. I don't remember its name and I confess to hoping, then and now, that it bombed. Years later I starred in a "Country-Rock-Western" musical for the Phoenix Theater. The *New York Times* praised my "fine, clear voice" and another critic pegged me, by the drawl I'd adopted to play a girl from North Carolina, as a "realie" from Texas.

For a long time I pondered my sin of putting on The Dog. I concluded that if I could just figure out how other people saw me and play *that,* I'd have this "be yourself" thing knocked.

John Springer did call me with a job offer, but it wasn't acting. It was typing. Radie Harris needed a secretary, her regular girl was sick, and she was on a deadline. If I took a cab to her East Side address immediately, she'd reimburse my fare.

I was yelling "Taxi!" in a New York minute.

Radie Harris was the gossip columnist for the *New York Post!* I read her column faithfully, because in those days the *Post* was a fine, credible newspaper, with Pete Hamill and a host of other literate liberals on its editorial page. This was before Rupert Murdoch bought it and put three-inch screamer headlines on the front page, like "SAM SLEEPS!!!" above a fuzzy blow-up photo of the serial murderer napping in jail.

The cab dropped me off in front of a cinder-block East side high-rise just like the one in which my sister lived with a bunch of fellow-stewardesses. I was amazed; I'd thought all people connected to show business lived in regal splendor, or at least bohemian charm! I'd never pictured Radie living in what I thought of as "Stewardess Building" architecture. I had a lot to learn about the newspaper business.

I took the elevator to Radie's penthouse floor and rang the buzzer on her apartment. The door was opened by a tiny woman with thin, wispy hair, nylon leopard-print lounging pajamas, and false eyelashes, one of which was becoming unglued.

"You must be Mimi," she rasped. "You got here fast. I'm not even finished dressing yet. Come on in." She led me into a cream-colored living room. There was no one else in evidence so I assumed she must be Radie, and that columnists didn't always change their pictures every decade.

"Listen, I have to go in back and finish dressing. Would you mind answering the phone? I know you just got here, but—just say it's Radie's line and take a number for me to call them back."

I've heard humans blink every few seconds without noticing, but when you're watching someone with an errant false eyelash strip you notice every blink. There were no polite euphemisms for alerting the victim to the problem, like there were for men's open flies or crumbs on someone's cheek; I could only hope Radie would catch the problem herself.

"Sure. I'll answer it," I replied, thinking, how much more fascinating a phone could I ever hope to answer than a New York gossip columnist's?!

"Have you read my column?" she asked, giving me a no-nonsense glare.

"All the time," I assured her. I would have said more, but Radie's look cautioned, Can the adulation, honey, you're a secretary, not a fan. She said, "I left a column by the typewriter so you could see how I do it." With that she shuffled down the bedroom hallway in her mules.

I looked at the column and saw I'd read it, so I felt free to look around. The place was airless as a bell jar. I was dying to crack open the sliding door to the patio. Why, I wondered, would anyone live high on Manhattan's canyon wall and not let in the breeze? Later, when I lived in a stewardess building myself, I found out the answer: at that altitude, the breeze carries enough soot to turn your place black in a week. Air conditioning filters the carbon, so one's decor merely browns and curls—a slow, Manhattan-antiquing process well underway in Radie's living room. But these beiges were not exposed to the ravages of fresh air.

The phone rang. I saw one on the glass dining table and picked up the receiver.

"Radie Harris's line," I chirped, feeling like I was in a thirties' movie.

"Is she there?" demanded an angry woman with no time for etiquette.

"Yes," I lilted in return, "but I'm sorry, at the moment she can't come to the phone. I'm taking messages for her—may I ask who's calling?"

"What are you?" the woman sniffed, "some kind of secretary?"

This seemed unnecessarily impudent, I thought, but it alerted me to the fact that this might be a Big Celebrity. They didn't need the common civility by which we ordinary slobs ingratiate ourselves to the world. I couldn't afford to alienate anyone on Radie's behalf, so I maintained a pleasant tone, thinking, Who is this? and, If gossip is a sin, as *The Baltimore Catechism* taught, then maybe a gossip columnist's wages of sin were to always deal with people at their worst.

"I'm a temporary secretary," I cooed. "But if you'll leave a message, Radie said she'd call you right back."

"You bet she will," snapped the woman. "Tell her it's Zsa-Zsa calling and she needs to speak with Radie right away."

Zsa-Zsa! There was no accent on the line, so I presumed this was Zsa-Zsa Gabor's secretary. And I was Radie Harris's secretary! Life! I marveled. One minute I'm nobody on 100th Street and the next I'm high in the sky, bearing messages to and from the gods!

"Of course I'll tell her," I soothed.

"You bet you will. Zsa-Zsa will be waiting."

She gave me a number and hung up.

I tried to calm myself, even though I held a star's personal phone number right in my hand! I had to think clearly. Was this message urgent enough to interrupt Radie's toilette? I looked down the hall where she'd disappeared and heard running water. Something told me the privacy of a gossip columnist was very private indeed, especially one of a certain age. I decided to wait. It was a good thing I did.

The minute Radie re-appeared I unburdened myself. "Zsa-Zsa Gabor called," I said in what I hoped was the proper mix of secretarial detachment and respectful urgency.

Radie never paused in her slow shuffle across the room "Ucccckkkhhhh," she replied expansively. She turned at her study door. Her appearance had been given a considerable lift by a wig that made her look like her picture, and securely-tacked eyelashes.

"Did you get a chance to read the column?"

"Yes."

"Good. Let's get to work."

She motioned for me to follow her into the room, which was small and littered with newspapers. I couldn't rest the matter until I'd conveyed a smattering of the impatience that had been foisted upon me.

"I think it must have been her secretary," I added apologetically. "And she sounded upset. She said Zsa-Zsa would be waiting for you to call back."

Radie was clearing papers off an easy chair and indicated wordlessly for me do the same with the hassock at its feet. Beneath the papers I found a phone, which I laid carefully on the floor.

"She's just mad about something I printed," Radie finally muttered, "which she says is untrue, but nobody else does. She's going to want a retraction, but if I print one the person I quoted will wonder why I didn't believe her and *she'll* want a retraction and the thing will go on and on and on and nobody cares except Zsa-Zsa. She just likes to see her name in the papers. She'd like to get as many mentions as possible out of this thing. I'm sorry I ever printed it."

Years later, when Zsa-Zsa was behind bars for slapping a Beverly Hills cop, I remembered Radie's words and hoped the star found consolation, in jail, in the amount of ink the incident generated.

I sat on the hassock with a straight spine, sitting tall to take dictation from a woman who snubbed the stars. Contempt for celebrity, as every careful publicist knows, is a contagious thing, and once it starts, it's hard to stop. Zsa-Zsa Gabor, I found myself thinking, minutes after speaking to her secretary with a pounding heart, Big deal. What's she ever done? I'd never seen her act in anything. She was known mostly for that damnable trick of being yourself so prized by certain people in show business. I rejoiced to see it evidently didn't impress even a gossip columnist, who was supposed to care.

The first item Radie dictated was about David Merrick, the producer; it was too business-oriented to intrigue me, other than knowing I knew something before the rest of New York did. I speedwrote it automatically until Radie said "Dot. Dot. Dot." That almost knocked me off the hassock.

Ellipses were Radie's trademark punctuation. I was intending to insert them between items; it had never occurred to me she'd dictate them, but she did, gravely, with emphases ranging from thoughtful consideration of her next topic to triumph in having gotten through the last with a spicy blend of fawning and cynicism. With a final, satisfied "Dot!" Radie ended the session and directed me to the typewriter on the living room's glass table, where I was to beat out a draft while she took to her phone behind closed doors.

Who was on the other end of her line? I wondered as I typed. If Radie spurned Zsa-Zsa, whom did she solicit? Before what stars, if any, did she grovel? I knocked on her door to deliver the draft, which she proofread and returned to me with a few corrections. She told me to leave the revision on the typewriter, but as I typed she reappeared to slip a fifteen-dollar check beneath a vase on the table and tell me to let myself out when I was through. She went back in her study and I didn't see her again.

Seven years later, I stood beside Zsa-Zsa Gabor in the opening sketch of "Three Girls Three," a television show in which I starred as one of the three girls. I whispered the scripted line to her, "Has anyone ever told you you're attractive?" to which she batted well-glued false eyelashes in response. The comic premise of the sketch was that three unknowns—Debbie Allen, Ellen Foley, and I—were picked from a chorus line over three celebrities—Zsa Zsa, Carol Burnett, and

Florence Henderson—to become stars of our own show. Everyone played them-selves.

I'd won the part, out of 250 girls auditioning on both coasts, by singing a par-ody I'd written of Helen Reddy's "I Am Woman." It was called "I Am Dog," and I sang it in Ms. Reddy's nasal, pseudo-Southern, Australian accent.

"I Am Dog and I am brown
Leave my mark all over town
Love the feelin' that I get from running' free.
…This is no craze
Here come the dog days
I am strong, I am invincible
I am DO-O-O-G!!!"

See? I'd been being myself all along. It just took me and everyone else a while to find out; after that we found me more convincing.

19.

Sleaze

Twice in my life I faced casting couch proposals. Neither was blatantly quid pro quo, but both were unmistakable. I turned down the first one, and that led to success.

It came from the director of a Long Island production of *The Diary of Anne Frank*, whose casting notice I answered those first months of reading the trades. I'd sent my picture and resume to an address in Manhattan's west sixties, then had been called there to read. I did errands on the east side before the audition, planning a brisk fifteen-minute walk crosstown. I was shocked when I saw Central Park at that latitude. I'd forgotten about it. That's how green I was.

The director complimented my cold reading for the role of Margot as "absolutely one of the best I've ever heard," then asked if I'd like to stick around, maybe have some dinner, and sleep with him. I was dumbfounded. His apartment was cluttered, he was a mess, and his production was on Long *Island!*—I couldn't believe he thought his package was even remotely seductive. I said no. A year later a playwrighting duo from the village called to say that this very director had given them my name as a good cold reader, and would I like to audition for backers' readings of their new play? I got the lead, and read for several audiences, one of which included Ken Waissman and Maxine Fox, the producers of *Grease*, the fifties' musical that had just moved from the village to Broadway. Because I looked like one of Ken and Maxine's favorite original cast members, Katy Hanley, they asked me to audition as a cast replacement, and I went down to the Royale Theater, where I sang "Born Too Late," the old Ponytails' hit. I wasn't cast immediately, but my picture was starred and put on file, and a year later I was called in again to audition for the National Tour. That led to a job as a tour cast replacement, which led to playing "Jan" on Broadway, which led to television's "Three Girls Three," my first signed agent, and fame.

But first, I accepted the second casting-couch proposition, and what I'd taken for a shortcut took me, instead, on a long and painful detour.

It happened during the run of my first non-Equity play, which I'd landed, fair and square, through a casting call in the trades. The play was a four-character love-quadrangle named *Asses*. "As in 'donkeys'," I was quick to explain when telling people, lest they think I'd be showing mine Off-Off Broadway, where nudity was all the rage. Sally Kirkland had just won fame by crouching naked all night on a platter as a roast turkey. I would be clothed as "Marta," even in the one scene where I'd wear only a black bra and garter belt.

"And it's not connected to Yoko Ono's film," I told friends hip enough to think it might be part of her documentary about rear ends and be disappointed to find out that it wasn't. I didn't want any disappointment marring the news of my New York debut. My role, a young hippie woman who loves both an older man and his young, bisexual boyfriend, was a good one; I was in almost every scene. "I didn't think you were enough of a hippie," the director cautioned when he phoned to say he'd cast me, "but the writer loved you, so you've got the part." With this caveat, it was confirmed that I'd achieved my first New York goal within mere months of my arrival—I had a role in a non-Equity play! Now I'd proceed with the second launch phase: attracting an agent.

The Dove Company presented their plays in an Episcopal church in Chelsea that still functioned as a house of worship and was therefore architecturally intact, with altar, pews, choir loft, and stained-glass windows. It felt odd to cavort in my underware, even for half a scene, behind the communion rail, where all my life I'd seen men in chasubles. But at Smith we'd learned theater developed from religious ritual, so I tried to think of my dishabille as part of theater evolution.

The "Dove Company" title was a bit misleading, since the company seemed to consist of only two people. They were our leads in *Asses,* a married couple who, in the best actor-manager tradition, produced plays mainly to star themselves. They'd once been called "Off-Off Broadway theater-of-the-bizarre's Lunt and Fontanne," in print, an accolade they cherished, mentioned often, and strove continually to deserve.

The woman hated me. She vehemently disagreed with my approach to my role, which I thought should be naive and sincere, since the director had wanted a hippie. She wanted me nasty and manipulative, which was exactly how I saw *her* part. We squabbled, with decreasing civility, using the director as our intermediary. He managed to agree with everything each of us said without every betraying a glimmer of anxiety that the two views were hopelessly opposed. This sort of equivocation is a skill many directors employ to save themselves when they cannot save a show.

During one night's rehearsal of the foursome restaurant scene, I'd just finished explaining why I thought I should sit down when I entered, rather than hover menacingly above the woman, as she wanted me to do, when she blew up at me.

"I have had ENOUGH!" she spat, eyes ablaze. "You know what you are? You're nothing but an uppity ingenue! You'd better learn to shut that mouth of yours, girlie, if you want to work in this town—" to her credit, she did not say "again!" knowing her power didn't extend beyond the communion rail— "and from now on, you'll jolly well start taking some direction!"

The men's frozen faces made it quite clear who I'd be taking direction from. Afterward, I played my scenes with her diffidently, coolly, as if to say, you must have confused me with someone who cares. She was very pleased. This process of provoking your fellow player's emotions in real life to produce certain results onstage was, I soon learned, very popular and widespread, but I found it cruel and confusing. So did an actor friend of mine who told me that once, on a movie set, he saw the film's star take a fellow actor by surprise by slapping him hard, in the face, between takes, to goose the scene's anger level. "He coulda just told the guy," my friend griped, "I hate that shit." Me too.

Meanwhile, by day in the aqua living room, I plotted my personal publicity campaign for *Asses*. With the trades' agency listings spread out before me, I circled names of agencies I'd heard of and ones whose names I liked. These I called to solicit names of particular agents who handled Off-Off Broadway; to them, and to contacts like John Springer and Radie Harris, I sent a flyer, picture, and resume. I also included a cover letter announcing my New York debut.

The letters were meant to be simple, but I got carried away in some of them. Writing on yellow legal pads out of loneliness and fervent wishing, I began to detail my family history, educational background, and long-range goals. This struggling-actor's equivalent of the college admissions essay was sent out into Manhattan, willy-nilly, to ambush perfect strangers.

Two found their mark in ways I hadn't intended.

The first smote an eminent theater reviewer with whom I'd corresponded at Smith College as part of an acting class assignment. Mr. Fisher had told us to choose a critic, follow his or her work for a year, and report at the end on his or her preferences and prejudices, and whether or not we trusted the reviews. I'd written this man to advise him of my scrutiny and invite comments, if he cared to send them, about his work. He'd responded with a gracious letter. I'd met his son afterward, on a Caribbean beach while I was on a family vacation. We'd chatted for a while before trading names. When I'd heard his, I'd commented that it was the same as a famous critic's. "You know him?" the boy asked incredulously. "That's my father!"

I hadn't seen the boy again, but in the aqua living room, I considered this history with the critic enough to warrant a letter and an invitation to *Asses*.

He'd arrived unannounced on a night when, blessedly, there were more bodies in the audience than onstage. This was not always the case. Many nights we four played for three and two, and I approached the state of Zen enlightenment wherein one knows the sound of one hand clapping. I spotted a man sitting off by himself, and guessed right away who it was. No one so like my father in age and appearance had come to our show. He lurked in the center aisle afterward, waiting for me, hunched in his suburban trenchcoat and clutching his fedora. I realized it had probably been a long time since the unfashionable addresses of Off-Off Broadway had been his beat. When I introduced myself, he asked me if I wanted to go for drinks to discuss the play. I said yes, thrilled at the prospect of conversation with a famous reviewer.

His critique of the show was diplomatic: he declared me the best thing in it. That established, we talked about Smith, and the coincidence of my meeting his son. "When I got the letter you sent from college," he explained, "I sent it to him, thinking surely it was his—he had to send it back!" We laughed together—aaah, life!

When he insisted on seeing me home in a cab, I felt fathered and protected. When he made the cab driver wait while he saw me to the door, I thought him unnecessarily cautious, but sweet. When I entered my foyer I was surprised to feel him slip in behind me, but what happened next really surprised me. As I turned to say good night, I was mashed against the mailboxes, with a whoosh! of raincoat and a toppling of fedora, which brushed my cheek on its way to the floor. The man planted his lips on mine for a long and hungry kiss.

It seemed to go on forever. While he twisted and gnawed, I had plenty of time to think about the moment when he'd back off. How would I handle it? "Yuck!"— my wholehearted impulse—seemed unnecessarily cruel. He must, I thought, have felt I wanted this. If he didn't, then his blatant usage of me was even more disgusting than his urgent, uninvited passion. Was the black underwear scene to blame? I wondered. How could a famous writer be so desperate? Were all old men like this?

These were my thoughts. This was before the term "sexual harassment" had been coined to help clarify such situations. I hadn't been trained to be assertive with men; had I been, I'm not sure what I would have asserted. A kiss wasn't so bad. I'd been warned not to be a cockteaser and felt somehow I'd failed. I'd heard that older men, in general, felt cheated out of the sexual revolution. Maybe the critic thought he'd found, in me, a free-loving admirer who wouldn't mind being hit up for his brief moment of inclusion.

The kiss finally ended. The man immediately stooped for his hat, so I was spared acknowledging the first moment of disengagement. When he straightened up, I saw his eyes; they were so bleary, so blinded by need, that I doubted he could have said my name if asked. Images of alcoholic, middle-aged magazine writers, from sources as disparate as John Cheever and *Mad* magazine, rose up before me: Disillusion. Despair. Unhappy marriage.

"Thank you for coming to the play and seeing me home," was how I handled the moment. "It was wonderful to meet you. Good night!" I climbed the stairs, and he let himself out the door alone, walking back to the cab, fedora in hand.

That was the warning shot. The casting-couch proposal came from an entirely different source.

Another of my letters intrigued an agent. I'd addressed it to him directly, as suggested by the receptionist at his massive agency. I was delighted to hear his secretary answer my follow-up call with, "Yes! I remember your name—Joe specifically said he wanted to meet you, and if you called, I should give you an appointment. He can't see your play, but he'd like to see you." All the other agents' secretaries had said that their bosses were not "taking on new clients at this time." Water seeks its own level, I reminded myself—I have attracted the best!

I arrived at the agency's offices and thrilled to their low-key buzz. I couldn't believe my luck—my foot was in the door!

Joe turned out to be as avuncularly middle aged as I'd pictured him. His face shone while he stated that my letter was one of the most intelligent he'd ever read, which clearly showed me to be different from most young girls who wanted to be actresses. I'd secretly hoped this was true and was delighted to hear it from such a knowledgeable source. Joe was most impressed by the fact that I supported myself with typing and dictation. That showed self-respect, he said, which was the reason he'd be willing to help me, if he could; I should feel free to check in with him "every couple of weeks" for possible auditions. We shook hands. As he walked me back to the reception area, I saw Sally Kellerman kissing her agent, European-style, on both cheeks. My God, I thought—I'm at the same agency!

Too excited to sit on public transportation, I flew home on foot. I approached a couple; the man nudged the woman excitedly as I passed, saying, in a low voice, "Patty Duke!" Oh my *God*, I thought joyfully—I even *look* like a Star today!

Twice more, I met with Joe in his office. He was unfailingly enthusiastic, impressed, and solicitous, suggesting at one point I write a play about three girls sharing an apartment in New York. He said people would be interested in that. I nodded, thinking he imagined it as far more interesting than it was, and swallowing the disappointment I felt whenever anyone suggested I do anything but act.

We were scheduled to meet one day when his secretary called to apologize because he had to be out of the office. "If you'd rather not cancel," she said, "he said he could meet you at four o'clock, before he goes to dinner and the theater." She gave me the name of a midtown bar. I didn't want to cancel; I said I'd meet at his convenience. He was the busy one; I'd be in the bar at four.

Joe apologized for changing venues. I said I didn't mind, and he relaxed. He asked if he could order me a scotch. I said yes. I missed cocktails, our grown-up ritual at home in Rochester. Liz, Sherry, and I didn't have them in the aqua living room, or in the neighborhood restaurants we patronized with the guys next door. Over drinks, I told Joe all the responsible things I'd done to advance my career since last we met. He beamed approval.

After paying the check and helping me on with my coat, Joe announced that he had to pick up a script from a client who lived upstairs—a Broadway composer, had I heard of him? I hadn't. Well, come up with me anyway, Joe said, while I get the script.

I went. In the elevator, we chatted about composing. I told Joe I wrote songs, too. Maybe you and my client could get together sometime, Joe enthused, and you could play him some of your songs. I concurred, thinking it sounded a bit daunting, but wanting to rise to the level of Joe's cheery expectations.

The elevator opened on a little hallway where Joe knocked on a door. There was no answer. "Guess he's not home," he said, perplexed. He lifted the mat; there was a key. "Sometimes he leaves the key when he has to go out," Joe explained. "I bet the script's inside." He opened the door and we went in. On the mail table in the dim hallway was a manila envelope and a bottle of scotch.

"Son of a bitch!" chuckled Joe. "He knew I might want to have a drink, the son of a gun. Well— you want to have another drink? Do you have the time?"

I had all the time in the world. But somehow I felt things were taking a turn. I came from a culture where it was perfectly normal for middle-aged men to drink at the end of the day in pleasant company—which, in Rochester, usually included men's wives. Where was Joe's wife? Did he have one?

"Sure," I said, telling myself I was being paranoid. Joe shed his coat. I kept mine on.

He took the bottle to the kitchen, returning with two lowball glasses filled a bit too generously, I thought. But I accepted and glanced around the apartment while Joe chatted about the occupant's credits.

I did not come from a culture in which middle aged men dropped their pants in pleasant company at the end of the day and started moaning. Which is why, when it happened, I didn't know what to do. I turned to see what was going on, and there was Joe, his shirttails luffing beneath his jacket like windless sails. Between them poked the wayward mast: Pinocchio's tell-tale nose.

I'd defended my right to be sexual so forcefully against my own savage repressions that any conventional notions of sex, which might have sent me screaming from the room, were effectively silenced. I looked in Joe's face to reestablish some sense of normalcy, but the sight above was almost worse than the sight below. His muscles were tight with passion, his eyes rolled upward in his head. He held himself and said there was something about me that got to him, damn me.

My God, I thought numbly, flattered and repulsed, I'm this irresistible in my *winter coat?* Joe's pants pooled around his socks and shoes as he beat off into his handkerchief.

Things had definitely taken a turn. But I was embarrassed and unwilling to shame him. The last thing I wanted to do was make things worse. I wanted it to be over. I tried to keep a respectful, "Oh, Wow," look on my face. When Joe was finished, he tidied himself up, shaking his head with a sheepish smile, folding and refolding his handkerchief. When he did look at me, he shrugged as if to say: My crazy, impetuous dick! Your wild, stimulating presence! And that was that. He'd gotten away with it. We would pretend it didn't happen, every time it did. It would always take us by surprise, so the only thing to do would be to go through with it. He didn't touch me.

The only agent I'd been able to interest had just presented his bill of commission. Or else a fond, foolish old man had just won access to some surreptitious sexual adventure. With that thought, the old showbiz maxim that had gotten me into trouble in the first place—"It's not *what* you know, it's *who* you know"—suddenly expanded, and I realized, with a sinking feeling, that it was also "what you *know* about who you know." This thought tipped the scales for a confused, naive, ambitious young girl. I didn't need Joe as an enemy before I even got started in show business. I decided the incident inaugurated a relationship.

Joe rinsed the glasses and washed his hands at the composer's sink. Then, tucking the script under his arm, he took me downstairs, where we waved pleasant goodbyes on the street as I got into a cab. Anyone seeing us might have thought we were father and daughter. Or maybe I was the only person in Manhattan too stupid to recognize the situation as exactly what it was.

Sex for a man is just a physical thing, my father had once told me, but for a woman it involves her whole self, because she invests her emotions. I'd been in high school when he'd told me that, and I'd been hoping he was wrong. I wanted men of my generation to be more like women. Now that I was an ambitious young woman involved with someone my father's age, I found myself hoping that, by their old standards, I could be more like a man. My emotions would not be involved.

"I'm sure it's a very intellectual relationship," deadpanned my mother, when she heard of Joe's interest. What does she mean? I thought. Does she know? Does she think it's par for the course? In hindsight, I realize she was asking herself the same questions: What does this man's interest in my daughter mean? Does she even know? Does she think it's par for the course? In the no-man's-land between the romantic ambitions we'd harbored and the price we knew some people paid to achieve them, my mother and I declined to scrutinize the facts.

Joe was only too willing provide distraction. He insisted on meeting my parents when they came to town, and we had drinks together while he reiterated to them what he'd said to me: I was an exceptional young woman with an excellent chance of making it as an actress. That's what prompted my mother's "intellectual" comment, afterward, in private. She suspected. She hoped not. But if it were true, I was on my own.

I did play my songs for the composer. He approached me at the piano, repeating one of my lyrics—"'Loving makes me real,'" he mused, "I like that. What do you mean?" His hands went to my shoulders, then up my neck beneath my hair. I twisted my head and leaned away. He was philosophical about the rejection.

Joe sent me to a music publishing company where I played five of my songs. One of my listeners said my lyrics were "the best" and teamed me up with a composer whom she also called "the best." I knew Clint Ballard from his hit for Wayne Fontana and the Mindbenders, "The Game of Love." "The purpose of a man is to love a woman/And the purpose of a woman is to LAHve a man/So come on baby let's start today/ Come on baby let's play/The game of love(love)love(love)la-la la-la-la love!" He'd succeeded on his own, but his publishers were looking for a lyricist with more depth.

Clint composed something for "Long Hard Winter," my song about an era of peace and love ending with an emotional and social deep freeze. It was a cry from my own unhappy soul:

"You're sitting by the fire, there are tears upon your cheek

Your body's bent with weariness, but still you cannot speak

And now I know your sadness and the reason why you weep

It's gonna be a long, hard winter."

The last verse had campfires lighting the dark road on which "gentle people everywhere are trying to get home."

I preferred my original three-chord melody to Clint's fussy, Vegas-style one, but I was collaborating with an established composer in the Brill Building; it was not my place to second-guess. The song never sold.

At last, Joe sent me on an audition. I knew it was legit because he gave me a bona fide script to read, the first screenplay I'd ever seen in my career. An appointment was set for me to meet the actor/director, whom I'd never heard of, though he was soon to be a big television star.

My proposed role's description was daunting: The Most Beautiful Young Girl In The World. It wasn't a speaking part, so I couldn't win by acting. The Girl stood on a windy hilltop, from which she haunted the protagonist at various points in the script.

I, who'd had qualms about marking myself "attractive" on a college computer dating form, doubted I could face a lens with conviction as The Most Beautiful Young Girl in the World. But this meeting was an all-important acting-career payoff for my disturbingly compromised, unsigned, agent relationship. I mustered my self-esteem to face it.

I was stunned, when I entered the conference room, by the contrast between the beauty of the Manhattan skyline and the strangeness of the actor's looks. Women would soon be sending him their keys in the mail, but he was definitely an odd duck. We shook hands.

He asked what I'd been doing lately. I felt the blood rise in my cheeks as I wondered, could he possibly know?—letting the agent who sent me here masturbate in my presence.

An Off-Off Broadway play, I said, and Smith College. I explained that I was just starting my career.

He nodded, staring intently. I squirmed beneath his gaze. "I'm afraid I'm not exactly right for this role," I demurred.

He opened his hands. "Why not? There's no right or wrong here. She could be any-young girl. There just has to be something about her, something that haunts the man."

Something you can capture on camera, I thought.

"Well…if she's supposed to have ethereal beauty—I don't know—like, sometimes my skin's not very good. And things like that." Having said what was on my mind, I drifted into silence. The scattered whiteheads on my face became a raging case of Dickensian smallpox, African yaws.

The actor raised his hand. "Please, *please*. We don't have to talk about pimples. We're *artists* here."

I considered his appearance and found him credible. I was reassured, but not cast. I don't know if the movie was made; I think his TV show came along to pre-empt it.

The meeting had gone well enough, though, for me to consent to being the dinner date of another of Joe's clients, an aging star. We're *artists* here, I thought. Maybe I'd finally reached higher ground. It was a group occasion, a restaurant celebration for some young actors in whom the star took an interest. Being thrice-divorced, and only briefly in town, he needed a date; Joe thought I'd add just the right zest to the company. I should have suspected something when Joe said my "intelligence" is what prompted him to think of me as the perfect escort for the man.

The evening went fine. There really was a group of young people; afterward we went to the star's apartment, and he played the piano and sang for us. I was the last to leave, and as he helped me into the cheap crushed-velvet maxi-dress I used as a topcoat, he complimented its charm and mine. He said I reminded him of two of his ex-wives. They were famous, so I was flattered.

The actor told Joe he'd found me delightful. Next time he called me directly, asking me to dinner at a star-studded restaurant.

I wanted to see glamorous New York, not just dine on Comidas Chinas y Cubanas on the upper west side. I went to dinner, and wasn't really surprised where I ended up. We returned to his apartment to sing. He brought aperitifs to the piano and began to kiss my neck. I didn't say no. I was no longer the injured party, the violated innocent; I knew by now that flattery was old men's foreplay to sex with young women, and I didn't care about the sex. Sex without love was just power. And I wanted very much to feel powerful, to feel the illusion that finally, *I* had something somebody wanted, instead of always being the needy one. I was a woman of the world, with my portable diaphragm. I could dispense my sexual favors as I saw fit, and I saw fit to groom this aging actor's ego, and feed mine, by going to bed with him. I doubted he could ever help my career, and he never did.

In the midst of things, I began to cry. The man didn't notice, and I kept it quiet, completing the sordid picture: Girl Prostitutes Self and Hates It. After he rolled off me, he said, with belated sensitivity, "You don't enjoy this as much as I do, do you?"

I stopped "checking in" with Joe regularly and began paying attention to men my own age, hippie graduate students as penniless and powerless as I, or young professionals whose egos didn't automatically expect sex in return for food and attention. It wasn't as glamorous, and it wasn't entirely celibate, but I could live with myself.

There was still enough sleaze on the audition scene to challenge my severely impaired moral judgment and preoccupy me with the difference between opportunistic and sincere sexuality. I answered a casting notice in *Backstage* announcing a non-Screen Actors Guild film to be made in India about love and peace. The actors would tour India by bus. I approved of love, peace, India, and bus travel; I went to the published address, a downtown loft. It was wall-to-wall with actors waiting to be seen. In the huge audition room, a skinny long-haired photographer was conducting individual portrait sessions with the actors, interviewing as he shot. When I entered, he directed me toward his white backdrop and told me to pose "however you feel comfortable." After I'd struck a few stiff poses, he asked if I'd feel comfortable taking off my shirt.

"It's not because we're necessarily going to be doing nudity, or anything like that," said the hippie in soft, reassuring tones. "It's just that we're going to be traveling in close company for a lot of weeks and we're looking for actors who can be really free with the script and with each other. We need a group with a lot of trust. So right now, see if you can let go with me a little and be as free as you can."

Uh-huh. The kind of "free" that the actors in *Hair* were every night, singing their way through Act I's finale and weighing how much they could use the extra $15 they'd get if they took off all their clothes at the end. An extra $125 a week was a big deal to chorus kids, and nudity wasn't supposed to be a big deal to the young, the hip, and the free.

I'd been on nude picnics in college with my friends, and I knew we hippies were supposed to trust each other. I shed my bra and curled up like an armadillo to be photographed, feeling completely unfree.

"You're really sensuous," said the photographer.

I recently met an actor who swears he recalls a low-budget movie that was actually made in India by actors in a bus at that time. Maybe. Or maybe there were non-SAG auditions for hippie Indian bus tours every time some photographer needed a quick batch of skin shots.

I went into a camera store on lower Fifth Avenue to buy a black leather port-folio like the ones I saw carried by other girls whom I thought were actresses. I thought we were all expected to build portable collections of different looks. I didn't realize the girls I saw were primarily models.

The clerk was a portly, bearded young man who asked me a few questions and sympathetically gave me a discount on a better type of portfolio than I could af-ford. Then he offered to shoot some head shots for free. He was a photographer, he said, but didn't yet make his living at it, which is why he worked in the store. He said he'd be grateful for the practice.

I was so stupid I went. We did the session in his grandmother's apartment in Queens, where he lived because he was separated from his wife. I don't know where grandma was; the place smelled old and was deeply depressing. He took the shots I needed, then asked for some he wanted; I agreed to pose topless, draped in his grandmother's lace tablecloth. We took a break lying side-by-side on her lumpy double bed, where he moaned about his bad marriage.

I got nothing useful from the session; his lighting was ridiculous. Looking back, I know how lucky I was that he wasn't either more of a creep, in which case I might have ended up dead, or a better photographer, in which case I'd have ended up facing actual photos of myself published somewhere, looking awkward and uncomfortable in some poor grandmother's relic from the Old Country.

It was a long, hard winter. In the spring, when the ground cracked, so did I.

20.

Cracked

I awoke late one morning, alone, to find Liz's huge Afghan hound smelling so foul I took him into the shower with me. Black gunk poured off his body onto mine; I shampooed us both and toweled him off, then wrapped myself in my robe and began to brush my teeth. As I looked in the mirror over the sink, time stopped; I disappeared down the tunnel of my own eyes. When I returned, I found myself in suspended animation, motionless, toothbrush in mouth. I wasn't sure how long I'd been away; it seemed like about fifteen minutes. I dressed and did two things: I made plane reservations to fly home in a few weeks, and I traveled on foot to the Psychiatric Walk-In Clinic at New York Hospital.

At the clinic, I sat in the waiting area facing an empty space where several corridors met, the perfect place for us disturbed to project our own entertainments. A large, impeccably dressed black man sat beside me.

"I notice your ring," he said in an accent that wasn't American.

I looked down at what my sister had called a "slalom ring" when she'd given it to me. She had one like it, a V-shaped gold band; she'd bought them both on her Pan-Am stewardess travels.

"It is from Africa," he said.

I said I wasn't sure, that my sister had bought it abroad.

"Africa," he insisted. "I know. I have the same." He lifted his hand to display it. "I am the son of the President of"—he gave me the name of an African country, Liberia or Gabon or the Cote d'Ivoire; I didn't retain it because my geography wasn't good enough. "I had to leave my country because all the girls there, they want to marry me. Five hundred girls! Because I am rich! I am crazy because they make me crazy!" He threw back his head and laughed richly. "That is why I am here! And you?"

I looked at him: ebony, clean shaven, beautifully dressed, plump and shiny as an apple. He was almost credible, except we were meeting in a Psychiatric Walk-In Clinic. I told him some general, untraceable things about myself before being summoned to my intake interview.

I sat by the social worker's desk while she read my form.

"Smith!" she said, delighted. "I'm from Smith. I went to the School of Social Work!"

She said this with a smile, as if we were meeting at a Smith club luncheon. But we weren't. She had a job helping crazy people, and I was a walk-in crazy person. I'd squandered my intellectual inheritance. I burst into tears.

She sent me to a doctor who diagnosed me that same day as anxious and anorexic. He gave me some pills. I didn't want any pills.

"Your trouble is you don't want to depend on anyone or anything, even some pills," he said. "But sometimes you have to. You need help."

Depending on people hadn't worked out well lately; they kept asking for things in return that hurt to give. I took the pills, hoping they'd be safer than people. They were orange and lasted two weeks. I never knew what they were. But I noticed they did stop me from reading advertising slogans as personal oracles and decision-making tips.

Then I flew home. It was late spring, which is always beautiful in upstate New York. My mother and I spent long hours talking on our back porch. I didn't dare tell her the unwise and creepy things I'd done. There were other ways to talk about New York, and we did; she sensed the sickness in my soul, the terrible disillusionment. She soothed. But she didn't probe. I was a grown woman now. Some sorrows had to be borne alone. That was the message.

Did it come from the legacy of her own wrenching separation from her mother and sister, when Daddy moved her upstate after the war, away from their nurturing love? Was it a remnant of our split over Jonathan, when she'd tried to urge chastity and had been cruelly rebuffed? Was the silence on certain matters a legacy of her own mother, my Nana, who'd declared adamant marital independence from her domineering mother? When I was little, my mother had always soothed my childhood tragedies saying, "It's hard to grow up." Her words had worked, because the sadness in them seemed greater than any sorrow I'd ever felt, growing up in the sunshine of her love. Now I realized some growing up only happened once such love seemed very far away. Knowledge of that distance was what had made my mother sad.

21.

To Tell the Truth

When I got back to New York, a master's-degree student from Smith, Don Marcus, called me to say he was forming a repertory company to play Dartmouth College that summer. He was using people he'd known at Smith and wanted to audition me.

He and Jerry Zaks came to the aqua living room. We read some scenes from Oliver Hailey's *Who's Happy Now?*, Jerry playing the six-year-old boy and I playing his mother, Mary Hallen. Don listened as we concluded the reading on a satisfyingly deep, emotional note. Jerry looked at me and said, "That came too easy."

I guess that's how it looked. But to act with friends, freely and for pleasure, unsullied by any covert agenda, had simply released the best in me after a mean and sordid year. We hugged; I was invited to Dartmouth, joining the great Smith actresses Sarah Harris and Ellen Parks, and actors Bill Sneichowski and Bill Cwikowski—Snicks and Cwiks. Snicks and I drank a jug of wine one night, talking about his Polish Catholic father. He'd told Bill,"If you become an actor, I will never think of you as a man." The story was so sad, I was so drunk, and Bill's wound so deep, that I threw up in empathy. Bill and I sobbed while he held my head over the toilet. That's how close the company became.

We lived in a fraternity house, ate brown rice casseroles, and put on three plays as the New Theater Ensemble. One morning, while I breakfasted as usual in the Dartmouth Student Center, I opened the *New York Times* to find my own smiling face staring at me from the summer stock listings in the Arts and Leisure section. It was a total surprise; Don had sent the times the company's 8-by-10's without telling us. Mine had been published: "Mimi Kennedy appears at Dartmouth in the New Theater Ensemble's production of *Who's Happy Now?*"

I was.

❀

I returned to New York that fall, going back to temporary secretarial work and non-Equity auditions. I didn't have the guts to cut Joe out of my life completely, but I saw him less frequently and no longer expected any professional good to come of it. I decided to contact Cousin Ruth. She was long-divorced from the man who'd been our family tie, and she'd become a huge star on "All My Children," but I thought she'd remember me. Soap operas employed lots of young actors, and the jobs weren't easy to get. I knew this even before the incident with Candy Early, which occurred years later, when we were dressing-roommates in *Grease,* but which is so instructive I'll include it here.

Candy was playing a sixteen year old on Broadway. She was, in reality, mid-to-late twenties. The producers of "All My Children" called her in to read for the role of a sixteen-year-old prostitute. They loved her reading, but judged her too old for the part, and cast a younger girl. They had the writers interview Candy to write a part tailor-made for her. When it was ready for the story line, Candy came in to read a few scenes informally, and the producers thought, uh-oh, she's not really right for this. They really wanted her to be the teen prostitute. So they gave Candy's role to someone else, fired the teen prostitute, and gave that role to Candy. She remained "Donna" for over a decade, going from Bad to Good and Poor to Rich, becoming one of the most highly paid, popular characters on the show, a soap success just below the stratospheric level of her colleagues Susan Lucci and Cousin Ruth.

Ruth was delighted to hear from me. She invited me to lunch on the set, where I found her flame-tipped and vibrant as ever, still creating disturbances in the electromagnetic field wherever she went. She walked me into her producer's office saying, "Give this girl a job!"

So the producer did. Not on the soap, but on "To Tell the Truth" a venerable game show then thriving in syndication. She gave my name to a production coordinator who hired me as a segment impostor.

The object of "To Tell the Truth" was for celebrity panelists to find out which of three mystery guests was really the person all three purported to be. Each segment opened with three silhouetted figures, on pedestals, in a wide shot. Lights revealed the figures in successive close-ups as the announcer asked them to state their names:

"I am Marie of Romania," Number 1 would assert.

"I am Marie of Romania," repeated Number 2.

"I am Marie of Romania," insisted Number 3.

All three then abandoned their pedestals to walk onto the set, sit at desks, and be grilled by the panelists trying to suss out the liars.

I was to impersonate a Goucher College graduate who'd taken electronics and car mechanics. That was the whole gimmick worthy of national TV: a girl who knew about cars!

A prime example of the mechanically challenged stereotype, I knew nothing about cars. Or electricity; but "To Tell the Truth" held preshow cram sessions to help impostors lie credibly, and the coordinator assured me I'd learn. The one caveat, she said, was that when I'd be asked to give my real name and identity at the end of the show, I couldn't say I was an actress. They didn't use actresses. I'd have to say I was a secretary. "That's true, isn't it?" she said.

This was in the days before home videotaping, even on Betamaxes. My national exposure would be as fleeting and evanescent as a stage performance, and I'd have to waste it hiding my real identity, even at the moment of truth! Still—it *would* be national television! Yes, I said. I supported myself as a…secretary.

I reported to the session, where I met the realie and my fellow decoy. We demolished a complimentary deli platter while enjoying highlights of Auto and Appliance Repair. I listened with the rapt attention of an adult determined to get that lost education. In high-school general science, I'd watched nuns chase ping-pong balls around the floor during silly experiments whose principles I not only failed to glean but whose wrong hypotheses had, I presumed, sent the experiment awry. What stuck with me from the "Truth" session was this news: broken appliances often aren't really broken and don't need expensive repairs. This confirmed years of suspicion, on my part, that unscrupulous repair were ripping me off at every turn. I eagerly imprinted the home remedy: plug replacement. You cut the old plug off the appliance cord, stripped some of the cord insulation, and attached bare wires to a new plug's terminal screw.

Dress rehearsal, where we were interviewed by a dummy panel, went well. I got all the votes, including host Garry Moore's, who couldn't vote on-air. He said he'd dated Goucher girls in his youth and unless his memory was playing tricks on him, Number 3 was one, if ever he saw one. I was 3.

In performance, after our dramatic opening, we guests took our seats to watch the panelists be introduced and take theirs. Henry Morgan, a surprise substitute, scared me. He reminded me of my father, who had an unerring nose for a lie.

Sure enough, in the midst of the proceedings, he turned on me like a hissing cat:

"Number 3: do the numbers one-eight-four-three-six-five-seven-two mean anything to you?"

Not only did they mean nothing to me, they so boggled my mind I couldn't think of a credible lie. So I did the next best thing: I tried to make Henry Morgan's question look stupid. "No," I replied, in a tone that said, such numbers have nothing to do with car or appliance repair, and I'm sorry for you if you think that they do.

"Number 1?" he snapped instantly at the other decoy.

"Dose're deh firing ordeh of deh pistons," she replied.

I could have killed her. She was from New Jersey and had made a big show of commiserating with me backstage about retaining too little from the cram session.

The panelists scratched busily on their pads. Henry Morgan smirked at me. No one else asked me anything.

Four hundred bucks, I thought. If the dress rehearsal had been real, I'd have won four hundred bucks!

Peggy Cass asked me a final question before the vote. Either she felt sorry for me, or she'd been coached to get the following exchange on camera:

"Number three," she began, "say I have a broken toaster and I bring it to you. How would you help me?"

Saved—this was the technicality I remembered!—I bent to the microphone to redeem my credibility.

"Most appliances aren't actually broken," I began instructively. "The first thing I'd do is change the plug."

"Oh," she said innocently, "How would you do that?"

Warming to my Mr. Wizard role, I elaborated. "You cut off the old plug, strip the wires, and wrap them around the new plug at the terminal screw."

There was enough of a pause for me to realize what I'd said. I could see the panelists sparring psychically for the privilege of a retort. Peggy won; she'd elicited the setup.

"Ooh! What's that?" She winced. "Terminal screw! That doesn't sound good!"

The place erupted.

Thus, my television debut repeated the lesson of my childhood radio debut. In the moment when I was most proud of having the right answer and delivering it, double entendre turned me unwittingly comic. "Funny is money," the comedy writer Eric Cohen used to advise me later in my career, but it wasn't on "To Tell the Truth." Still, the laugh felt good. Perhaps, I concluded, it was the best I could expect in a game won by lying. I always lost at those.

My deepest consolation came in knowing at least I'd fulfilled the New York mandate, "Be yourself." In my television debut, no one had believed me as anything but.

Before I left the studio I asked the New Jersey decoy how the heck she knew the answer to Henry Morgan's diabolical question.

"Oh," she said, "I was eatin' with my family last night and my brother offehed to take me outside 'n' show me undeh deh hood, but when I sawr it, I jus' said, feggeddaboudit, it's too complicated. But just befoah he closed deh hood his flashlight hit dese numbehs, an' I asked him what they wehe, an' he sez, 'Deh firin' ordeh of deh pistons.'"

Living at home beneath the family roof, I saw, gave young adults all kinds of support when it counted. Let her have the money, I thought. I couldn't have done it for the world.

❍

A new tenant moved in at 308 West One Hundredth Street above the cute guys. She was not only an actress but a working one in the cast of *Hair*. I could visit her by going out my living-room window, climbing over the two front balconies, and entering hers.

I attached myself to Ursuline Kairson, spending days in her apartment, listening to her stereo on her groovy loft bed, cooking, talking into the wee hours, staying overnight. I hadn't had a girlfriend like that since I'd been in high school. I saw *Hair* many nights for free, meeting the cast and becoming friends with Ursuline's friends. It was from her I learned about the nudity paying $15 nightly. From her, too, I learned valuable beauty and health tips. She was a vegetarian and had all kinds of natural lotions and perfumes. Because she was dark African-American, all her tricks didn't work on my Irish coloring, but she'd been on her own a lot longer than I had, even going to boarding school, and was the first fellow-actress I knew on a daily basis. I loved my roommates, but their livelihoods didn't depend on their looks; if they didn't shave their legs, no one cared. I absorbed what Ursuline knew, most importantly the steely self-respect her mother had instilled in her to protect her from the ravages of racism. The casual integration young actors knew in New York theater in the seventies was one of the richest benefits of those times for all of us. I, who'd grown up privileged, had been devastated by the effects of just one year outside my protected cocoon. Ursuline's inner strength was what I wanted to learn most of all.

When the cute guys who lived below Ursuline left to travel in Europe for a few months, Liz and Sherry announced that they would do the same. They disappeared for weeks without sending back word. Then one day Liz walked in our door wearing an embroidered Afghan shearling coat, followed by her boyfriend in an identical vestment; they took up residence in our tiny back room. Sherry arrived with her boyfriend days later, and they began sleeping together in the double bed across from mine in the big bedroom. Everyone knew the arrangement was temporary; soon the couples had found places of their own, and that was the end of the aqua living room.

My sister hooked me up to her stewardess housing network. I found a place with a flight attendant named Lu and her roommate Tina, who worked for Mayor Lindsay's administration. Thus I began life anew, on Manhattan's East Side, 80th Street between York and First, in the high-rise confines of a Stewardess Building.

At first I missed my psychologically sophisticated, political-intellectual friends. Tina and Lu read paperback best-sellers and distrusted me. I heard Tina tell her friends at a dinner party, to which I'd declined an invitation in order to compose on my guitar in the back bedroom, "She's on some kind of ego trip."

They also objected to my cleaning contribution, which was nil. Liz, Sherry, and I had cleaned in spontaneous bursts, or when something spilled—sometimes not even then. Once Liz had bumped my cardboard nightstand as she walked by, causing the little alarm clock on which my life depended to fall to the floor and shatter. "Oops, broken," she'd said, heading out to class. I was miffed, but it wasn't a deep transgression in the aqua apartment. Personal possessions were held in common, and Liz always shared her clothes.

Tina confronted me: "Is it possible you just don't *see* the gunk in the bathroom?"
It was more than possible; it was true.

Tina moved out to live with her boyfriend. Lu and I remained, splitting the extra rent. I found Lu at the living-room dinette one morning, crying into her yogurt and granola. I asked what was wrong. She told me she hadn't been out on a trip. She'd just returned from having an abortion. I was stunned. I'd thought Lu was responsible and mature, with a wonderful life and a serious, political-appointee boyfriend. I'd lived with her half a year and never guessed there could be trouble running deep beneath that smooth blonde exterior. I had been on an ego trip; Lu was as lost and lonely as I was.

"We've never talked very much," she said that morning. "But I've always really admired you. You seem so free. You're really going after what you want. I'd like to do that, but I've never had the guts."

And I, who had the guts, was losing heart.

●

That year I waitressed, having grown sick of office work.

I answered an ad in the *Times* from a Second Avenue ice cream parlor that promised waitresses up to $250 a week part time. The day I applied, the owner directed me to a store to buy a black leotard, fishnet stockings, a cellulose dickey, and a bow tie. He'd provide the skirt, he said. I reported to work the next night, and he escorted me to the upstairs patio, ordering the overweight girl working there downstairs. She glared at me as she left. I was swamped all night; every table was full. Overwhelmed, I dropped a sundae in a customer's lap.

The next night, I was assigned downstairs. It was much less lucrative. I assumed it was because of my clumsiness and was frankly relieved to learn the job at a slower pace. The man dismissed the other waitresses at closing and had me finish up. Then he offered me the patio station permanently if I'd accompany him upstairs now. I couldn't believe it. It was bad enough feeling compromised for the sake of my acting career. Whoring for a waitress station was out of the question. I was relieved to discover a sexual line I would not cross, even one below sea level. I said no. After two weeks, my tips had shrunk to nothing and I quit, realizing the only way to earn anywhere near $250 was if the man arranged it. I was profoundly sad, knowing some girls, possibly the one on the patio who got booted downstairs every time a new girl came to work, said yes, convincing themselves it was a relationship. I told everyone I could about the guy, except the *Times.* I didn't think of that. The ad kept running.

I applied at Schraffts and was assigned the lunch shift at Thirty-fourth and Park under the aegis of a manager who coached the waitress staff as if we were a girls' sports team, with peppy talks and pithy maxims. The senior waitress was a big-boned Irish woman named Maisie, who was so unassuming someone else had to tell me Maisie'd worked there seventeen years.

My mother loved Schraffts. When I was little she'd take me to the one on Madison and Eighty-sixth for hot fudge sundaes and boxed marshmallow fudge to go. Schraffts no longer sold the marshmallow fudge, but they served the sundaes, and as I made my first, I was lost in pleasant reveries of the sweetness and abundance of my mother's love. Then the manager walked by, eagle-eyed. "Too much!" he rebuked. "*Way* too much! *One* scoop of ice cream! *One* ladle of hot fudge!"

Delivering those stingy sundaes broke my waitressing spirit. I could see the unspoken question on people's faces as they looked at the meager fare in the silver dish: Did these used to be bigger, or was I just smaller? I found myself apologizing. Sometimes, my heart pounding, I'd sneak two scoops, two ladles to customers I couldn't bear to disappoint.

In 1972, I had to pay my taxes for the first time. Harry Linton, the actor's taxman, advertised in *Backstage,* so I went to him. I'd made $300 over the poverty line, and I had to file. I learned about deductions from the actor's taxman, who used his nurse-daughter's life to illustrate the detail he expected in accounting for fiscal expenditure. "I saw her rinsing out her stockings and uniform by hand one night. I said, 'How much does a bottle of that stuff cost you? How many bottles do you use a month?' See? For her, that's a business expense."

I didn't use Woolite for work, but I rented a piano for musical auditions. At $15 a month it was my biggest deduction. I got a refund of about $200. I was audited. I've always suspected it was more about Vietnam War politics than $2,600 in wages and tips. I was terrified; the auditor was nasty. He homed in on the piano. It didn't matter I'd used it to *prepare* auditions, he said, if I hadn't made any money doing musicals. He disallowed it, and I had to write a check for $32. Which at the time, I recall, was a big goddamn bite out of my bank account.

○

I still had relatives in Manhattan on my mother's side. There was her mother, whom I called Nana; Nana's sister, Ethel; and George, their brother, the last of my mother's four bachelor-uncles known, collectively, as "The Boys." George lived in the Eighty-sixth Street apartment between Park and Madison where he'd spent his adult life with mother and brothers. One by one they'd died, leaving George to sit alone all day, steeped in newspapers beneath an ancient floor lamp that had aluminum foil taped to the shade to keep the glare out of his eyes. An Irish housekeeper saw to his needs; housecleaning was not her priority.

He was a shy gentleman and he always had been. But a taxi accident in Central Park at midlife had crowned his meekness with loss of both his mental acuity and his Park Avenue ear-nose-throat practice. George had been a gifted artist as a child, but The Boys had to have professions, and the matriarch pegged those hands for a doctor's.

Whenever I visited, no matter where our conversation began, it always ended on a Navy ship during World War II.

"I was the only doctor on the boat, y'see, and everybody, when they meet an ear-nose-throat man, thinks *eye*-ear-nose-throat, y'see, but I wasn't. ...So when this boy came on board with his face half blown off—geez, it was something terrible— the officer came to me and said, 'Doctor! Can you save the eyes?' And I tried to tell him, 'I don't know anything about eyes, I'm just an ear-nose-throat doctor.' But I was all they had on board, and the officer in charge said—oh geez! I'll never forget it—he said"—at this point in the story, George jabbed a finger at the empty space in front of him, widening his eyes and growling—"'Doctor! I'm *ordering* you to operate!'" George's finger would fall. "Just like that!" Then George would hunch his shoulders and be Yiddish, for comic relief: "So...vat coult I do?" Then he'd let his shoulders fall. That was the only laugh. "I had to operate. But when I tried to begin, my hands were like this."

This was the central action of the story: George raised his hands off his knees and made them quiver as he stared. Then he'd let them drop. "They were shaking, just like that. Geez, it was awful. I thought everyone could see. The head nurse said, 'Doctor? Are you all right?' I had to say I was, but geez, I was scared! I stitched the poor guy up the best I could, but I didn't know much about what I was doing, a' course. Geez, that was awful!"

George would get to the end and blink, amazed to find himself having lived through the nightmare once again.

"Geez," he'd wince. "That was the Navy."

And that was the story, recurring helplessly whenever he talked aloud, that explained why Uncle George spent his last decades in a chair, hands lying limp on his knees, resisting further orders to do what they would not, and could not, do.

Nana and Ethel were livelier; they'd been the family rebels. Nana had married upstate—tantamount to eloping—and Ethel had married a Protestant. Nana moved in with Ethel, insisting it was temporary, refusing to give up her own apartment, and I used to visit the two for cocktails or lunch. They followed Cousin Ruth on "All My Children" and delighted in show business gossip, or any indications of my future success. They believed in me.

As they sickened—Nana with heart disease, Ethel with undiagnosed symptoms of uterine cancer—they grew fearful. Nana shook her head once as I was leaving, saying bitterly, "I don't know who I am anymore." It struck dread in me. I was just beginning my life, trying to Be Myself. Once I'd found myself, would I lose me again, in a darkness at the end of life?

When Nana finally admitted she couldn't live alone anymore, my mother came to New York to close her vacant apartment. My sister and I helped her; Susie had lived there the first two years of her life. Mother had lived there as a career gal, a war bride, and a young mother. I'd stayed there during my first magical visits to New York.

The place was thick with oily dust and grime. We had to throw out all the bedding and lace curtains. I moved through the rooms, remembering Nana in them. She'd ironed and cooked in the kitchen, smoked and commandeered her phone in the dining room. She'd loved, and lived fully, her middle-class New York existence there, with the clubish ceremony at the end of every day—cocktails with The Boys and the matriarch next door. My reverie was shattered by finding a glass in her kitchen cupboard filled to the brim with something brown. It was hundreds of dead cockroach carcasses.

Ethel died in a dark room in New York hospital. Nana died a few years afterward, the day after Christmas, in the arms of her youngest daughter, Sue. George died later, after I'd moved to California. My mother used to say a play about her family's lives would make *Long Day's Journey into Night* look like a Marx Brothers comedy. She said it from Rochester, where she'd created a life of more light than shadow.

I'm sure my maternal relatives knew light, too, when they were young. It's hard to judge lives from their endings in lonely and sick old age, particularly of people who believed, as my New York relatives fervently did, in keeping up appearances. Their shadows haunted my ambitious beginnings in New York, my mecca. Most young people keep the dying at arm's length if they can. I was grateful to be around the old people, but it scared me too. After Nana died, I realized for me a happy life would have to include dealing regularly and frankly with the cockroaches in the cupboard. I didn't want ugly things building up in the dark to be discovered when I was gone. I didn't want to be paralyzed by shame about my failures, which would occur, I knew, despite my best efforts. I wanted to be able to forgive myself, even if I turned out to be something of a fraud.

22.

Andy Warhol

The notice in *Backstage* announced open non-Equity auditions for roles in *Pork,* a new play by Andy Warhol. I couldn't believe lowly nonunion actors had a shot at a project by the man who'd invented Pop Art, and the phrase, "In the future, everyone will be famous for fifteen minutes."

Auditions were held at Cafe LaMama. It was exciting just to be in that renowned emporium of avant-garde theater. Or *almost* in; I spent most of the day hunkered outside with a group that was the last to be seen. When we were admitted, we filled theater seats warmed by a day's worth of previous actors and watched each other read onstage for the director and the fascinating, impassive Andy. He sat facing the house.

The part I was right for was "Helen Hell." I knew I'd read much better than the other girls, but most of them looked weirder than I; I feared defeat because I wasn't a Warhol type. By five o'clock half the group, including me, hadn't read, but the director looked out and said, "Thank you all for coming. We're sorry we can't read everyone, but Andy's exhausted. He wants to thank you all and hopes he can work with each of you sometime in the future."

The crowd was too cool to groan, but the release of tension into disappointment created an almost palpable heave. Andy leaned forward in his chair, saying something to the director. His voice, even at close range, was so soft I never heard it. The director listened, then announced, "There are a few of you whom Andy would like to stay!"

Few of us had moved anyway; desperate hope for something exactly like this had kept us glued to our seats. The platinum elf's skinny arm floated upward; the director tried to follow as Andy began to point: Him. Her. That one. Him. Her. Up there. The final wavering point was at me.

"Thank you," the director said again loudly. "Please leave your resumes at the door, but unless I speak to you, you can all go home." He approached some people in the front, then made his way up the aisle stairs and stopped at my row. Actors filing out paused for a split second, hopeful, but the director was looking at me.

"Andy wants you in the play," he said. "He likes your face." He took my name and number and gave me a script.

•

Pork, the script's introductory note explained, had been created from the taped conversations of Andy and his friends.

The rumor at the audition was that the tapes were made while everyone involved was on acid—LSD. Reading the script, I believed it. The only thing I understood was a whimsical monologue about pillows flying through the air and coming through the windows; the rest of the script was incomprehensible. And an inch-and-a-half thick.

Well, that will be the excitement, I told myself; watching the mise-en-scene clarify Warhol's fascinating world and bring it to life!

We were a strange and motley crew that gathered the first day of rehearsal in a loft on Great Jones Street. I was far and away the most traditional-looking person there. There was a vivacious gay man called Wayne County whom I loved immediately because he was friendly to me and because Wayne County is in upstate New York. Andy was there, staring silently over the director's shoulder during the director's opening speech:

"I want to welcome you all on Andy's and my behalf, and let you know how excited we are about the play and all of you. There will be some changes in the script, depending on what happens in rehearsal, but for the most part, this is what Andy wants to see onstage. It's based on the life of Bridget Polk, one of his good friends." Lots of people nodded; they knew her.

"Sometimes," the director continued, "people drop out of my plays, for whatever reason. I'm warning you now, I don't take it well. If you drop out of my play, I will snub you when we meet in the street, I will tell everyone I know never to work with you, and I will say nasty things about you behind your back forever. So I would caution you strongly against doing anything like that."

I swallowed hard. The script had given me pause. But it was Andy Warhol. People would come to see it no matter what. The work possessed the seed of genius, regardless of whether it bloomed.

We began rehearsal, and the opening scene was set: Pork, played by a short, overweight woman with boyish hair, is discovered waking up in the morning in her bed at home. The actress would be spread-eagled nude toward the audience, the director explained, with a dirty sanitary napkin between her legs. Our star, wearing a gray sweatsuit, splayed her legs open and got a big laugh.

The actors playing her parents come in and argue loudly above Pork's head. She argues back. Other characters, figments of Pork's imagination, walk in and out of the scene with odd bits of dialogue. We rehearsed this scene all day and went home. I had not yet been assigned a part. During a break, I'd opened a door looking for the bathroom to find the director passionately kissing a man he had pressed against the wall. He turned around to see who was disturbing them and sneered. "Excuse me," I said meekly. "I was looking for the bathroom." They waved me down the hall. "Thanks," I said, in a bright way that was meant to reassure them, and me, that the sight of their passion was an everyday, ordinary thing.

The next day, we began again with the opening, Pork reclining on her rehearsal-module bed, the actors playing her parents taking their positions. They'd just begun when the director said, "Wait!"

Everybody stopped.

"This isn't enough for the opening," he said. "I want…hmmm…" His eyes raked the circumference of the rehearsal room and found me. "You haven't done anything yet, have you?" he asked. "Have you been assigned a part?"

"No," I said, coming away from the wall to stand straight, ready to serve, but already experiencing some trepidation at having to be in the scene with the bloody Kotex.

"Okay," said the director, "You'll come into this scene from stage left, and stand there, like a statue, in red high heels, you know, like those alien chicks in those fifties B science-fiction movies?"

I walked into the scene, downstage left, and struck an imperious pose.

"Perfect!" he laughed. I was pleased I'd delighted him.

"And you'll be nude. You don't mind nudity, do you?"

There was a brief pause. "Can we talk about that later?" I asked.

A voice rang out from along the wall: "She'll LOVE it!" I turned to see it belonged to the spike-haired blonde who'd been wrapping herself around a girlfriend for most of the rehearsals. They laughed at me scornfully. I felt like I was in hell.

"Yeah—so you'll be nude, wearing high heels, and you'll be carrying a glass plate of steaming human shit. That pose is PERFECT. Okay, let's go on."

The speaking actors resumed their dialogue as I stood with my imaginary plate of shit and my imaginary no-clothes, thinking: Now I can't even ask my sister to come see this. She was the only person I was going to ask. I knew I couldn't invite any theater professionals. I'd gotten into enough trouble wearing underwear in a conventional, well-made play. I wondered if this director would let me wear underwear.

"Move up." The director yelled to me.

"Up?"

"Yeah. Go to Pork and hold the plate directly above her head. Give her room," he told the other actors.

I slipped between the bed and the actress playing the mother, to strike the sci-fi, high-heel, alien-queen pose again. I could tell it'd made a hit. Who knew how big my part could grow, from this opening, standing naked, center stage, with a plate of shit?

"Great! That's great."

The actors finished the dialogue, and the director moved on.

I never got to hear the scene about the pillows. I bought a manila envelope on my way home that day and used it to mail back the script with a letter that said I was sorry, but I couldn't do the play, though I wished the company well.

I felt I'd finally done the right thing, even though I'd done it partly for a venal reason: when I won fame, I wanted it to last longer than fifteen minutes.

Part Four

LESSONING

1972–1977

"Do you hear that? That rage? That rage is meant for you."

Doris Roberts, 1972

"Go to acting school."

Sid Caesar, 1972

"No actor can act a role he hates."

Stella Adler, 1972

"My secretary, went to Smith, right? *Dumbest fucking human being* on the face of the earth!"

Boss at Viacom, 1972

"At this point I usually tell students to go into therapy."

Curt Dempster, 1973

"I've been a fool. I love you. I love you. I love you."

Me to Larry Dilg, 1974

23.

Sid Caesar

Across the hall from my apartment in the Stewardess Building lived an American Ballet Theater dancer named Jackie. It was an incredible relief to find her; Lu, my flight attendant roommate, was sweet, but we were emotionally incompatible. Stewardesses had to keep a grip. People's lives depended on their equilibrium in situations guaranteed to unglue every performer I knew: severe turbulence and engine failure.

Jackie, being in show business, shared my view that mood swings and self-dramatization were normal and even attractive human behavior. When her roommate left New York at the same time Lu transferred to the Midwest, Jackie suggested I move in with her. I accepted. I knew we'd get along in every way when I saw her wet-mopping her living-room floor, saying, "Don't mind me, I love to clean."

I admired Jackie and her dancer friends. For one thing, they wore wonderful makeup. Lucia Chase, ABT's director, liked her ballerinas wide-eyed, so the dancers applied mascara until it clumped, a fashion "don't" for ordinary women that looked fabulous on them; their lashes were thick and stiff as toothpicks. Their physical discipline was awesome; daily, they danced in pain, onstage and in arduous classes.

But the best thing about the dancers was that *they* admired *me*. "You actors get to use your *minds!*" a featured soloist once sighed enviously to me. He was eating lasagna at one of Jackie's potluck suppers, which she hostessed regularly in our apartment with the fervor of a minister's wife. I was amazed at the amounts of ice-cream and Mom's best-recipe casseroles consumed by those lissome bodies at our communal table. Jackie had told me how any weight gain was shamed in dance class and could mean the loss of a dancer's featured roles. For this reason, she finally admitted, most of the guests at our suppers went home and threw the whole thing up. Dancers, I learned, were in terrible thrall to their bodies, and I think many of them binged in an attempt to placate their hungry and desperate minds.

On the day I was to leave my old apartment, I'd packed my earthly goods into a closet, out of the painter's way, but I couldn't move them until afternoon. My morning was consumed with an audition for my first Equity job.

Joe, the agent who'd never officially signed me, knew of a last-minute opening on Sid Caesar's tour of *Last of the Red Hot Lovers*, by Neil Simon. The actress
playing Elaine Navazio had dropped out of the show after its run in New Jersey,
and the producers needed a quick replacement for the bookings already set in summer stock. Joe sent me in to read, saying, "Look older." We both hoped I'd get this
job, so we could get on with our lives and leave the seamy past behind.

I arrived at the Eugene O'Neill theater stage door wearing falsies, a tight red
turtleneck, a pencil-slim skirt, spike-heel boots, and a wig. The doorman directed
me to a chair in the wings; someone eventually arrived to take my picture and resume. By the time I was called onstage, my heart was pounding. I could see a line
of people, mid-theater; they shouted friendly hellos. I greeted them back and was
told to read the opening scene with the stage manager. I launched into it, using a
brassy New Jersey accent that made me feel very self-assured. The reading went
well. At its end, someone called out, "How old are you, Mimi?"

"Twenty-six!" I belted back, hoping distance made my extra three years as
credible as the bust and the wig. They viewers thanked me and said I'd hear one
way or the other by the end of the day.

By the time I got back to the apartment, the telephone had been buried beneath a newly laid ground cloth in the bedroom. I rescued it, placed it near the
bedroom door, and went to tell the painter I was an actress who'd just come from
an important audition and was waiting to hear whether or not I'd gotten the job.
I asked him to please alert me if the phone rang while I was across the hall.

Thrilled to be deputized for such a glamorous vigil, the painter introduced
himself as Sidney. He sounded Cockney. I thought he was right out of George
Bernard Shaw—James Doolittle in painters' whites.

A short time later, as I walked in from carrying a load to Jackie's, I found
Sidney standing in front of the long living-room window, beckoning me.

"Yew've told me yoa secret," he said, "naw oi'll show yew moine."

He took a knotted handkerchief out of his back overall pocket in suspenseful
silence, untied it, and laid it in his cupped palm. He folded back the corner to reveal a pile of glittering diamonds.

"Doimands're me 'obby," he said, stirring them with a fond forefinger. "'Ow
much d'you think these 'ere 're worth, off the top o' yer 'ead? Eh?" I told him I'd
no idea. "Sixteen thousand," he murmured, removing his finger, tying up the ker-
chief, and tucking it away. "That's what oi'm carryin' t'day." He winked at me
through the thick lenses of his black-framed National Health glasses and went
back to work.

Was he somebody's walking safe? Were diamonds the painters' portable pen-
sion plan? Some New York stories remain unsolved mysteries.

The phone didn't ring until late afternoon. I was sitting on the bedroom ground cloth beside it, trying to read, listening to Sidney's roller clittering up and down the living-room wall, drawing ever closer as the day, and my hopes, faded.

"I've got an answer for you," announced Joe's secretary so breathlessly that I suddenly suspected she knew my situation with her boss and appreciated that this news brought deliverance. "And the answer is...YES!!!"

She screamed it with all the joy I felt. I dropped the phone and danced, screaming too. I'd be getting my Equity card; I'd landed my first Equity job on schedule, two years after college graduation. Though, by my own standards, I'd cheated, and I'll never know what that cost me.

I picked the phone back up and heard her tell me she'd call back with details about rehearsals, which began in two weeks. I said I'd have to call her, for I was moving, that very minute, across the hall. We hung up.

Sidney stood in the doorway, blinking.

"You go' it then?" he chirped. "Aoww, I knew yew would! Yew've 'ad a glow about chew since oi first saw yew this morning!"

I would have hugged him, if it hadn't been for the paint. I shook his hand vigorously instead, thanking him for his vigil. Then the only thing left to move was me, so I went. As I passed, Sidney gave me a pat on the shoulder saying, "There yew go! A bi' o' pint!"

I craned to see what he'd done to my good audition turtleneck, but he was already brushing the spot. Whether he was removing or increasing the evidence, I never knew, because the mark, when I saw it, was ghostly, but he'd boasted:

"'Aven't yew heard? Whenever a pinter pats yew and leaves some pint, it's good lahck!"

Thus spake Sidney, with a pocketful of stars. He winked one owlish eye at me through its thick, paint-speckled lens and said, "Yew're on yowah waiy!"

●

The first day of rehearsal, I had to submit a biography for the tour's playbill. I agonized over how to explain my dearth of professional credits and finally came up with the ridiculous statement, "Miss Kennedy has acted extensively at community theaters around the country." That's how I turned the bio in and that's how it was published.

The company at Showcase Studios was heady: Sid Caesar, Doris Roberts, and Jill O'Hara. I tried not to be terrified, but it wasn't easy, especially after the director gave the following speech:

"If you want to change something you've been doing or want to work out something new, this is your chance. I'm just a traffic cop. I'll stop you from bumping into one another, but please—*please!*—don't ask me about your motivation. If you do, I'll just say what the director told the young actress who said she couldn't cross downstage unless he gave her a motivation. He said, 'You want a motivation? I'll give you a motivation—your *paycheck!*'"

Everyone chuckled as if they'd heard this story before. I hadn't, and four years of college training flew out the window. We'd taken motivation seriously at Smith. But I chuckled too, as if I'd heard the joke extensively at community theaters around the country. Where, of course, actors didn't get paychecks.

Acts I and II needed brush-up rehearsal; most of the week was devoted to the Act I duet between my Elaine and Sid's Barney. I knew my lines, but I jotted down the blocking in my script. I learned movements Sid wanted to keep that he'd worked out with the previous actress. I was nowhere near ready to discover any of our own. I spouted the text in a brassy voice and went where I was told, with a sexy swagger. At Smith, our training had emphasized "developing the instrument," and I was playing mine for all it was worth. Unfortunately, I was doing a student solo while sharing the stage with one of the greatest comic improvisers of all time, the acting equivalent of a jazz musician. Sid was gentlemanly. He played the notes as written. Ladies first. I was learning the number.

At home I worked feverishly on character. In rep the previous summer, I'd explored subtext with Curt Dempster's protégés in a group, sharing ideas, building characters as an ensemble. Now that I was an Equity pro, a hired gun, there'd be none of that touchy-feelie stuff. I'd have to bring it with me when I came. Unfortunately, I brought talent, guts, and determination, but very little technique.

The little I knew, I used. I wrote pages of backstory for Elaine that I'm sure would have mystified her creator, Neil Simon. I developed a psychological gesture. This technique had been described in our Smith freshman acting text, *To the Actor*. The author, Michael Chekov—the great playwright's nephew—believed character could be summed up in one physical move, a brilliantly distilled mannerism that could center one's performance in an instant, whenever it was repeated.

Working feverishly in Jackie's and my living room, I discovered I felt Elaine's impatient allure most vividly when pacing and flicking my nails, in a standing position, or, when seated, crossing, recrossing, and jiggling my legs—and flicking my nails. These stunningly unoriginal and tediously time-consuming motions became the basis of my physical performance. My lines I approached the same way I had at age twelve in community theater: I stitched together readings into what I hoped resembled an organic and seamless whole.

Sid, a genius to whom work was play, watched my work and made no comment.

We opened in Connecticut to good reviews. I was critically praised, a fact that led some members of the company to mutter about "cow-town reviewers." I'm a cow-town girl, I thought to myself. Maybe that's why they like me.

My performance, glued together by the pressure of opening, came apart the following week. I felt myself losing laughs, so I tried to milk them back. Sid started playing around, to relax me. Onstage, in front of the audience, he'd wheedle and coax, bark and cajole, stick out his tongue and cross his eyes at me. I had no idea what to do with this. The audience did; they laughed. I stood by, flicking and jiggling, until they stopped. Then I resumed my dialogue.

It was like letting the air out of a tire; by the end of Act I, Sid was driving *Last of the Red Hot Lovers* with a big, wobbly, flat. Jill O'Hara's Act II had a bumpy start, and eventually she figured out what Sid knew: Elaine Navazio had slashed a wheel. It took everyone else's energy just to get the play moving again. This did not make me a popular member of the cast.

One day Jill and I were looking at a map of where we were in Ohio. Forgetting my lie in the playbill, I'd exclaimed, "Wow. Would you believe I've never been west of Buffalo?" "No kidding," Jill replied dryly, and I knew then that no one had believed my story, and Jill wasn't even surprised to find out I was too incompetent an actress, offstage as well as on, to sustain it.

At the end of Act I, Barney pours out his heart to Elaine in an aria of midlife male doubt and insecurity. She responds with the question: "And for this you wanted to get laid?" It's vintage Neil Simon: funny, inadvertent, and bittersweet— in the right hands. Mine were not the right hands. Too much nail-flicking, for one thing; for another, I'd never said "get laid" in my life. I thought it sounded coarse, so I played it coarse. In my hands, the line, after the mammoth leg-jiggling pause with which I preceded it, had all the charm of an axe murder.

I knew something was wrong when, nightly, the laughs grew weaker.

"You've got to be more of a woman and less of a girl," Sid sputtered in frustration, early in the summer, when he was still speaking to me. I was helpless to translate this suggestion into specific performance adjustments, so I just got broader—became more of a broad.

One night I was invited to go to dinner with the rest of the company. This was unusual. I'd gotten used to eating fast food alone in my motel room.

"Anyone worth anything in this business has been fired," Sid proclaimed over the repast and proceeded to regale us with a hilarious story about a time he was sacked. Others chimed in with their own riotous stories of dismissal. Only I, clinging to my first professional gig, didn't have one.

I realize now this dinner was probably planned to prepare me for a blow that never came. And it never came, I suspect, because of Doris Roberts. Doris, a magnificent actress and human being, could take no pleasure in another's misfortune, even if she did greet me at half hour in the tour's first weeks with, "Did you take your talent pill?" I took comfort where I found it, and her gentle dig hinted that though she realized I didn't know what I was doing, she thought I had talent, at least intermittently.

After the group dinner, whether on her own volition or at someone else's last-ditch request, Doris began to coach me. She accosted me backstage as if she had time on her hands and nothing else to do.

"Show me how you're doing that moment," she'd say, and I'd act out the one in question. She'd make suggestions to improve it. Why are you saying the line that way? she'd ask. Don't you think Elaine would care more about that?

It helped, but not enough to avert disaster one night in a barn theater. Sid had finished his monologue. He looked over at me for my line. When he saw the leg-jiggling and nail-flicking begin, he arched backward on his hassock, gave a loud moan, then sank forward in a lifeless slump.

This was unusual; I knew something in Sid had snapped, and the prospect was terrifying. I stopped jiggling and adjusted my body language to deliver my line, but in those seconds, Sid's posture changed. His silences were eloquent. This one said, "At last! Something to do while I wait!"

He'd found a barn moth dive-bombing his head.

Sid followed its flight pattern, crossing and uncrossing his eyes. He craned his neck slowly to one side, then the other. The audience loved it; this was "Your Show of Shows" Sid Caesar! Sid and the moth shadowboxed. I sat stock-still, ready to speak, but it was too late. Sid was fully engaged. He'd found a playmate, which I hadn't been all summer. After a while, the audience grew anxious, knowing moth-play couldn't be part of Neil Simon's story in a New York apartment. It was a distraction—but from what? Sid, sensing their restlessness, brought the interlude to a close. He killed the moth.

Bringing his hands together with a resounding CLAP! he made the creature disappear. There was a shocked silence. No one wanted to believe they'd just seen the death of the delightful living thing. This wasn't some awful experimental play in the village, this was *comedy* in summer *stock*. But when Sid wiped his hands on his trousers, grimacing, he erased all hope that the moth would be returning for the curtain call. Several people groaned. Sid turned to me, expectant and cross-eyed.

I said my line. About three people, who must have woken up when Sid clapped, laughed. The rest of the house was as quiet as a crowd at a car crash.

My exit line that night—"Please GOD, let there be a machine in the lobby!"—was even more desperate than usual. I fled downstairs to my dressing room and cowered behind the door.

Act I's curtain applause began, and Sid barreled downstairs as if he were bouncing off the walls. After his dressing-room door slammed, a knock came to mine.

I opened it to find Doris posed silently, tapping her index finger on her left shoulder as if she would point to her left, but discretion prevented her. I followed her implied direction to Sid's dressing-room door, from behind which came sounds of garbled yelling.

"Do you hear that?" she said.

I nodded that I did.

"That rage?" she clarified.

I nodded again. There was a huge crash, and Doris's eyebrows went up.

"That rage," she cautioned, " is meant for you."

We stood, transfixed, as the crashes continued, diminishing to a series of small bumps before they stopped. We would learn later that Sid had turned his dressing-room chair into firewood.

"So whatever you're doing in Act I that Sid doesn't like, I suggest you change it," she concluded, then melted away as quietly as she'd come.

The next afternoon, she showed me how Elaine, a frustrated smoker, could search for cigarettes everywhere on the set *as she spoke.* This would build comic suspense without bringing the play to a grinding halt. I shudder to think such a simple activity so liberally suggested by the text had never occurred to me. But it hadn't. At Doris's urging, I reverted to my childhood habit of picking up cues, and nine toilet-flushing minutes fell off the act. *Last of the Red Hot Lovers* began to hum coolly along from curtain-rise. By the end of the summer, I was on speaking terms with the rest of the company.

Sid's final words to me—and he took the cigar out of his mouth to enunciate them—were *"Go to acting school."* He gave me a stern look from beneath those bushy brows and nodded, before chomping back down on the stogie with a wide grin.

24.

Stella Adler

After I returned to New York and filed my first unemployment insurance claim, a milestone in any actor's life, I began looking for an acting teacher. I didn't have to go far. The trades announced that Stella Adler would be conducting acting classes on Fifty-seventh Street that fall. She was revered; I phoned for information. The classes were almost full, but Stella interviewed all applicants, I was told, so I was given an appointment. At her studio near Carnegie Hall, I found other nervous aspirants waiting to see her. This rattled me. Somehow I hadn't imagined getting into a class as quite so competitive.

When my turn came to enter the theater, an assistant waved me toward the door, and I entered alone to see Stella across the room, seated, eyes shut, with her leonine head thrown back against what could only be called a throne. As I approached her, she tilted forward and opened her eyes, reluctantly it seemed, to study me. I introduced myself, and she asked why I wanted to be in her class. I explained that I'd just come off a summer tour with Sid Caesar, which had been difficult for me because I didn't think I'd ever found my character. She nodded and asked me what I would do for my audition.

I panicked. Somehow I'd missed the information that an audition would be required. When I stated this, Stella merely shrugged and said, "Show me something from that role you just finished."

I knew my flawed Elaine Navazio would probably scuttle my chances for admission. Thinking of those waiting outside, I said, "I'm afraid it's not very good as an audition piece. I sort of hate it by now."

Stella's eyebrows arched. "Well no wonder. No actor can act a role he hates."

What unequivocal clarity! What simple truth! I was desperately wanting Stella to teach me just as she began, I thought, to regard me as if I might be too stupid to learn.

"Let's see; show me," she commanded, jerking her head toward the stage.

I did Elaine's final speech, a wonderful speech that I'd rarely gotten right. I'd been too broad, or not broad enough. I'd missed the mark because I'd never aimed from inside. At the end, Stella ruled crisply:

"I see. Your problem is, you're a very good actress, so that's all anybody tells you, and nobody's ever helped you."

Yes! Help me, Stella!

"I can help you. If you'll let me."

Of course I'd let her! Why not?!

"Tell them outside I'll take you," she said, leaning back against her chair, laying her palms on its polished carved arms. I'd been dismissed. Years later I would hear people say that Stella Adler either took to you or she didn't. To me, she didn't.

There were about twenty of us in class. Students couldn't work every week, so performance time was precious and nervewracking. I was impressed by a woman who looked like a well-manicured Long Island housewife because I found out she was married to French film director Jules Dassin, and I thought her courageous for taking a class, starting a career at the bottom instead of trading on her husband's fame. But Stella was as hard on her as she was one me. The young men, naifs recently arrived in New York from the provinces, were her favorites. After one young-lug type did his Biff scene from *Death of a Salesman,* Stella rose from her chair to step majestically onstage and embrace him, then announce dramatically to the rest of us:

"*Here* is an *actor!* Take a good look, everybody!" We did, and saw a boy blushing to his hair roots. Stella turned back to him. "Your heart, your soul, your *honesty...* is what I saw in Paul when he was young." She meant Newman, we knew. "Sit down," she said softly. "Very good."

This was the benediction we all sought, the acting-class equivalent of God the Father's "This is My Beloved Son, In Whom I Am Well-Pleased." The young man lumbered back to his seat, thinking, I'm pretty sure, what we all were: High praise for a raw, uneven monologue.

"The reason Marlon was so brilliant," Stella instructed, "is because he always knew *exactly* who he was talking to!"

This was one of the many bon mots about Great Acting that constructed the Ideal toward which the class strove, by trial and error, seeking Stella's encouragement, avoiding her admonishment, in our scenes offered up for her judgment. I performed three. Each of them pushed the Ideal further from my grasp.

The first, *Talk to Me Like the Rain and I Will Listen,* I did with a partner who was from some mythic cowboy state, Wyoming, or Montana. He'd asked me to work with him. He lived in a dreary, cheap motel room just like the setting of the piece, and we rehearsed there. I thought we'd successfully absorbed its atmosphere of broken dreams for our presentation. Stella liked the boy's performance and gave him adjustments to make, which she praised. She said very little to me; its gist was that I shouldn't try to play such characters. Next I crafted a monologue from Olivia's lifting-of-the-veil scene in *Twelfth Night;* Barry Keating, a director friend of mine from Smith-Amherst summer rep, helped me rehearse it. I thought I'd achieved something playful, self-assured, and flirtatious, but Stella was unimpressed. She had me perform some adjustments on a few lines before she lost interest and told me to sit down.

Finally I brought in *The Crucible*. Because I identified with Puritan religiosity and self-denial, I thought I'd really connected to the monologue, performing it honestly and simply, without gimmicks. When Stella rose from her chair and walked toward me, I dared hope, for a moment, for the blessing bestowed on the lug. It did not come. As she neared me, I could see Stella's eyes glittering like obsidian.

"You're the kind of actress who plays the costume, aren't you?" she said accusingly. Then she sighed. "You can do that if you want to. Go ahead. But it's not the kind of thing that interests me, and I can't help you with it. I can't, I'm sorry. I've tried, but I really can't help you, anymore." Her final look to me suggested I'd taxed her beyond endurance. She walked back to her chair, leaving me to drip offstage.

Several classmates told me afterwards they'd liked the scene and found Stella's criticism too harsh. But Stella, true to her name, had shone clear light on two truths: I was an intuitive actress who relied almost exclusively on externals to shape a performance, and she couldn't help me. She offered no technique to supplant reliance on externals, possibly because she was so swayed by them herself. One day she gazed at us in steely silence as we filtered into class. When we'd taken our seats, she ranted.

"I look at you and wonder why some of you ever even *thought* of becoming actors. You think just because you have temperament you can be actors. Well, lots of people have temperament! It doesn't mean a thing! To be an actor you must be an *artist!* Some of you will *never* be artists! You're too damned *middle class!* What even brought you to the theater in the first place?! I see you come in here, week after week, wearing those *terrible* middle-class clothes...! Why, *why* do you wear them? Some of you—really—you look so damn bourgeois you make me *sick!*"

I looked down at my class uniform—playing the costume! I'd devised it to look regal and bohemian, from an empire-waist, ankle-length, sleeveless purple smock buttoned top-to-bottom over a white blouse with its own floppy self-tie. Now I realized Stella had always seen it for what it was: a polyester secretary's blouse and a housedress from Gimbel's. I never wore either again.

Stella devoted most of the last class to questions. I, in jeans and leotard, raised my hand, hoping for a talisman to take away from my time with her: a word or look that might convey I'd amused her, if not inspired fondness or respect. But as the final minutes ticked down, Stella took a question from Linda, a willowy girl with skin like peaches who'd been gawky and inaudible in all her scenes.

"Oh, all right, Linda! What do you want to know?" the legendary actress mock-groused, spreading her arms toward the girl. "Beauty must be served," she explained to the rest of us, giving Linda a bow.

Another reason why I've been at the back of the bus, I thought. If Stella liked you, you cherished the things she taught. If she didn't like you, you tried to forget what you'd learned—that you were a conventional slug with no business taking to the stage, which Stella had once ruled with her extended family.

I air such stinkingly sour grapes admittedly for the satisfaction involved, but mostly to warn actors that in the matter of a teacher, reputation may be important, but "Different Strokes For Different Folks," and "Chacun A Son Gout" must be your guide.

In the early spring, I rode the bus downtown and crosstown to Eleventh Avenue, then walked so far west on Fifty-second Street I could smell oil and dead fish on the Hudson River. After climbing three flights of stairs in a warehouse I found Curt Dempster, founder of Ensemble Studio Theater, in his tiny office behind a stack of scripts.

"What are you doing here?" he asked me.

"I'm finally ready to take your class," I replied.

25.

Curt Dempster

My unemployment ran out; I had to take a day job to support my training with Curt. He didn't allow students to do outside acting while they studied, except television commercials, which weren't an option for me. I wasn't in Screen Actors' Guild and didn't have an agent, not even Joe anymore. I envied the girl in Curt's class who made a mint doing Pampers spots; I had to fall back on my typing.

I applied for permanent secretarial positions with regular hours, so I could be in class promptly at 6:30 P.M. twice a week. Curt saw tardiness the way therapists do: as a lack of commitment. If it happened more than twice, he said, he'd kick us out of class.

I narrowed my job choices to two: one at Viacom, Inc., and the other at *National Lampoon* magazine.

The *Lampoon* was my favorite publication, and that was the job I wanted to take. My interview with P.J. O'Rourke, in which he dictated an ad from the magazine's back pages, made working on the humor rag seem potentially more like *Men's Hairstylist and Barber's Journal* than I cared to believe, but P.J. assured me: once you worked for the *Lampoon*, you eventually got to do everything. The ad he dictated mentioned girls' nipples looking good in wet *Lampoon* T-shirts; I speed-wrote through it thinking, God, all men are alike. But after my furtive, shame-tainted sexual experiences with older men, the sniggering, puerile scatology of the *Lampoon* seemed healthy as vitamins. I was devastated when P.J. frowned at the idea of my leaving twice weekly at 6 P.M. "I don't think we can handle that," he said. "When we put the magazine to bed, everybody needs to be here at all hours."

I was an actress. I'd committed to class. I couldn't work for the *Lampoon*. I walked onto Madison Avenue feeling the tug of a road not taken.

Viacom was no media giant then, but a mere syndication arm recently severed from its CBS corporate head because of FCC rules against networks developing their own programs. Two men, Phil Howort and Merrill Grant, were looking for a secretary who could "be on our team." That was the job description, because, as Merrill put it, "Even we're not sure what we do. The main thing to know is that it has nothing to do with anything else that goes on around here."

Once in the job, I found out that what Merrill and Phil did was develop television shows to sell to television networks. I'd never heard of this work, which would one day be the vehicle of my own destiny.

I enjoyed typing business letters and flawless versions of pilot treatments, which is how I divined the mystery of my bosses' occupations. The rest of my time was spent talking to the other secretaries, eating bialys, and perusing fashion magazines. From these basic activities, I regarded the ringing telephone as an annoying distraction. I did thrill to some of the callers, like Don Kirshner, who developed "Rock Concert" with Viacom while I was there. The late-night show was a hidden evolutionary link between "Shindig"/"Hullabaloo" and MTV, and Kirshner was a legendary rock producer whose name was all over my forty-five record collection. He actually called me "doll"; it charmed me to hear Damon Runyon's term in daily usage, being applied to me. But I'd been generally handicapped by Katherine Gibbs Secretarial School of Boston's total inattention, in its summer crash-course, to the secretarial skill most vital to my bosses' work: Giving Good Phone.

I was ignorant of the crucial subtleties, and creative variety, of telephone one-upsmanship: who calls whom; the return, the ill-timed return, the nonreturn; the levels of excuses, ranging from respectful to insulting, for a boss's inaccessibility; the ploys by which a good secretary overcame such excuses when given to her.

At first it didn't matter. Phil and Merrill piloted their own instruments, unless they wanted to impress someone or play a joke, in which case I was expert at going along. But after Phil left Viacom to become an agent—he was later one of nine at ICM—Merrill worked hard to expand his contacts. He shmoozed overtime, took trips to LA and did tennis dates, power breakfasts, and parties. He built relationships outside the office and largely beyond my ken. I had to be in the office, suddenly, early enough to cover calls from the coast, but otherwise I was ignorant of Merrill's ascent to a level at which my phone skills proved sorely inadequate.

I found this out the day he returned from lunch in an ebullient mood. He stood over my desk to ask, "Any messages?" in his usual offhand manner.

"Frank called," I replied, in Kind, handing over a "While You Were Out Slip" with exactly that written on it.

Merrill's breath sped up as he read the two words. "Frank? Frank who?"

"Just...Frank." I waited for the light of recognition to click on in his eyes and saw the beginnings of frenzy there instead.

"He said it like he knew you really well," I added weakly. "I'm sorry."

"Frank" had managed, brilliantly, to convey that any probing into his last name would prove an embarrassment to us all.

"He said he'd call you back. Or you could call him."

Merrill's voice quavered as he fought for self-control. "'Frank' from *where?* Did he say from *where?*"

There was a list of phone numbers posted above my typewriter by Merrill's previous secretary, a woman of obvious efficiency despite the rumor she'd left to go on a rock 'n' roll tour. I glanced at it now, confirming my uneasy suspicion that there were important "Franks" at all three networks.

"Um, Frank from ABC? Or CBS. I think. One of those."

Merrill turned on his heel to enter his office, where I heard him sigh prodigiously and flap his suit coat loudly on the couch before picking up his telephone to begin the delicate business of tracing down "Frank."

"My secretary," I heard him say sotto voce to someone. "Went to Smith, right? *Dumbest fucking human being* on the face of the earth!"

I fled to the ladies' room and sobbed, but I emerged a phone dragon. No more juvenile power games on *my* watch: I didn't care if you were Fabian, Cher, or the frigging *Pope*, I got your last name. My "While You Were Out" slips were as detailed as tax returns.

Two years after I'd taken wet T-shirt dictation at the *Lampoon*, I was back in its offices singing a song I'd cowritten for *The National Lampoon Show* tour. Ellen Foley and I were acting the roles on tour that Gilda Radner had created in New York before going on to "Saturday Night Live." The *Lampoon* editors liked "Bad Girls" and put the song in the show, giving me my first showbiz writing credit. Neither P.J. nor I mentioned my secretarial audition; I'm sure he didn't remember it. But I did. His assurance had proved true: Once you went to work for the *Lampoon*, you eventually got to do everything.

❂

Curt began his classes with a group relaxation exercise. We spread out on the stage, lying on our backs, and were guided through muscle contraction-release and deep breathing until our spines melted into the floor. I loved being on the floor, where chalky dust got into my hair and onto my skin. Secretaries didn't lie on floors. On the floor, I was an actress again.

Afterward we took seats in the raked semicircle house and watched one another work. There were students at all levels of training; that first evening Curt guided someone through an "Emotional Preparation." She took a seat onstage and he coached her from his chair in the audience, sure-handedly leading her through the labyrinth of memory to the precise emotions she needed to make her scene objective more urgent. Other actors did scripted scenes. Some actors did solo activities; others did improvisations with partners. These began with one partner onstage, doing a solo activity to achieve an objective, and continued when the second partner entered with an objective of his or her own that required the first actor's help. Dueling objectives created fascinating encounters.

"Objectives" were what we wanted: situational outcomes, specific behavior from another person, desired objects. "Activities" were concrete tasks, devised by us, which we performed onstage to achieve our objectives. "Relaxation" consisted of deep breathing, and muscle contraction-release and was done before going onstage along with Emotional Preparation, a meditation that made our objectives feel urgent. Curt coached students out loud through any portions of the technique with which they needed help.

The second week, Curt assigned me the acting partner I'd have for the duration of training—Richard. He was a new student, too. He was tense, angry, narcissistic, and smiling, just like me.

Partners were directed to meet frequently outside class to practice some basic exercises. The first of these was "Mirroring," in which partners sat in opposing chairs and mimicked everything each other did. At first the lead was assigned, but as partners mirrored each other's tiniest impulses, the lead flowed back and forth until it became impossible to tell who led and who followed. Unless someone fought to retain the lead. Which at first, most of us did.

The "Repetition Exercise" added words to Mirroring. Again seated in opposite chairs, partners mimicked voice and body language, with the lead assigned. Eventually, Curt allowed spontaneous verbal impulses into this exercise, which shifted the lead to whomever expressed one. Partners who were fluent at Repetition moved on to the "Word Game."

To this day, I don't think I understand the Word Game and fear I never played it well. Or maybe it's just hellaciously difficult for everyone. When Richard and I practiced at his one-room apartment, his wife had to find errands to occupy her on the streets of Hell's Kitchen for an hour or so. At mine, Jackie had to leave, or at least sequester herself in the bedroom while Richard and I set up opposing chairs in the living room to trade screams, imprecations, and stinging personal remarks, which comprised the Word Game as played by terrified beginners.

What I knew about it was this: it began with both partners, eyes closed, seated in chairs, doing a quick relaxation exercise. One of us counted to three, then opened our eyes and whomever had been designated to begin made some spontaneous verbal observation of the other. The other responded in kind, briefly and directly, to the partner's look and sound. This began a free-associative exchange of verbal impulses based on mutual scrutiny. That was the idea; but since staying focused on one's partner and verbally brief was difficult for most of us, the Word Game rarely flowed. It jolted, sputtered, and stalled, punctuated by screams of frustration and calm interventions in class by Curt. Swearing and "discussion" were taboo. Because much of our daily language either masked our spontaneous feelings or vented them with curses, we found these exclusions stifling. Our ability to make honest, direct, succinct emotional utterances had withered. Curt's coaching reminded us to stay focused outward, so as not to drown in self-consciousness.

"Concentrate on him," he'd urge. "Did you see him smile when you said that? Why? Was her voice mocking just then? How did it make you feel? What's that mean, when he rubs his hair? Did you notice his foot stopped jiggling?"

The universality of our impediments was humbling: it seemed all of us were angry and denied it. We preferred to smile and conceal—the affable actors! We weren't angry! We never had nasty thoughts! Only when we admitted we did, and expressed them—all the way to wishes to annihilate everyone else, to which they usually led—were we free from the most stubborn obstacle to good work.

Another humbling universal epiphany was that most new students' objectives failed because they reduced them to unspecific urges to "win." Curt insisted on details: *what* did we wish to win? What desperate lack would be filled if we *did* beat the other guy, annihilate everyone else? When we searched our pasts for the answers, constructing objectives and activities based on private details, our work became mysterious and fascinating. We got beyond annihilation. We became focused, not scattered. We were able to get what we wanted. We weren't frustrated, powerless infants. Great Acting, I saw, happened when actors were secure enough in their objectives to observe everyone and everything around them. Great Acting was not an impossible, distant Ideal; it was a process that started simply and gathered strength as it flowed.

Curt insisted on relaxation. He maintained he'd once seen an actor in a highly praised performance who was so tense he'd actually tried to sit down in a chair being occupied by another actor. Curt thought most acting was bullshit.

I had trouble expressing my anger, like everyone else, especially the female students. I began to picture "my anger" as a preternaturally dense metal chip in my stomach, compacted by years of denial. I feared dissection would set off a fission chain reaction that would destroy me. This fear, Curt suggested, was the universal basis of Bad Acting, which I feared more than rage or death. Dutifully, I began to explore my anger.

"Switchblade fantasies," I jotted in my notebook, "the power to kill. To defend myself.

FUCK IT ALL

FUCK IT ALL

FUCK IT ALL

UNCLE ALBERT ON THE BUS WONDERING WHAT PAUL MC-CARTNEY WAS SO SORRY ABOUT."

Around the time I wrote this, I ended a guided group relaxation in fetal position, sobbing at a corner of the stage. Following Curt's suggestion to go to a happy place, I'd arrived, mentally, in the corner of my childhood bedroom where my brother had built a cardboard castle for my dolls. We'd spent long, happy hours there, playing doll dramas. But the scene had switched abruptly to the head of our front stairs, from which I watched Danny below me, walking out the door to go to kindergarten. He'd left me alone in our universe, and he'd never come back to stay. It was the first time I'd revisited this goodbye, and it unleashed a profound grief that swamped me.

"At this point, I usually tell students to go into therapy," Curt advised me privately at the end of class.

I called a therapist, Mr. Brockman, whose name I'd been given at the New York Hospital Psychiatric Walk-In Clinic a year and a half earlier. I stayed with him almost a year, until I went on tour with *Grease*. He listened in classic silence to my dreams, stories, complaints, and fantasies; the relief this gave me was massive. I hadn't heard my mind out loud since the days of Confession. Then, I'd talked to erase the past. Now I talked to reclaim it, to find out what I wanted and why. I learned that beneath my fear, competition, and anger was a deep, unexpressed grief. I didn't learn, until I became a mother, that my own mother had taken a three-week cruise when I was six months old to break the mother-child bond and reestablish the primacy of her marriage-bond. Such trips were customary in those days, for this reason, among upper-middle-class couples. They're a terrible idea for the baby. "I used to leap out of bed for joy at your two A.M. feedings," Mother had once said of my first months, "just for the chance to *see* you again!" Our bond had been a strong one and that early separation was like death, removing my mirror, disintegrating my fledgling baby-self with consequences no one understood. With Mr. Brockman, I identified my lonely autonomy in New York as a threatening rerun of other experiments in independence that had gone awry and left me lonely and terrified. Memory flooded me. My work in acting class became rich in detail. I developed a "fuck you" attitude. I could annihilate without guilt. I felt invincible.

"I've discovered I'm not expendable," I told Curt after a few months. "I used to be afraid that if I expressed my true feelings, they'd run out. But the more I express, the more there are. They never stop."

He told me that was an important thing to know.

A writer friend, David Rimmer, had given me a novel by Larry McMurtry, *All My Friends Are Going to Be Strangers,* and I was nearing its end on the bus to class one night. I continued reading as I walked down Fifty-second Street, passing the warehouse, even though I knew it would make me late to class. I couldn't stop; the protagonist's plight had me transfixed.

Danny Deck was drowning his novel manuscript, at night, in the Rio Grande, because he'd come to hate words. They made him so lonely, reminding him of all the people he'd loved and lost. "The door to the ordinary places was the one I had missed," he thinks, before pushing his manuscript to the bottom of the river and turning it to pulp. He surfaces in the dark current and turns South to "go see rivers." Only they can assuage his grief. "Such a wonderful thing, to flow. I wanted to so badly. It was all I had ever wanted to learn."

I was doubled over on the hydrant where I'd perched to finish the book, sobbing, when a passerby gently touched my shoulder and asked if I were all right. I told him I was, that I'd just come to the end of a sad book and was on my way to acting class. The stranger smiled and waited for me to collect myself before he went on his way.

Even before reaching the warehouse third floor, I heard Richard raging. Entering the theater, I saw him in the center of the stage, dominating a group improvisation. He was hitting the work light on its long chain and screaming nonsense invective. When the bulb's wide arc escaped his swipes, Richard's fury increased. Redoubling his efforts, he'd attack with more venom when the bulb swung back.

It wasn't hard to see myself as that bulb, or think that I'd been locked in a screamfest with a partner who liked to rage and punish as much as I did. Richard's tense grimace contrasted miserably with the kindness I'd just received from an observant stranger on the street. Or the flowing of rivers. I wanted to flow, too. I whispered to Curt, "I can't do this anymore," and left, without ever taking off my coat.

A classmate later said that Curt had told the group I'd panicked. Maybe I had. But Danny Deck drowning his novel in grief and rage, the stranger's touch on my shoulder, and Richard's abuse of the lightbulb combined that night to deliver a powerful epiphany: emotions could destroy and create, and I was tired of sham skirmishing. I wanted to work.

I walked fifty blocks back to my neighborhood, but before going home I went to Elaine's, a literary and show-business boite I'd always been too scared to enter. It was full of angry, smiling, creative people talking about themselves and their work. I sat at the tiny bar, ordered a scotch, neat, and drank it. That was my graduation. I flowed out of the frying pan, into the fire.

26.

Larry Dilg

The vehicle of my return to the off-off Broadway stage was a rock musical version of *Das Rheingold* with music by Jim Steinman, directed by Barry Keating. Barry had also directed Steinman's original musical, *The Dream Engine* at Amherst College while I was away my junior year in London. I'd returned to Smith to hear I'd missed the best college production of the decade, as well as my Perfect Computer Matchmate, Larry Dilg, in the lead.

Joe Papp optioned *The Dream Engine* for the Public Theater. Though he never produced it, Papp's enthusiasm gave Steinman a reputation as a wunderkind, which made Mercer Arts Center, a multistory hive of Off-Off Broadway theaters near the Public, agree to produce *Rheingold*.

I auditioned to be a Rhinemaiden: "Swimmin' in the Rhine and it's fine, so very fi-ine." But I was cast as the goddess Freia, alternating with an actress named Annie Bardach. I was happy; I loved the gothic-rock score, and I got to sing most of it in the chorus. We learned some of the songs from tapes Steinman had recorded in LA, where he'd gone on other business at the start of rehearsals. On these tapes, Steinman addressed another voice as "Larry."

"Is that Larry Dilg?" I asked Barry.

He said it was.

"He was my Perfect Computer Matchmate," I told him.

Barry passed this amusing tidbit to Steinman, who in turn told Larry that his future wife was doing *Rheingold* in New York. This hatched a fantasy among the men that Larry would come East, marry me, and settle in Connecticut with a trench coat, two kids, and a station wagon.

Wendy Wasserstein, who'd been at Mt. Holyoke when *The Dream Engine* rocked the five-college area, choreographed *Rheingold*. She was struggling to establish herself as a playwright, but the Pulitzer Prize was years away; she too had been taught to have "something to fall back on." Hers was dance, thanks to her mother. She made the Rhine seaweed sway and the Niebelungun dwarves dig coal in rhythm. I entered the Niebelungun cave scene on my hands and knees bearing half the weight of gospel/rock singer Andre DeShields on my back.

One night, my fellow goddess Freia, Annie Bardach, took a bunch of *Rheingold* actors to the show her husband, Gary Goodrow, was doing at the Village

Gate. It was called *National Lampoon's Lemmings*. I knew I'd like it because it came from the *Lampoon,* but the Woodstock parody I saw was so brilliant I went back several times. The audiences always screamed for more, and eventually, we got it, as "Saturday Night Live."

John Belushi played Joe Cocker; Chevy Chase portrayed an acid-tripper too stoned to support his head on his hand as he lay lounging on a tabletop, propped on his elbow. His head rolled off his hand a few times, his elbow frequently collapsed, and in the end his whole body rolled off the table. Chris Guest, whose later career was arguably the most original and eclectic of the three, struck me as funniest with his James Taylor impression, after being announced, "This guy has CHARISMA, and that's what show business is all about!" Chris, as James, in the spotlight, went into a slow nod over his guitar and collapsed on the floor.

Rheingold enjoyed far more modest success, though it, too, was culturally germane, containing seeds of music that later turned up on "Bat Out of Hell," the Meatloaf-Steinman collaboration that became one of the best-selling rock albums of all time.

Months after our show closed, the Mercer Arts Center fell down. It crumbled to the ground without warning or explanation in the wee hours of one Manhattan morning. Perhaps a decade of vibrating rock scores had weakened the old structure; perhaps it reached critical mass of struggling actors' anger and imploded. What's certain is that everyone who ever played the place had the same thought, hearing the news: We brought the house down.

●

It was ego, ironically, that made me decline the acting offer that came my way while I was striving to improve my image at Viacom as Merrill Grant's Secretary From Hell. Jackie directed a call from our apartment to my desk; it was the casting office of *Grease.* Months before, I'd auditioned for the show at the invitation of the producers, who'd seen me do an Off-Off Broadway reading. On the strength of that audition, I was offered a job as understudy on the National Tour.

I pictured myself in a strange hotel room, in a strange city, waiting for some full-fledged member of the company to sicken so I could go onstage after hearing the audience groan at the news of my substitution. *Grease* understudies, in fact, led happier lives than this; they went on so often they were regarded as regular cast. But I couldn't imagine that, when I told the casting director no. She said she understood and would call back when a suitable role opened up. Months later, "Jan" on the national tour did, and I jumped.

Merrill Grant was so happy to hear I was leaving that he never bothered to clarify why. I was going, that's all he knew, and he'd never have to be the bad guy who fired me.

Four years later I was gamboling up an NBC soundstage ramp in Burbank, California, lip-synching the title song to "Three Girls Three" when I saw two men watching us from a distance; I recognized one of them, from the drape of his trousers and the angle of his shoe, as Merrill Grant. Years after that I recognized the back of his head from forty paces; he was the only permanent office boss I ever had, and I think I imprinted on him like a duck.

That California day, Merrill and I grinned broadly to see each other in such mutually successful contexts, his as a producer being squired around NBC by an executive, mine as one of the season's pilot hopes.

"I never knew you wanted to be an actress!" he squawked. "One of the temps who replaced you told me the other girls called my secretary's seat the 'Chairway to the Stars' because both you and Phyllis left to go into show business! That's how I found out what happened to you! When you said you were leaving to go into *Grease*, I'd thought you meant Greece the *country!*"

Ah. I joined in his chuckling. Knowing we'd been equally clueless took the sting, at last, out of having been the dumbest fucking human being on the face of the earth.

○

In the old days, when touring was called "trouping," it was often a harrowing experience. Being "a trouper" once meant you went on with the show despite theater fires, canceled bookings, hotel evictions, and managers who'd skipped town with the company payroll. Actors' Equity solved most of these problems, and the modern national tour of a Broadway hit can be a high point in any actor's life, especially if that actor's traveling free and unattached.

Grease had run a while at the Shubert Theater in Chicago before I arrived, and it stayed for three more months, during which time I got to know the Windy City under ideal conditions: with money to spend and friends to spend it with. Restaurants and bartenders welcomed actors because we provided color and gossip for the locals. Merchants fawned on us; I did my first expensive shopping, buying in trendy boutiques like the one with a single style dress done a hundred ways with different antique silk remnants.

Other actors passed through town to join our rolling party. William Devane and the since late, but truly great, Leonard Frey came in with *One Flew Over the Cuckoo's Nest;* Ben Gazzara arrived in Eugene O'Neill's *Huey*, with Peter Maloney. Peter was my fellow-Rochesterian, whose father had acted with my mother at the Community Players. Another old friend, William Roerick, my father's college roommate, came through with *Night of the Iguana*. Long ago, he'd taken me on his knee, bidden by my father to discourage me from acting. I was five years old. "If you can have any other kind of life," the actor had lectured, "choose that." I'd nodded. He'd said to Daddy, "It's no use, Gerry. She's going to do it, if that's what she wants." I'd scooted away. There he was on a Chicago bus, going to his matinee, as I went to mine; we recognized each other with wide smiles, and I sat down beside him. It was a sweet moment, making that journey together; it seemed predestined, as if we'd always foreseen it. "Your father's very proud of you, you know," he'd said that day, his blue eyes watering. George Hearn, David Selby, and Tom Atkins were doing *Henry IV, Parts I and II* at the Goodman Theater. We did so much partying I got nodes on my vocal chords and had to sequester myself in my hotel room to rest my voice. Even that was fun. I wrote short stories and a screenplay that our stage manager Lynne Guerra shot on the Michigan Avenue beach with a rented camera. Starring Ray DeMattis and his boyfriend, it ended up in a small film festival and won some sort of nomination. On Sunday nights I discovered the "National Lampoon Radio Hour," which featured most of the *Lemmings* actors and a hilarious new guy named Bill Murray.

Grease closed in Chicago. In Toronto, we did the last stand of the tour's long run. After it closed, I returned to New York with enough experience to attract an agent and enough money, at last, to rent a place of my own. I found Jackie, on my return, curled up on our living-room couch under an afghan, reading Rollo May's *Love and Will*, red eyed, those waterproof, doll-like lashes wet with tears. She was drowning in painful memories of childhood; her New York adventure was drawing to a close. She stayed with Ballet Theater a little longer. Then she moved to Toronto. Last I heard, she'd married a Christian dancer and become part of a religious dance troupe in Canada and was nourished at last—body, mind and soul.

o

The Eighty-seventh Street studio, overlooking First Avenue, had five windows, including one in the bathroom. The sunlight alone was worth $210 a month; I grabbed it. On the day I moved in, with my orange crates and tablecloth-covered footlockers, my sister hung nylon voile curtains she'd presewn and helped me install bracket shelves. At the end of the day we opened a split of champagne and toasted my latest step up the ladder of maturity. I was a Head of Household.

I reopened my unemployment claim and began contacting agents. In those days, graduating from a youth ensemble musical gave actors the sort of instant credibility enjoyed by graduates of Ivy League colleges. The hippies from *Hair*, sincere clowns from *Godspell*, rockers from *Jesus Christ Superstar*, and high-school hoods from *Grease* were professionals, tried and true. Agents and producers were interested.

Because the portable black-and-white television set in my apartment was old and got terrible reception—Manhattan second floors didn't fare well without cable, which I couldn't afford—I didn't watch television and had no idea what "look" was desirable for television commercials. But I had it; my Buster Brown page boy and flat upstate accent made me the sort of ordinary person then in vogue with advertisers. Doris Mantz at ICM began sending me out on auditions.

I booked my first spot for Peppermint Patties. The audition was easy; I had to eat candy, enjoy it, and deliver the scripted reaction with genuine enthusiasm. I came across as authentic and original. On the set, these qualities, for which I presumed I'd been hired, were quickly buried beneath a mountain of more pressing concerns.

The first dozen takes were devoted to getting my line up to speed. Once I talked fast enough and had gone rigid with velocity, my facial expression was scrutinized. None I tried were right, which didn't surprise me; most of them verged on "how's this?" The director finally showed me what he wanted: an eye-roll. Imitating it made me feel phony and slowed down my words again. That cost several takes to correct. The director finally took me behind camera to show me on a monitor that he was flipping my image upside down midtake. "See?" he said. "That's the gimmick. I need the eye roll ri-i-ght—" he paused the tape— *"there!"* I nodded and returned to my mark, thinking of the German director Max Rheinhardt. Mr. Fisher, my Smith acting professor, had told us Rheinhardt was so precise he'd leap to the stage while actors were rehearsing and set the angle of separation of their fingers as he wanted it. I'd shuddered to think of trying to act under such circumstances; now I felt I was in their modern equivalent. The camera was Max Rheinhardt, a demanding tyrant. I finally got the eye-roll to the director's specifications. Then the clients stepped out of the darkness, where they'd been pacing the set's periphery all day, and asked the director to "restore her original freshness."

The commercial, when I finally saw it on TV, looked adorable. It went by in a flash, and you couldn't tell I was suffering. Years later, on "Homefront," I became a crew favorite for my ability to finesse a scene, performance and blocking, in one take. The pride I took in this skill was directly traceable to my first day acting on camera, when my agony mounted with every take, and the takes went on forever.

My second spot was for Cascade. I think I got the job because my faith in the product was profound. My mother used Cascade exclusively, and to this day I can't name another dishwasher detergent. But I was chosen for the "Honey, I'm Ho-ome" spot because I looked unthreatening enough to portray the first working woman ever to use Cascade. Desi Arnaz's classic greeting was *my* line. *I* came through the door to find my husband cooking, a bag of groceries at his side. Later, emptying the dishwasher, I see spots on the glasses. "Did Cascade do this?" I ask my spouse, incredulously. No, he confesses, because he got a cheaper brand of detergent. "Great," I say, "You saved a few pennies but we got all these spots!"

Tension gripped the set as we shot this segment. Director, agency, and client feared wifely chiding of a husband good enough to do the goddamn housework in the first place was tantamount to ballbusting, henpecking, pussywhipping; it would erode the nation's social fabric and—worse—the brand loyalty of traditional Cascade households. Having never lived with a man, I was blissfully unaware of the cultural minefield through which we strode. The married actor playing my husband offered suggestions, based on his home life, about how to eradicate all taint of emasculation. They were eagerly embraced. "*You* saved a few pennies" became "*We* saved a few pennies" so the predicament was mutual, less isolating for the man.

I let them do the sociology; I was concentrating on acting for the camera. I'd seen those corny Cascade "before" and "after" shots all my life, where actors, photographed through glassware, frown at spotty glasses and smile at spotless ones. I happily mimicked what I saw clearly in my mind; I understood *why* the glass had to be no more than three inches from my nose, no higher than my eyebrows, no lower than my chin.

In Curt's class, getting the acting right—specificity, simplicity, flow—was all that mattered. In film, no acting mattered that didn't get on camera and into the can. As I matured in experience, cinematographers, camera operators, and directors often approached me to warn about technical details that could make or break a shot. Having watched as great acting moments went down the tubes while everyone waited for the actors to solve a problem by serendipity, they knew I'd rather know about it than labor on in vain. Working unaware of camera requirements is as frustrating for the actor, ultimately, as the opposite situation: being blocked for the camera's needs without ever having rehearsed the scene for its acting values. Of course, often it's necessary, and good directors ease the pain, but actors don't love it.

○

Walter Hill's statement on the subject is the last word, as far as I'm concerned. He directed a *Tales of the Crypt* in which I played the part of a murder victim's sister. It was a tiny role played at the top of my lungs, accosting a defendant as he strides into court surrounded by bailiffs and lawyers; I break through them to spit on the man and scream, "MURDERER! YOU KILLED MY BROTHER!" The group barely acknowledges me; it keeps on moving.

We'd done about three takes, timing everyone's simultaneous movements to their marks, when a crew member approached me to say that if I could lean a little to the right during my outburst, it would be helpful.

I'd gotten the job because the show's casting director was my friend and neighbor, Karen Rea. Our sons played together every day. She knew I needed the work at a time when my career had slowed, and I'd wearied of acting, but needed to supplement my husband's teaching income. The original line for the character, "MURDERER! YOU KILLED MY SON!" brought me to tears at the audition, thinking of Karen's and my little boys. Walter Hill was moved by my performance on videotape, and cast me. On the set, the line changed to "MURDERER! YOU KILLED MY BROTHER" because Walter refused to exploit the death of a child if it wasn't a plot point. I thought that was profoundly moral and proceeded to find desperate grief in the death of a brother, committing myself to the moment with equal passion. I was enjoying acting for the first time in months when the crew member asked me to lean during the chaos. Suddenly, I was acutely aware of being a day player, whose job was to deliver the shot, not a great performance, and I was embarrassed to think I'd gotten carried away.

Until Walter Hill appeared at the man's side to throw a chummy arm around his neck and muse aloud, "You know, we must never forget that film is both a photographic medium—and a *performance* medium." The man smiled apologetically and slipped away. Walter whispered, "I love what you're doing, and I know that can't be easy to come up with every time. Just keep doing it." At a crucial moment in my life, he reminded me that it was important to get the acting right, because his work, he humbly knew, depended on actors who could.

○

Grease was revived at Coconut Grove Playhouse, Florida; I went down to do it with a revised National Tour cast. Robin Lamont, the actress who'd had a hit record with "Day by Day" from *Godspell,* was the new Sandi Dumbrowski. We became roommates and best friends, spending idyllic days by our condo pool and yachting the turquoise ocean with local admirers.

I became smitten with a hippie sailor named Brian. When the show ended, he invited me back to the Grove for January so we could drive up the coast together for his annual crafts convention in New York. I'd never driven up the coast; it sounded wonderful. By accepting, I was able to part from him with a lighter heart.

Back in New York, two things happened quickly.

I was offered a job, for February and March, as a member of a touring children's troupe for Indiana Repertory Theater. I'd never been able to get arrested in regional theater; the offer was an important one to me. It came from a man who'd staged managed one of the summer theaters on the Sid Caesar tour. I was grateful he'd remembered me. I accepted the gig.

Next, Jim Steinman told me Larry Dilg was driving back East from California and would be arriving at his home in Long Island within days. Jim and David Rimmer arranged for the four of us to meet at The Haymarket, a bar on Eighth Avenue, on a night I already had a ticket for *Equus.* They'd meet me, they said, after the show.

I arrived to find Jim and David in a booth, but no Larry. I sat down facing the door and waited. It was December, and chilly; I kept my coat on. My mother had bought it for me at Lord & Taylor on her most recent visit to New York; I'd admired hers, which was just like it, and she'd wanted me to have one of my own—a proper, dress-up, theater coat.

Larry said that when he saw me, he couldn't believe how old I looked. If I'd known this, I would have killed myself, or at least the coat. But he also says that this first-impression-maturity turned him on. His former girlfriend had dressed in T-shirts, jeans, and huarache sandals. Merino wool with gold buttons inflamed him.

I was equally struck by Larry's outerwear, a Hudson Bay jacket that looked like a picnic blanket my father used to carry in his car. He looked ridiculously young, like a schoolboy. The smoldering brunette who'd sung "I Shall Be Released" at an Amherst fraternity house, and walked away from my coy self-introduction, now sported a loopy grin that welcomed me. When I saw him, a voice inside me said, "This one's mine." Larry has since reported that *his* inner voice said, "I know who this is."

The possessive nature of my thought embarrassed me. I'd thought I was cooler than that. I think my genes cried out, my body recognizing what my mind didn't yet: this is my husband, father of my daughter and son, cocreator of a family in the long chain of marriage and reproduction that brought us into the world.

We four drove around that night in Larry's van, traveling to the Cloisters in Fort Washington as I sat in the middle seat with David Rimmer, looking at the back of Larry's head. This is a primal view of a potential mate, replicating, as it does, indelible images of parent-at-the-wheel. Larry fared well in this light, appearing confident but not domineering. The next night he and I had a movie date, going to see John Cassavetes's *Woman under the Influence.* The subject was family dysfunction and its impact on women. Our mutual empathic response was a revelation whose significance was not lost on either of us. We bonded.

Larry drove me home and, parked in his van opposite my building, we began to kiss. After a while I said, "Someday you'll have to come up and see my apartment."

He replied, "Why not now?"

I couldn't think of an objection. He came upstairs for two days.

I still had my plane ticket to Miami. I decided to follow through with the trip. It was wise, I thought, to view this whirlwind matchmate affair from a distance. Larry's sanguinity with my decision was almost alarming. "I know when you see that guy you'll realize you don't love him," he explained. "You love me."

I remembered blonde, pony-tailed Brian as pretty hot stuff. I had to admire Larry's guts.

My plane landed early in Miami; Brian wasn't at the gate. When I found him in the terminal bar, grinning over a margarita, I knew it was going to be a long week. After we hugged, I ordered a margarita, too. That night we slept on his friend's boat because Brian's was being repaired. There were separate sleeping compartments, which made romance impossible. Even in my relief, I was a little miffed; Brian didn't know I'd met Larry. What if I hadn't? Did he really think a woman would come all this way for a truck trip?

We started up the coast, sustaining our pretense of chummy adventure. At the first gas station, I called Jim Steinman. I didn't know Larry's number on Long Island. "You've got to get a message to Larry," I begged. "Tell him everything's just as he said it would be and I can't wait to get home."

Brian and I got to Manhattan in record time, arriving at night in my apartment, where he crashed immediately. I apologized for having to make some phone calls to friends I'd promised to alert—for reasons I kept vague— the moment I got back in town. He grunted and went to sleep. I called Steinman, who surprised me with news that Larry was at David Rimmer's apartment, a mere ten blocks due south of me. The reason Larry was in town horrified me; he was leaving Manhattan at seven the next morning with a vanload of modern dancers whom he'd be driving around the country for the next three months. He'd taken the job, Steinman explained, because he'd needed the money and had despaired of seeing me again until I returned from Indiana in the spring.

Fighting hysteria, I called Rimmer's. Larry answered. "Come see me," I begged. "I have to say goodbye." He said he'd start walking uptown immediately. After hanging up, I told Brian I'd just found out a dear friend was leaving unexpectedly for Europe in the morning, and I *had* to say goodbye. He said, "Oh. Okay." I assured him I'd wait downstairs, so he could sleep. He already was sleeping, I think.

I stood in my doorway, eyes glued south on First Avenue. When I saw Larry, I ran, like Maria to Tony in *West Side Story*, and stopped his mouth with a kiss. Not that Chino, sawing logs in my apartment, would have given a damn, but even in winter, behind closed windows, conversations from the street could be heard up there, and I didn't want Brian to hear this one.

"I've been a fool," I whispered."I love you. I love you. I love you."

We took an unforgettable walk around the block, stopping in every doorway to kiss and grope. By the time we were back to mine, I knew Larry loved me too, and that he would come to Indianapolis to drive me home. Then we'd move in together and never be separated again. I climbed my stairs and got into bed beside the dreaming Brian, who drove off the next morning for his crafts convention and vanished.

○

The first day of Larry's and my cohabitation, I awoke in the grip of a physical joy that had budded in the night, the nesting and nurturing instincts. Now that I had a man, I wanted to feed him.

Larry was a vegetarian. I had no fruits or vegetables in the house. This was not because I'd just gotten off the road, but because I didn't keep fruits and vegetables in my kitchen. The produce in New York supermarkets was not tantalizing. The upstart Korean sidewalk stands offered better, but the sad truth was, I didn't know what to do with fresh fruits and vegetables. My mother had fed us the boxed, frozen variety. I'd failed to even stock Bird's Eye in my tiny, frost-filled freezer compartment.

I did, however, have Bisquick! I knew vegetarians liked home-baked breads, and Bisquick biscuits were the beginning and end of my knowledge of home-baked breads. I set about making some while filtering Melitta coffee the way Robin had taught me in Coconut Grove. When the biscuits were done, I arranged them in the covered, china vegetable dish I'd inherited from Nana and placed it on the Portuguese tablecloth-covered footlocker between two mugs of coffee. I woke Larry with a kiss, saying, "I've got breakfast!" I was Earth-Woman, Source of All Bounty.

He smiled, rose, and went to lift the cover off Nana's vegetable dish. After a pause, he asked, "What are those?"

Making them, I'd run the classic bridal biscuit scene in my head: the biscuits are too hard, the coffee's too weak, the postnuptial breakfast is a disaster. I'd realized I might be setting myself up for a potential living-in-sin version of that corny flop, and here it was. Larry saw my face and knew he'd made a mistake.

"No, these're great!" he said, downing two biscuits and drinking the coffee. He waited an hour before suggesting we go check out the breakfast menu of the coffee shop across the street.

He ate a cup of corn with pimentos in it. It looked canned. I watched him in despair, thinking, I would *never* have thought of *canned corn* for breakfast. This thought unleashed others in rapid succession: Why do I want to feed this man? Do I have to? Does he want me to? Will he feed me? What's at the bottom of this? In that moment I realized I'd fallen in love with a man who would challenge as many of my instincts as he'd satisfy, and that I wanted it that way.

It turned out Larry was adept at feeding himself. He taught me how to stir-fry vegetables. He did most of our cooking, if we didn't eat at Farm Food kosher dairy restaurant or Papaya King, whose two stands in our neighborhood served great hot dogs and pina coladas. Larry's vegetarianism was not strictly orthodox.

He got a job driving a taxi, and I got a job as a Broadway understudy after walking down Forty-fifth Street and being spotted by Frank Marino, a former *Grease* tour stage manager. "Mimi!" he said, "What are you doing? Want a job?"

He was stage-managing *All over Town* at the Booth. The show needed an understudy for Jill Eikenberry and Pamela Payton-Wright. I was thrilled to audition. I'd submitted my picture and resume more than a year ago, when the show was first casting. I'd known, seeing the announcement in the trades, that I didn't have much chance of being auditioned, without an agent, for a Broadway-bound Murray Shisgal play directed by Dustin Hoffman. But I'd tried. I'd been working at Viacom then, living with Jackie, and hadn't held my breath for the call that never came.

After I auditioned for the understudy role, Frank called to tell me I'd gotten the job, saying excitedly:

"They *remembered* you! When they were first casting, Dustin picked your picture out of a pile of submissions and said, 'Let's see her.' You were one of the only ones he wanted to bring in! But they could never contact you!"

I thought back, wildly, to those days. I'd canceled the Actors' Answering Service because I'd been working full time at Viacom. Jackie and I handled each other's calls, she by day, I by night. We were good about writing things down, but, when I did *Rheingold,* or Jackie did errands, we were both out of the apartment. Had the call come then? Had Jackie forgotten to write the message down? This is a nightmare from the dark days before the dawn of the answering machine.

All over Town sputtered to a close that summer. I auditioned for the national tour, but didn't get either role I'd understudied on Broadway. I was secretly glad. Larry and I were happy together; the prospect of separating was unbearable.

My theater commitment over, I was free to see the show I'd been dying to check out at a midtown club: *The National Lampoon Show.* It was a new script featuring John Belushi and Bill Murray, from the Radio Hour, who tore up the place with a brassy Broadway number called "Lunch," shrieking the finale, "LUNCH! LUNCH! L-U-U-UNCCCHHHH!" in an absolute fever of belter's hysteria. Another brilliant addition to the Lampoon ranks was Gilda Radner. At last, I thought, a girl who matched these preening guys at every step!

Steinman told us that Meatloaf, an actor-singer he'd worked with at the Public Theater, had been offered the Belushi role in a proposed college tour of this show, and he himself had been offered the gig as pianist. He thought it would be great if Larry and I auditioned, so we could all tour together. The other roles were open, Steinman assured us, because most of the Lampoon cast had been hired to do some new TV comedy show.

Larry and I auditioned and were cast. The director, Martin Charnin, also hired Ellen Foley, a magnificent singer. We split Gilda's parts between us, but I got the one I coveted: The Girl in a bar pick-up scene who gets to call Meatloaf's character an asshole.

During our New York rehearsals for the Lampoon tour, Steinman and Meat took a day off to audition for the TV show Gilda and Belushi had already been hired to do. It was known around town by then as "Saturday Night." The producers were seeing every young comic and actor in town for one marathon day at Nola Studios, and Steinman told me that if I tagged along, he'd play for me to perform the two parodies I'd written to amuse my friends, "I Am Dog," my version of Helen Reddy's "I Am Woman," and "I'm Having Your Baby," my answer-song to Paul Anka's "You're Having My Baby."

Nola Studios, when we arrived, was in chaos. It was crawling with actors and comedians, practicing their bits, doing relaxation exercises. I approached the woman gatekeeper to the audition room and told her I didn't have an agent or an appointment but that I would like to be seen, if possible.

She looked at me incredulously and waved her hand at the swarm around us.

"Do you see these actors? *They* all have agents. *They* all have appointments. And I doubt we'll be getting to see all of *them!*" Then, as if she'd heard something in her own voice that disgusted her, she softened. "But you can wait if you want. I can't tell you not to."

At 9 P.M., after the last actor left the audition room, the gatekeeper said, "They know you've been waiting all day and they'll see you. But they're exhausted and ask you to please keep it short. Just one piece of material."

I retrieved Steinman from where he'd been composing in one of Nola's piano studios, and we entered the room. The atmosphere was palpably punchy. Lorne Michaels, Chevy Chase, Michael O'Donoghue, and Anne Beatts were sprawled in chairs that I seem to recall as college desks, the type with writing surfaces attached to the arms. I'm not sure who else was there. I lit into "I Am Dog."

"More! More!" they yelled when I was done, sitting up in their seats. "What else have you got? Do everything!"

I did "I'm Having Your Baby":

"I'm having your baby/ You're a creep you're a coward and I wish that I'd never known ya/I'm having your baby/ And looking back now I wish I'd only blown ya."

There was a chair-scrape and thud following this lyric; I noted with pleasure that Chevy Chase had toppled to the floor upon hearing it.

Lorne told me to see him in his office first thing in the morning. Anne Beatts, a former *Lampoon* magazine editor, followed me out of the room to ask for the lyrics to my songs so she could include them in her anthology of women's humour, *Titters*.

Good audition.

I arrived at Lorne's office the next day to find him discussing with Chevy Chase whether or not Chevy could, or should, act as well as write on the show. I offered the unsolicited observation that Chevy's acid-tripper had been a highlight of *Lemmings*. "See?" said Chevy to Lorne, before leaving us to our discussion of my future on "Saturday Night." Lorne was sure he wanted to use me, he said; he wasn't sure how. If I stuck around, he'd find a way. I told him I was contracted to leave town in two days with the Lampoon tour. Lorne thought for a moment, buzzed his intercom, and said, "I'm coming to your office with someone I want you to meet." Then he took me on an elevator to another floor, where things looked more mahogany and green.

I performed an impromptu "I Am Dog" in the office of Dick Ebersol, who said to Lorne, "She's very funny," and to me, as if translating, "You're very funny." The two men agreed to talk later. Lorne shook hands with me at the elevator and said he'd call me that night.

It was one o'clock in the morning when he did.

"I've just gotten out of our meeting," he said. "As far as the repertory group is concerned, Dick is afraid you're not white bread enough. Here's what I know. If you stay in town, I'll use you. But I don't know...you seem committed to your relationship with this guy you're going out on tour with, and...I don't know... maybe that's what supposed to happen. We'll put 'I Am Dog' on the first show— I've already checked with the tour, I know I can get you out for that—so when I see you, we'll talk more then."

I went out with the *Lampoon* cast. We didn't have a show on the day I drove to New York for my costume-fitting with Frannie Lee, who chose a long brown T-shirt dress for "I Am Dog," very Helen Reddy and very canine. I did a college show in Connecticut Wednesday and was due back in New York for 'Saturday Night's' dress rehearsal, when a call Wednesday night from Anne Beatts changed everything.

"This is awful," she said. "We can't do it. Helen Reddy and Jeff Wald won't let us have the rights to the music."

She explained that she'd written a last-ditch, woman-to-woman letter reminding Helen that feminists were constantly accused of having no sense of humor. Let's prove the critics wrong! Anne had urged. The plea hadn't worked, perhaps because it didn't go woman-to-woman. The final "no" came from Jeff Wald, who felt the song was too important to women and their movement to endure parody. For every woman like Anne or me who thought the ability to laugh at oneself was a sign of resilience and maturity, Jeff evidently imagined millions of women whose self-esteem would collapse if they heard someone making fun of a popular song.

Lorne, utterly without leverage because nobody'd ever heard of "Saturday Night," apologized and booked another comedienne. There's been a law passed since, making parody legal without expressed permission.

When I was a child, my father used to take us on car trips every August to vacation attractions around New York State. On our way to "Frontier Town" and 1000 Island's Boldt's Castle, I saw farm vistas and small towns that seemed so incredibly lonely they gave me nightmares. In one such town, I was overcome with hopelessness. Our car stopped at a red light. The five-and-ten red-brick anonymity of the downtown intersection and the dull people crossing in front of us crushed me. The moment seemed eternal. I got on the floor of the car and asked what town it was. "Oswego," said my amused father. "I hate Oswego," I said. "Tell me when it's over."

That fall in Oswego, New York, I watched "Saturday Night Live" and realized the defining moment of fame had arrived for our generation and I'd missed it. I was standing, with the *Lampoon* cast, in the deserted student union of the state university there. The students were all watching in their dorms. I remembered the moment on the floor of our family car and felt it had been a foreshadowing.

I also remembered Maureen Stapleton soothing me on the set of an AFI film for which I'd been volunteer prop girl and she the volunteer star. After hearing I'd narrowly lost the part of Sonya in a regional theater production of *Uncle Vanya* to Julie Garfield, a fine actress and John Garfield's niece, she made a special trip over to the prop table to say, "Don't worry. It's happened to all of us. You know what to think. Everything happens for a reason. You're being saved for something better!"

Deeply honored that the great actress would go out of her way to console me, I thanked her, knowing that if she in her wisdom could repeat the old saws, there must be some truth to them, and I should take heart.

"And all that crap," I heard her mutter softly as she went back to her mark.

27.

Seeing Stars

As a child, I'd yearned to become a professional actress. At twenty-seven I'd achieved that goal. As a child, I'd also wanted to become a saint. That aspiration had been considerably less well-managed.

By age twenty-seven I'd seen and done things that absolutely disqualified me from sainthood as I'd known and loved it. The largest category of female saints, Virgin-Martyr, was filled by women choosing death over sex. I was not only a sexually active woman, I practiced contraception, compounding my sin. Any dim hope I had of sanctity in later life as an old lady having married sex without birth control was newly threatened by a lust that gripped me so hard I thought it would never let go: the lust for Fame. Now that I was an actress, being an actress was not enough. I wanted to be a star.

Once upon a time, I'd thought all actors were stars. The magical beings Cousin Ruth and William Roerick had lit up my dull suburban living room like giant suns, though they would not have described themselves as stars at the time. Now I knew what they did then: in show business, some beings are more magical than others, and the most magical of these are Stars.

I'd taken to the stage because it seemed spiritually safe, a haven where I could live passionately without consequences and preserve my soul untainted for heaven. Sex had foiled my clever plan and committed me to this world. With heavenly celebrity a broken dream, it seemed I might as well go for it on earth and try to become a Star.

Stardom was not spiritually safe. It definitely had consequences. Acting was make-believe onstage, but stardom was make-believe in the real world. Stars imposed new versions of themselves on reality, and charmed, bullied, or conned everyone into acceptance. My church did not condemn stardom or fame; it boasted of Catholic celebrities. I knew, as a child, that Loretta Young, Ann Blyth, and Ricardo Montalban were coreligionists of whom I could be proud. President Kennedy lifted a generation of Catholics out of immigrant "ghetto mentality." Stardom, especially if used for philanthropy and advertisement of virtue, was good. Therefore, I reasoned, lust for Fame was not as wrong as lust for Sex and would involve less moral peril and emotional pain.

As I traveled the backroads of America's Northeast on the *Lampoon* college tour, my disappointment at having missed Fame on "Saturday Night Live" increased. It gnawed at me during the endless car conversations about how much Steinman, Meatloaf, Larry, and I would owe Barry Diamond by the end of the tour for wear and tear on his aging Buick. Nights I had to sew up the moist crotch-rip in Meatloaf's jeans, because I was the only trouper practiced in the domestic arts, I felt like Cinderella. I'd been invited to the ball! Where was my Fairy Godmother?

During a sound check at some college gym in the Midwest, Ray DeMattis, who'd played my boyfriend on the *Grease* national tour and was now on Broadway, called me to say the role of Jan was opening up in New York, and the producers were going to bring me to Broadway by Christmas.

Bibbity-bobbity-boo.

∘

Larry and I spent the *Lampoon* tour's winter break joined at the hip. When he'd go back on the road in January, and I'd stay in town doing *Grease,* we'd be separated for the first time since living together.

Which is why we both ended up in a West End Avenue apartment one morning for a photography session with our friend Jimmy Wykowski. Neither Larry nor I enjoy posing for pictures, but our careers were heating up, and we needed new head shots. The dual session seemed like a painless way to get them. Larry sat first; he had rehearsal afterward with Meatloaf and Steinman, who were working up songs for "Bat Out of Hell."

By the time Larry left Jimmy's, loaded with guitar and amp, I'd been posing a while, moving my chin on a constantly rotating axis to find its best minimizing angle. He'd been gone a few minutes when the door buzzer sounded. Jimmy sighed and abandoned the tripod to answer it.

The urgent whispers I heard at the door told me something was very wrong even before Jimmy turned and walked toward me, his face ghostly white. He laid a shaking hand on my arm. His palm was so clammy its chill went right through my sleeve.

"Mimi, d-d-don't panic. Th-this man says Larry's been h-hit by a c-car and is down in the street, alive, but h-hit pretty h-h-hard."

My denial instinct is so strong I smiled and went numb. Then I moved. Jimmy got my coat; I went directly into the hall, where the stranger who'd borne the news stood holding the elevator door. We got in. "Someone's already called an ambulance," he said softly. "The lucky thing is I was out in the hall to see him leave your apartment so I could retrace his steps and tell you. I'm sorry."

It *was* lucky. On the way down in the elevator, I bargained for more: don't let him die, God. Don't let him be hurt bad. We'll get married. I promise. I saw it was hubris, the way we thought time would go on forever. We'd never imagined death parting us *before* we took the vow.

I broke through the knot of people at the curb to find Larry, as advertised, in the street. One leg was curled upward like a question mark. At the end of it was his foot, lying by his ear like a telephone receiver.

"I'm here," I said, kneeling by him. "Larry, it's Mimi. I'm here." I touched his thick Hudson Bay jacket, wondering if it had saved his life. Behind his head the pavement was dark. Blood. I watched the stain carefully; it didn't grow.

Larry's eyes opened. Returned!

"What happened?" he asked.

"You were hit by a car," I said. "I think your leg is broken."

"My leg hurts."

I was glad he could feel. I gave in one iota to relief before he asked, "What happened?" again in exactly the same tone of voice.

Oh, Jesus, I thought, where's that ambulance?

"You were hit by a car," I said calmly.

When the ambulance arrived, paramedics loaded Larry on a gurney and into the back. I climbed in after him and was surprised to find benches along the sides. How thoughtful, I remember thinking, as if someone had just offered me a seat on a crowded bus.

I'd never been in an ambulance before. I feared them. I'd been taught to pray at the sound of sirens, for the poor, unfortunate strangers whose lives had just been shattered. Now the siren moved with us; X marked the spot of the poor, unfortunate strangers. We flew through the Manhattan blocks populated with enough people to fill a small town. I felt sure some of them prayed for Larry.

"My legs are incredibly crushed and broken," Larry said in a fake Latin accent.

It was a line from a rehearsal sketch so bad it had never made it into the *Lampoon Show*. We'd tried to mine comic gold from the dismal tragedy of *Alive!*, the book about the soccer team who survived a plane crash by eating some of its dead members. Barry Diamond's bad-accented leg line surfaced in every failed version of the sketch and became the comic high point. Once that happened, we abandoned the attempt, but the line lived on to remind us of our comic nadir. It was gruesomely accurate now. I was impressed that Larry could deliver black humor from the state of shock. I knew he was trying to say he'd be all right, and I chose to believe him.

We arrived at Roosevelt Hospital, where the driver had told me he'd be going because it had the best emergency orthopedics. I hadn't known ambulance drivers shopped. When we arrived, I saw why; the emergency team engulfed Larry like an octopus. I turned away inside, when I saw the nurse cut off his boots with a scissors, but I stayed in the curtained doorway until the doctor told me what I wanted to know: that the head injury was superficial and there was no internal bleeding. Surgery was scheduled. They doped him up and rolled him away. I couldn't follow immediately, for reasons I've forgotten.

I called his parents and Steinman. He must have called the tour's stage manager, Joel Tropper, who was first to arrive at the hospital. Joel may have dealt with insurance matters; to this day I don't know. Larry's parents came in from Long Island and drove me back to our apartment that night. I assured them I'd be fine on my own, and would get some sleep. When I went inside—the place seemed so utterly changed from the secure nest we'd left that morning!—the first thing I did was search for evidence that Larry had fulfilled his months-ago promise to me to get medical insurance. He'd made it after our bitter argument prompted by his parents' call asking whether they could remove him from their policy, now that he was on his own.

Posthippies didn't worry about future security. Insurance was considered slightly beneath contempt. I kept a framed piece of sheet music on my wall showing a cartoon of Aesop's fabled worker ants and the carefree grasshopper playing a violin and dancing to the song—"The World Owes Me A Living."

Larry's parents' solicitude reminded me that our financial disdain was a luxury paid for by others' anxious care. From my lofty position as a fortunate, fully insured member of Actors' Equity, I'd accused my lover of being a hypocritical mooch.

Now in the dim lamplight, I found evidence that Larry had let his taxi union medical coverage lapse without ever going on self-pay. I couldn't be angry at someone I'd almost lost, so I became terrified instead. I didn't know what our insurance status was with the Amalgamated Guild of Variety Artists of America; our AGVA contracts with the Lampoon were too new for us to know the medical policy.

Roosevelt's business office, and Joel Tropper, obviously knew more about AGVA insurance and New York's no-fault laws than I did. What I do know is that the hospital never discussed money with me prior to, or during, Larry's care. He got what he needed, including the $35 aspirins I remember seeing on Roosevelt's invoice.

Two months after the accident, Larry, in plaster cast and on crutches, and I visited a lawyer friend of my father's. Mr. Solomon—a reassuring name for a legal man—was a partner at the firm of Louis Nizer—another reassuring legal name, if it's on your side of the lawsuit. The firm's detectives traced the car that hit Larry. Its owner claimed someone had borrowed it without permission. The "someone" had given a false name to the police, was unlicensed, and had tried to flee the scene. Only the intervention of a heroic cable TV installer, who'd blocked the departing Pontiac with his van, had kept the culprit on-site long enough to lie to the police.

But the Pontiac was insured. Mr. Solomon said there was ten thousand dollars from which to claim Larry's lost wages, pain-and-suffering, and damages for irreparable harm done to his dance career.

Dance career? We couldn't believe our ears. But insurance companies don't believe their ears, they believe paper. Mr. Solomon had Larry's contract from AGVA

—the union that covered Las Vegas chorines—and bills from the surgery that put pins in Larry's leg to prove that the accident had harmed a hoofer who coulda been a contender.

Thus did our future rise like a Phoenix from the ashes of a dream that never was. Larry felt, as I did, that we'd received an ultimatum. Bodies, unlike love, wouldn't survive death, and now was our time to make something of both. We agreed that with the five thousand dollars coming to us after Mr. Solomon's legal fees, we'd buy a ring and a great French honeymoon.

o

My opening night on Broadway was a private celebration, with Larry being in the hospital, but a celebration nonetheless. I was showered with attention. Onstage, I had the laughter and applause of my first Broadway audience. Backstage, I had flowers, gifts, and telegrams.

I looked around my dressing room and realized I occupied that white-hot heaven I'd seen long ago through Tammy Grimes's dressing-room door. Then, I'd been a girl of twelve, visiting backstage at *The Unsinkable Molly Brown,* and driven by a dream. Now, I was twenty-seven. They were *my* bouquets in glorious profusion; *my* telegrams and notes taped around the sparkling bulbs. It was *my* face in the glittering mirror saying, welcome to a dream come true.

Larry had sent a dozen long-stemmed red roses. The card that accompanied them bore his message in the florist's looping hand:

"You're going to the top. May it be a long, slow ride so you can enjoy it all the way."

Larry's savoring of sexual pleasure was a charming quality in a lover, and one for which I was grateful. But Sex was not to be confused with Career. I resolved to tell him, when it would not impede his speedy recovery, that I intended to get to the top of the world, Ma, as quickly as possible, and stay there the rest of my life.

o

One night, Richard Burton came to *Grease.* The cast had been warned, and we were out of our minds with excitement. Peeking through the curtains in the wings as the audience filtered in, we saw him arrive: Hamlet! Mark Antony! Mr. Elizabeth Taylor! He was visiting us because he'd soon be replacing Anthony Hopkins in *Equus* down the street. He was touring the neighborhood and meeting the neighbors.

We couldn't believe a British actor of his stature would be interested in our rowdy, Chicago-born, high-school show. But he was more than interested. He *loved* it! We could see it on his face, as we snuck looks during the show. And he told us so afterward, backstage:

"You're all just marvelous!" he beamed, his voice inimitably Shakespearean, but his black turtleneck, winklepicker boots, and insouciant forehead curl suggesting a Teddy-Boy whom, I suspected, we'd just sent back to his Welsh working-class roots. "In England our greatest actors would give their eye *teeth* to be able to do what you can do. You can do it all—sing, dance, and act! In England, you'd all be stars!"

This puffed us up for days. Then things got even better: Burton sent us an invitation, which was posted on our cast bulletin board, to be his guests at Sardi's for an after-theater supper. We were in a collective tizzy for days, anticipating this event.

I fussed too much with my hair and makeup after the show, trying to mute my fifties' look into something sleek and seventies, and I arrived too late to sit at Burton's table. I found a seat at the small table holding the overflow crowd, but I didn't mind. Susan Hunt, Burton's new love, was its hostess, and I was curious about her, though her presence meant we probably wouldn't be meeting Elizabeth Taylor, as most all of us had secretly hoped.

Our boisterous party was the focus of the restaurant that night, and we basked. But midway through our meal, attention shifted to the front entrance as surely as if someone had picked up the room and tilted it toward the door. From the center of the commotion, news spread quickly: Elizabeth had arrived.

Susan Hunt rose calmly, excused herself, and disappeared as a knot of people hove toward Burton like a dust devil moving across the restaurant floor. At his table, the knot parted to reveal Elizabeth Taylor, larger than life, on Vincent Sardi's arm. Burton stood to greet her. With every eye in the room upon them, the legendary lovers kissed, European style, on both cheeks. Then Sardi escorted Taylor to a seat across from Burton—and right behind me. I had to adjust my chair so Liz could wiggle into hers. We exchanged giggling "Excuse me's" and "That's all right's." All serious conversation at my table ended. We chewed, sipped, and listened.

She'd had a terrible day. She'd been drinking Johnny Walker all afternoon. Could the waiter please bring a bottle of Johnny Walker Red to the table? He could and he did. I thought I'd read that Susan Hunt was helping Richard cut down on his drinking. I hadn't noticed whether or not he'd sampled any of the excellent wine he'd had poured for his guests, but in light of the rumor, Liz's behavior seemed pointedly provocative. No one opposed her. She proceeded, like celebrated male alcoholics I'd read about, to inebriate herself without anyone having the will or power to stop her.

The hour was late and members of our cast began to excuse themselves, regretfully, to go home to tea, bed, spouses, and lovers. I didn't. When Liz moved her seat to engage a group of remaining actors, I joined them.

She monologized for us; Youth Wanted To Know and She Felt Like Talking. We heard intimate physical details of her arduous day, spent within the confines of her hotel room. It had tested the limits of her endurance, but she'd survived it, and, like a trouper, she'd damned the torpedoes to get to Richard's little dinner party. She liked talking to young people. She was undeniably charming despite the vapidity of her conversation. Her lids grew heavy over her violet eyes. I left when she did and rode home on the subway, pondering the night's events.

I saw that all of us in *Grease*, that night, were happier than Elizabeth Taylor. Shining in constellation, as members of an ensemble, we possessed a joy she did not seem to have as a first-magnitude star. Even in the presence of the love of her life, Liz Taylor burned alone, without relief, in the center of her own vast firmament.

○

The good people at "Saturday Night Live" included me in their wider circle of friends and often invited me to the show and aftershow parties. I went to one that was John Belushi's birthday celebration.

As the crowd sang "Happy Birthday" John was presented with a cake decorated like a giant Quaalude. People squealed and moaned. He laughed and blew out the candles.

I spent most of the evening talking to coproducer Craig Kellem, who was yearning to return to his therapeutic community in California. What's a therapeutic community? I'd asked. I'd never heard of such a thing; Betty Ford was still just a former First Lady whose glazed look could be justified by her shock at finding herself in the White House when the last office for which her husband had campaigned was a congressional seat. She hadn't yet confessed her pain-pill addiction or established the center that made her name synonymous with recovery and taught us all about therapeutic communities.

Craig described his as a gentle utopia of mutual creative support. It sounded nice, but nowhere near as exciting and creative as "Saturday Night Live." I was about to ask him why he'd trade it all away when Gilda Radner came to kneel at his feet and rest her head on his arm.

"I just realized," she said, "that if this show's as big a hit as everyone says it is, I won't get out of my contract until I'm thirty-five. Thirty-five!" she moaned. "That's so old! What will have happened to me by then? What kind of life will I have?"

How, I wondered, could Gilda be worried about *anything?* She was brilliant, beloved, and triumphant! I'd followed so briefly in her footsteps, before hers led to Fame and mine to Oswego, that I identified with her much more than I admitted to anyone, knowing the comparison flattered me too much. Gilda on her knees, unhappy, gave me pause. If she were looking around for meaning at her lofty height, that meant I'd better start looking for some down on the ground, where I was. Fame, if it came, might not bring happiness.

The day I first learned of Gilda's illness I was standing in a supermarket line in Santa Monica with my two young children, feeling exhausted, overburdened, overweight, and anonymous. Such fame as I'd won had come and gone—if not in the minute warned by Perry Como's song, or even in the fifteen promised by Andy Warhol, at least by then. I occasionally felt sorry for myself, particularly when watching awards shows while sleep deprived. I was engaged in candy negotiations with my son, trying to keep my squirming daughter in the grocery cart long enough to write a check unencumbered, when my eyes fell on the tabloid headline: "Gilda Radner Near Death."

I froze inside. It couldn't be true. My daughter reached for me; I hoisted her onto my hip, grateful for such precious cargo of bone and flesh. Her hand stroked my hair. I nodded at my son's choice of M 'n' M's, which he proudly placed on the conveyor belt. My God, I realized, I'm the one that's blessed. Surrounded by life.

I'll do a novena, I thought. I'd never done a voluntary novena in my life, but I couldn't think of anything else to do. I didn't really know Gilda. I hadn't seen her in years.

When the story disappeared, I thought: She lived! I did the nine masses, almost in a row. The story eventually re-emerged in Gilda's own voice. Her book, *It's Always Something* answered some of the questions she'd asked Craig Kellem so long ago. What happened to Gilda was: on "Saturday Night Live" she created a body of work that will make people laugh as long as image-producing technology endures, and if it fails—Never Mind—will persist in the oral tradition. After "Saturday Night Live" she continued to work; found and married the love of her life; and, when time grew short, she turned illness to healing and wrote a book to banish her, and others', fear of death. It was her encore to an incredibly graceful bow from the world, after which her husband started a foundation to help others fight ovarian cancer. That's what kind of life Gilda Radner had. She accomplished, in my view, what no modern celebrity had yet managed. She made Celebrity look little-bitty-teeny-tiny-teensie-eensie-weenie compared to the Soul.

●

In my family's Catholic oral tradition, there was a travel dispensation from Sunday Mass. It meant that while you were on the road and couldn't get to Mass without ruining your vacation or disrupting your schedule, you were excused from going, without pain of mortal sin.

I'd considered myself on the road since college.

On Eighty-Seventh Street, I could see a Catholic church from my fire escape. *Grease* didn't have a Sunday matinee; I'd run out of inconvenience excuses. I began to show up, occasionally, for Sunday mass.

Larry came with me. His childhood Methodism had imbued him with a strong sense of social justice, but its Sunday practice was, in his words, "worship of the family" undertaken only by the well-dressed, in groups. Our Catholic congregation's motley impressed him. I told him Catholics looked like hell at church because they had to show up or go to hell; Sunday Mass was not an optional dress-up activity. But Larry saw in Catholic sartorial neglect some indication that it was What's Inside That Counts, and he wanted to know What's Inside. He told me he was thinking about converting.

This was good news for me, who'd been raised on the belief that a Catholic who made a convert got into heaven free. I no longer believed such pat assumptions, but I did know a dual-Catholic marriage would eliminate certain sources of friction. Larry and I were intellectually competitive enough without adding religion to the mix.

I contacted a Jesuit family friend in Rochester, Father William O'Malley. He'd met Larry on a trip to New York, and the priest's approval had blessed my attraction to my Computer Matchmate, helping launch the relationship into permanent orbit. I asked him for the name of someone Larry could see about instruction in becoming Catholic.

O'Malley put me in contact with Brother Rick Curry, who lived in a Jesuit Community, St. Francis Xavier, on Sixteenth Street. Rick had eyes like fire; he'd been born with only one arm, which had barred him from the priesthood. When he'd entered the Jesuits, ordination required two fingers on each hand for priests' sacramental duties. Rick became a Brother. He absorbed the limitation as he had an earlier one: growing up in Philadelphia as a handsome kid and a fabulous dancer, he'd wanted to dance on American Bandstand, where his mother worked in production. But it was feared Americans would go into cardiac arrest at the sight of a one-armed dancing teenager, so Rick wasn't allowed to appear. As his Jesuit apostolate, he's founded the National Theater Workshop for the Handicapped, which, like its model, the National Theater for the Deaf, trains talented people with physical disabilities to become theater professionals, so that disability is part of the stage and screen picture, something we're accustomed to seeing in the mirror.

Rick recommended Larry to Father Jack Alexander for instruction, and Jack—a wonderful teacher, as my husband was destined to be —gave Larry books to read, which the two then discussed. Larry emerged from this dialogue ready to make the leap.

With the priests and some of our friends, he was welcomed into the church with a Laying On Of Hands Ceremony. This was a legacy of Luci Baines Johnson, the president's daughter whose prewedding Catholic baptism threatened the entire ecumenical movement by enraging the Episcopal church, which had baptized her as a baby. The Catholic redo subverted Vatican assertions that all Christian baptisms were effective for salvation. The Catholic church had to apologize. It stopped overwatering, and the Laying On Of Hands was the happy result. It's very similar to a Tibetan healing technique called Reiki.

I worried, with all this, that I was simply hedging my bets, using the church as a psychic safety net in ways *The Baltimore Catechism* had made clear were insufficient. But my alternative was to ignore the church, and I couldn't do that, even as a sophisticated analysand. It was the repository of all my emotions about God. Whether or not they were displaced from human significant others who'd been found wanting, they were still my deepest connections to profound meaning. Catholic spirituality had been bequeathed as my birthright; it was the foundation of my entire education. If I abandoned it completely, I'd cut myself off from my deepest emotions about God. And that, I suspected, was what the doctrine of mortal sin was all about.

So Larry and I went to church.

The parish priest on Eighty-Seventh Street was determined to build a young adult community, much to the chagrin of Larry, me, and everyone else under forty whom he collared in the lobby and practically hurled downstairs to coffee and donuts after eleven o'clock mass. The priest's energetic bonhomie was impossible to evade, and sheepish reluctance to dampen it was what bound the young adults, in that basement, on Sunday mornings.

He loved actors and insisted on introducing us to one other. Struggling actors don't want to meet one another, but people presume we do. I was showered with the names of fellow fledglings during my early years in New York. I never called any of them. Knowing how many strove for the goal that eluded me was depressing, not cheering. Only the intimate bond of acting class, or working on a production, dredged the capacity for mutual support in my rivalrous heart. The day Father dragged Gwen Humble over to me, all I could think of was, oh God! Another actress my age who goes to Church on the upper east side—that means we're the same type! Only she's blonder and thinner! She'll get all the good parts!

But we became friends as young adults. Show business, as it turned out, had room for both of us. Gwen went on to have a nice career in costume miniseries, doing the kind of romantic roles I only got to play in sketch comedy.

None of the other young adults seemed to worry that Fame was possibly an unworthy goal. Going For It was good, and Making It was good, as long as one did both honestly.

I couldn't shake the feeling that for me, Fame was an apple of temptation. I wanted to bite, and I feared the consequences.

Part Five

HOLLYWOOD

1976–1982

"When you walk through fire, you shall not be burned."

Isaiah 43:2

"Honey, that show died a long time ago. It's been dead since last summer. Before the last three went on the air."

Bob Broder, 1977

"It's too late now."

Me, Bridal Jitters thought, 1978

"Don't mind me. I'm just monitoring my heart."

Nick Vanoff, Producer, 1980

"Birthing, birthing, birthing, so joyfully we birth!"

Peter Cook, 1981

"Why was I acting?"

Actor in Ingmar Bergman's Fanny and Alexander, *1982*

28.

Three Girls Three

The September I turned twenty-eight, I booked a daylong spiritual retreat at a convent I'd heard about near Gramercy Park, where nuns hosted private days of prayer and reflection. No sooner had I done so than Rick Hashagan, an ICM television agent who'd sent me out on one show at the suggestion of the commercial department, called me with an audition appointment on the day I'd just planned the retreat.

"I checked back with the people on 'The Fruit and Vegetable Show,'" he said, citing my previous outing, "and they said you were really good. So I thought you should go up for this show. It's sketch comedy, too. Called 'Three Girls Three'."

The audition was at nine fifteen; I'd planned to get to the convent at ten. Since I usually wandered through department stores after auditions, where mirrors and salespeople assured me I still existed even though I'd stopped performing, I thought prayer would be a nice chaser, for a change. I didn't cancel the retreat.

On the appointed Monday I arrived early in the gleaming lobby of the new Minskoff building. While waiting for the elevator to the second floor, I was joined by a skinny man with electric hair.

"Second floor?" he asked.

"Yes."

"You're an actress? Auditioning?"

"Uh-huh."

He had an affect so languid every gesture seemed to exhaust him and every sentence seemed the last he'd utter before dying of boredom. I found it very funny.

"You'll be auditioning for me. I'm Kenny. The producer."

"I'm Mimi," I replied.

"Mimi. Early, huh? The stars got later times."

He said this as if stars bored him to death. The elevator came and we got in. "Oy, I hope the room is open. I don't have a key. Did anyone else go up yet?"

"I don't know. I've just seen you."

"Oy," he sighed.

We got off the elevator. He tried the double doors to the studio; when they opened, he glanced backward and gave me an extravagant eye roll, then murmured calmly, "See ya, doll."

No one had called me "doll" since Don Kirshner. I liked it, and all its Runyonesque baggage. I couldn't wait to do "I Am Dog." I was confident Kenny liked me already.

The NBC casting liaison called me in.

"Hi, Mimi," Kenny said. "We know each other already, calm down," he explained to the liason, Cheryl. "What are you going to do, doll?"

"'I Am Dog,' a parody of 'I Am Woman'."

"I'm a dog?" he repeated, incredulous, showing the first glimmer of emotion, which unfortunately looked like dismay.

I nodded, and gave my music to the pianist.

As I sang, Kenny's mouth fell open. Cheryl gave no indication of her response.

"That's the stupidest song I ever heard," he said when I was done.

"I know."

"But you're funny, that's the main thing. Come back at four o'clock."

I got on the subway and made my way down to Twenty-third Street, showing up at the convent in lip gloss and my very best dress.

❂

"It might be helpful to us both if we started out talking a little about what brought you here," said the nun with kind eyes, and the sort of luminous, finely etched skin that comes from no makeup, sunlight, or cosmic angst.

Show business, I told her. I'd always wanted to be an actress, and now that I was, I seemed to be headed down a path that made spirituality difficult for me, if not impossible.

She nodded. After we talked a little more, she opened the Bible on her lap and said, "I'm going to read you some things, and then I'll leave you to pray as you see fit for the rest of the day. All right?"

Whether she had so many spiritually parched actors wash up on her shore, twenty blocks south of the theater district, that she knew this passage spoke to us all; whether it was a personal favorite she thought might be helpful; or whether, hearing me, she chose it because she thought it might be apt, what she read stayed with me the rest of my life. It was from Isaiah, and said, in part: "I have called you by name. You are mine. … When you walk through fire, you shall not be burned." By the end of the month, I'd be in Hollywood.

Sister closed the book and rendered a quiet opinion: "I think God may want you where you are, in show business," she said.

❂

At four, I returned to the Minskoff to find myself in the company of several other actresses, Ellen Foley among them. It thrilled me to see my old *Lampoon*-mate; after contemplating the big picture, I was stretched and generously saw room for *both* of us at the top! We were given sketches to cold-read in groups.

I did a Miss America sketch with an actress named Debbie Allen. She did beauty-pageant fatuousness hilariously. I loved her.

Gail Parent was there. Kenny introduced her as his partner and co-executive producer. She, like him, was languid, deadpan, and unerringly funny; I was awed, because I'd read her comic novel, *Sheila Levine Is Dead and Living in New York* and had seen her credit on *"Mary Hartman, Mary Hartman,"* the show that brought me back to television as a viewer. I began to urgently want this "Three Girls Three."

Debbie Allen offered me a ride home from the audition in her car. I'd never known an actor who drove around New York in a *car*. We cruised uptown like two high-school girlfriends. By the time we reached 87th Street, we'd shared the important details of our lives and felt absolutely destined to work together. We said goodbye with a high five: See you in Hollywood, girl!

Rick Hashagan called me backstage Wednesday after the *Grease* matinee.

"You're going out to LA for a screen test," he announced.

I screamed.

"So's Ellen Foley."

I screamed again. He didn't know about Debbie. She was not his client. But an image already took shape: the three girls would be Debbie, Ellen, and me.

"You have to come by my office and sign the test deal," he said.

I went to ICM the next day to sign the first test deal of my life without even knowing what it was. I sat opposite Rick, who put his elbows on his desk and leaned toward me. "It has come to my attention, " he said slowly, "that you are not officially signed with this agency."

"No," I said.

He spread his hands: an offer.

"Don't you think it's about time you had some representation?"

I wanted to leap across his desk for joy, but I asked him if I could think about it. He nodded, suddenly nervous. I had no idea it delayed the test deal. All I knew was that actors were never supposed to say yes to things right away. I made him wait a day, terrified the whole time his offer would be rescinded. Then I called and accepted.

And that's how I finally got my first signed agent, a week before I got my own television show.

●

I first saw Los Angeles on my twenty-eighth birthday. I flew out with Ellen Foley, who, being younger and hipper than I, was ambivalent about Hollywood glitz. Still, she wanted the show badly enough to be nervous about the test.

"Don't be nervous. It'll be fun," I said. "It's my birthday and I think we're going to get this." Only my blissful ignorance of the other contenders allowed me to actually believe this.

Ellen and I were driven to the Sheraton Universal Hotel by a cheery production assistant. I obsessed on the palm trees the whole way. "Palm trees!" I marveled breathlessly. "Look at the *palm* trees!"

I've since spoken to many New York actors who did the same thing, and I myself have heard palm-tree exclamations driving first-time visitors from the airport to their LA ground destinations.

Actors, if you go to New York City for a career, pack a bathing suit. You may never have dreamed of LA, but if you work, you will end up here, for some amount of time.

In 1976, the Sheraton Universal Hotel was a lone outpost. Today it's part of Universal City, but then the only thing sharing its scrub-brush slope was an eerily vacant parking lot.

I've driven by it now so many times, with carsful of children going to Citywalk, that my first memory of the place has faded utterly. The thought of my sobbing, shivering self in one of those upper rooms seems unreal.

After we'd checked in, Ellen excused herself to rest her voice for the next day's test. I followed the bellboy to my room and watched him deposit my bag, open the drapes, take his tip, and leave. Alone, I panicked.

The view he'd revealed of the Hollywood Hills, with its spiky cedars and other strange flora, was so foreign to me I felt as if I'd arrived in the Middle East. This was not a comforting thought in the mid-nineteen seventies. Distant houses looked like plane crash debris scattered through the darkening shadows. The Hollywood sign, which would have been familiar, funny, or at least a reality check, was on the other side; I hadn't seen it. This was no welcoming urban skyline, like Manhattan's, which had always inspired in me the happy, expansive notion: "Someday I'll own this town!" Before the Hollywood hills, I shrank. They seemed to be doing the talking, and the message was: Someday we could eat you and not even burp.

I'm not good with separation anxiety. I was the last child to be pried, bawling, off my mother's lap the first day in kindergarten. Now, at the Sheraton Universal, I felt a sob-a-thon coming on. I would have taken to the streets to prevent it, but there were no streets to take to in LA, as many people had warned me. I certainly hadn't seen any around the Space Station Universal. I could explore it innards, but I feared being met, as I wandered, by Stepford employees asking me what I wanted. What would I say? "Can you please stop me from being so scared?"

I didn't turn on the television. When I'm feeling acutely alone, the sight of human images appearing and disappearing at the touch of a button makes me even more depressed. I went to the telephone and called Larry.

The minute he answered I began to cry. He reminded me of all the good reasons I was in LA—I'd been chosen from hundreds of girls for a screen test, I had a job on Broadway in *Grease*, I was having a dream-come-true in Hollywood on my birthday. This was just a transition, he said, and those were always difficult. He was right. I curled up in a fetal position after we disconnected and hoped for sleep, but the phone rang.

I answered brightly, trying to disguise my stuffy nose. It was Kenny.

"Hi doll. So how's the hotel, how was the flight, who cares, what are you doing?" he said rapidly.

"This hotel is so weird," I said. "There's no life around it. I can't go out."

"So do you want me to come pick you up? I'll get you out of there. Listen, you're my favorite, you know that, don't you? I shouldn't tell you. Don't tell anyone I told you. What are you doing right now? Do you want to go to a party?"

I told him I did because it was my birthday.

"Well perfect. Because we're going to Michael Douglas's birthday party. What did you bring to wear?"

I inventoried my wardrobe, and he, already my producer, told me the right costume in which to meet him at the entrance in half an hour where he'd pick me up in a blue Cadillac convertible.

It was a big, bourgeois car. The sight of it delighted me. I got in, and Kenny immediately told me we had to stop at his friend's house to use a phone. He was trying, for the thousandth time, to locate Debbie Allen, whom he'd yet to book for the screen test.

"What?" I said. "She has to come! She's the best!"

"She is the best—she is, isn't she? Don't ask, I've called her five times, with the agent, at home, with the machine and the music, driving me crazy, she's supposed to be back, she's not back, where is she?—her agent thinks she's in Houston."

"So call Houston! You have to. She's the best."

We made the pit stop at Kenny's friend's. Borrowing home phones was common practice in the days before cellular. Kenny found Debbie, touching off a round of business calls that would land her in Hollywood the following day. We proceeded to Michael Douglas's.

I was flattered to find myself an object of curiosity as one of the girls "testing for the 'Three Girls'." Everyone seemed to know about Kenny's project, even Michael Douglas, who was standing on a balcony overlooking the glittering view of Los Angeles that by now is familiar, worldwide, from the movies. He gave me a hug upon hearing we shared a birthday. Then he introduced me to his father.

Kirk Douglas appeared both vibrant and totally orange. His hair, tan, and buttersoft leather jacket were all orange. His prodigious chin dimple was the only shadow about him. He was very impressive as my first indigenous movie star sighting on native soil; Michael's career was still the lesser one, being then a product of television. Wow, I thought. Good birthday present, God.

◦

The screen test took place on a set with a semicircle of stools on which we actresses sat and watched each other perform. It was a sisterly and inviting geography, like a support group. The luggage of one of the stars of *A Chorus Line* had been lost in transit, and my patchwork silk dress had been chosen by Kenny as her substitute outfit, so I was actually feeling supportive.

I myself was wearing a 100 percent polyester floor-length red strapless dress with an elasticized waist and bust ruffle. I'd bought it for forty bucks on Lexington Avenue and thought it was an incredible fashion find. Kenny told me later he'd wanted to rip it off my back.

Debbie sang "Magic" from *Pippin*, I sang "Freddie My Love" from *Grease,* and Ellen blew everyone away with a wailing, soulful "Blue Moon." The other women sang their signature numbers from their Broadway shows. It was amazing company for a girl who'd done her first New York musical audition singing "Seventy-Six Trombones" in the bass clef, without knowing the words.

I flew home on the red-eye with Ellen. "We're going to get this," I said. And we did.

◦

Bob Mackie asked me for my favorite colors. Thinking in showbiz terms, I said pink. I was looking at his studio racks, with the Vegas chiffons and feathers.

"I don't think I'll be doing the show in a pink palette," he said apologetically. "If you can't have pink?"

My polyester audition gown had done the job. I thought. Red conjured, too, Alexis Smith bringing down the house with "Losing My Mind," sung on the chiaroscuro set of *Follies*.

"Red," I said.

The red gown Bob Mackie gave me for "Three Girls Three" was, in my biased opinion, the finest dress he ever designed. It wed the image of Mary Queen of Scots to Las Vegas, which turned out to be a perfect union. The dress's tight velvet bodice presented my bosom in a way women are now buying the Wonderbra to do, and the waist descended in a deep V to a beaded chiffon skirt so heavy it made a pencil-slim silhouette. The beaded chiffon sleeves were caught at the wrist.

I shimmered and glowed and "bled" across the screen, giving the cameramen apoplexy during the opening number, in which trick photography "revealed" us in the dresses, magically transformed like Cinderellas, as the chorus boys who'd masked the change circled and swirled away.

Like Cinderellas, we didn't get to keep our dresses either. They vanished into studio vaults.

"We gave them to people who don't have any sequins," said Gail.

Years later, Kenny summoned us three girls for a rare reunion and gave our dresses back. I was thrilled until I tried mine on at home. The beads tumbled off through my fingers. The velvet bodice had been butchered, the skirt tacked on shoddily. It was a size nothing. I put it back in the bag, where it remains to this day. If I die tiny and desiccated, I can be laid out in it, but I hope to be rich enough beforehand to sponsor its rehabilitation.

The first comedy sketch I taped was with Bob Hope, in which I accosted him on a mock-up set of an NBC hallway and begged him to help three unknowns by doing a sketch on our show. Even as I studied the script marked "BOB" and "MIMI" an NBC executive was accosting Bob in "The Tonight Show" corridor, one soundstage away, doing exactly what I did in the sketch—begging. There was a rush of excitement in our studio when word came that Bob had said "Yes" and was on his way. He'd purportedly agreed to a cameo appearance for the receipt of an unmentioned salary that was probably more than all three girls made on all four shows, and "Mimi." It's an apocryphal story. Even if it's true, I'm sure it was just a Monsieur Beaucaire joke.

Bob rushed in declaring he had only fifteen minutes to spend, and we shook hands. Then the cameras rolled. We read cue cards at each other—duel of the deadpans. I didn't have to act. I had my objective in which to enlist my fellow player: Mr. Hope, please help make our show a hit. As usual, because I was desperately sincere, people found me hilarious.

Things went well until Bob interrupted the take.

"We don't need that line about me being one of the richest men in the world," he said. "It doesn't add anything and it's not funny. Let's get it outta there."

He waved two languid fingers at the offending cue card and it was gone.

I hadn't thought the line added anything either, until I saw his reaction. Then I was kind of sorry to see it cut.

After the final shot of the pilot, Debbie invited me and Ellen into her dressing room, locking everyone else out. She poured us champagne from the producers' gift bottle; we toasted one another and drank. Then Debbie delivered one of the finest sermons I'd ever heard, wailing a final admonition that we all "Stay close to nature!"

The congregation said Amen.

•

We taped the next three shows with guest stars, of whom the first was Steve Martin.

He didn't do much prime-time television. We'd seen him be really funny on "Saturday Night Live," but we had no idea how funny he'd be just standing around. By the time I taped a dating sketch with him, I had to spend a lot of time looking away from the camera because I couldn't keep a straight face. "I bought it from show people. Actors in *The Wizard of Oz*," was his off-camera line before we entered the set, which was a living room with a five-foot ceiling, beneath which we hunched for the entire sketch, flirting, sharing soulful glances, and dancing doubled over without mentioning a word about our physical discomfort. I buried my face in his shoulder while we danced, laughing so hard I cried.

Carl Reiner did the third show, and Flip Wilson the fourth. By then, we girls were offering comments and suggestions. Carl complimented us, and Flip's repeated exclamation was, "Good tele-thinking!" But our handlers were becoming upset.

"You girls are already getting a reputation," one of them warned us. "People are saying you won't take direction, that you insist on having your own way, and trying to push your own ideas. You could end up getting a reputation for being difficult. I'm warning you."

It scared us into silence. We'd only been trying to "stay close to nature." Because we played ourselves on the show, and the backstage sketches were based on our lives, we'd felt free to contribute ideas. Debbie's on choreography later made her one of the most creative choreographers in show business; Ellen's sense of her own vocal strengths gave her strong opinions about suitable material; and my comic timing was offbeat, different from what many people expected. But the right to have creative input, we learned, was a perk in Hollywood, awarded on the basis of seniority, power, and affiliation. To expect to have it as newcomers was the height of naivete. To insist on it risked one's career.

Kenny supported us; he'd found us, and he believed in us to the very end. And others told us good things:

"You're going to be such huge stars!"

"Look at that face! What a fabulous face!"

"Do you realize you three are going to grow up on national television?"

"I knew you were funny, but now I see you can *invent*, like Lily!"

Kenny took me to a party at Brenda Vaccaro's, whom I revered since seeing her in *Midnight Cowboy*. Her house was full of beautiful pine antiques and overstuffed chintz sofas long before the trend was popular. Paul Simon and Shelley

Duvall passed me in the hallway, and my eyes almost fell out of my head to see Julie Christie on the couch—Julie Christie, my favorite movie star.

I knelt on the rug and listened to her talk. When the conversation lulled I told her that I'd never forgotten the dress she'd worn to the Academy Awards, when she won for *Darling,* because it had looked like liquid gold.

"Really?" she said. "I can't remember."

I was amazed. How could you not remember the dress in which you won your Academy Award, even though photographs of you wearing it were plastered all over the world for weeks afterwards, and with diminishing frequency, ever since.

Fearing she'd been ungracious, Julie hastened to add:

"But how nice that you do! I'm afraid I was frightfully nervous at the time and don't recall a thing. But awfully nice of you to remember. Really. Marvelous."

Kenny took me to another party in a gated home in Bel Air. It looked like Versailles inside, with fresh lilacs and sparkling candelabra everywhere. Nancy Walker, at the long buffet table, confided, though she did not know me from Adam, that the place looked to her like a giant ladies' room. This remark took on a certain irony for me later when I realized I'd gotten my period and was wearing a white satin jumpsuit, but didn't feel comfortable enough to sidle up to any of the female guests, or the Perfect Hostess, to ask for help. I improvised.

At one point in the evening, the host bent over where I was sitting to deliver a sotto voce message to his wife. It was the only contact I saw between the two all night.

"Darling!" he said in a quasi-European Cary Grant accent, "You're the most gorgeous, incredible, ravishing creature at this entire party!" I was near enough to hear and get a noseful of his laundered shirt and exquisite cologne.

He kissed her on each cheek and sprung off his palms to back away.

"Excuse me," he said, lifting his underarm out of my face.

They'd been married a little over a year and rumours of their divorce were already circulating the party. Within a year, they'd prove true.

In the master bedroom, a group of people, including Diana Ross's husband, were watching the pilot of "Three Girls Three," which included a sketch wherein Debbie parodied Diana Ross. While my real self wandered the downstairs feeling awkward and provincial, the celebrated guests gathered in the bedroom to watch my talented, self-assured image entertain them. Sue Mengers chatted with Jeff Bridges on the stairs. They were the real Sue Mengers and the real Jeff Bridges, but they seemed like ghosts of their celebrated selves. Hollywood was full of ghosts, and I was becoming one of them. Our dense, unsatisfied bodies longed to inhabit our images again, the beings of light on the screen. Our physical selves drifted restlessly between scripted lifetimes.

I went into the hall and saw someone I'd known in my childhood, a cousin in a family I'd spent summer vacations with. I felt like I was hallucinating.

"What are you doing here?" I asked him. He wondered the same thing about me. I told him my story, and he said he was still writing songs, as he'd done in college. We danced. Or my ghost danced; my image was still upstairs, entertaining.

I reported highlights of these evenings over the phone to Larry, who particularly cherished the quote of the host. We haven't entertained since when he hasn't taken me aside and urgently declared me the most gorgeous, incredible, ravishing creature at the entire party.

During the taping of the final show, a phalanx of agents suddenly appeared outside my dressing room and walked me to the stage. "We want you girls to extend your option with the show," one of them said. I asked him what he meant.

"The original contract runs out in June, but the network wants more time to decide. We have no problem with extending, and Kenny and Gail want to, but you girls would have to remain under contract to the show until mid-November. Instead of June."

"Would we get paid any more money during that time?"

"No," one admitted. "It's just for the good of the show. To give it a chance."

I was all for it. I said yes.

Days later, I returned my rented Datsun and flew home.

Waiting contentedly for the March air date, I would take the bus and think, soon I won't be able to take the bus anymore because I'll be too famous. I washed dishes in our little kitchen, stir-fried our vegetables, scoured the bathroom, and shopped in the dismal New York supermarkets, savoring my secret, which soon the world would know.

I was a Star.

29.

Kim Stanley

K enny came to town. He invited me to a dinner party being given by
Brenda Vaccaro at Serendipity, a restaurant in my neighborhood. How
glamorous, I thought. What a wonderful new life! Larry didn't go; he was
playing in a band at the time, with a regular gig in Canarsie where the only de-
pendable patron was a man who came in every night with a bag of money for the
cash register.

It was a large dinner party, I saw as I entered the restaurant and glimpsed a
long, bustling table. Kenny came toward me to host the introductions with
Brenda. The first person they brought me to, much to my delight, was Maureen
Stapleton.

We'd met on Jeff Bleckner's AFI Film, where I'd been the prop girl and she'd
been the star. It had been a difficult shoot, especially the day on the chilly bluff
overlooking Manhattan bay when Maureen had growled, "If anyone ever says to
me again 'I have a grant…!'" Maureen either remembered me or pretended to,
equally gracious. I was glowing as Brenda steered my attention to Maureen's dinner partner, a woman with long, straight white-gray hair spread over a rough,
olive-green shawl. I'd noticed her when I'd come in. She was striking.

"And this is Kim," Brenda said.

"Hello Kim," I said politely.

Then I looked into her eyes and saw to whom I was speaking.

Once, when I was home in Rochester for Christmas during my days as Curt
Dempster's acting student, I'd turned on the TV to find the Actors' Studio version
of *The Three Sisters* in progress. Shelley Winters as Natasha, the young Sandy
Dennis playing Irina—I was glued. But it was Masha who arrested me. The
minute she appeared on the set, it was impossible to watch anyone else. Who was
this solid woman with the penetrating gaze, I wondered. She was riveting. She
broke my heart, effortlessly. Curt taught relaxation, focus, and truthful response,
all of which this actress did better than anyone I'd ever seen. She seemed to stare
through her own mask and penetrate others' as if human guises, onstage or off,
were heartbreaking necessities of which she'd grown weary. Her name, I saw in the
credits, was Kim Stanley. Before *The Three Sisters* I'd never seen her. After, I hadn't
known what had become of her. Here she was.

"*Kim!!*" I repeated suddenly, squeezing all my admiration into one syllable and feeling my face dissolve in a huge smile, "I am *so* happy to *meet* you!"

Kim looked into my eyes, horrified, then screwed up all her facial muscles and sing-songed at me: "*We*-ell, I'm so happy to meet *you-oo, too*-oo!"

She dropped her grimace and turned to the rest of the table.

"God," she shivered, "what a phony smile!"

There was a moment of shocked silence. Kenny took my elbow and led me away. People began to talk. I heard Brenda behind me.

"It's a wonderful smile, Kim. That's her smile. You've just never seen it before. It's the way she always smiles!"

Kenny tucked me at the end of the table, opposite George Grizzard. Maureen and Kim were kitty-corner to me. "Kim that was completely uncalled for," I heard Maureen saying in a low voice. "That was very, very rude."

I assured my dinner companions I was fine and picked up my salad fork. Kim went quiet. George Grizzard told some wonderful stories. A little while later, Kim said to Maureen:

"Boy, you're really playing the game tonight, aren't you?"

"I'm not playing a game at all," Maureen said irritably. "I like these people. They're very nice people. They're my friends and they're yours too!"

Laughter bubbled from other quarters. I ate.

Maureen sighed and smoothed an errant strand of Kim's hair out of her face. Kim looked sad and said:

"You're doing my hair. Are you *that* angry with me?"

This simple observation struck me as so true it took my breath away. I was instantly transported to childhood, standing next to my towering mother, dressed up to go somewhere and hoping I met her approval. Instead, I got hair brushed out of my face. Are you that angry with me?

That was Kim Stanley. Everything she did had an emotional logic so deep it seemed to spring from the universal soul. It occurred to me Kim Stanley couldn't lie; for her, dishonesty was an emotional impossibility. It's what made her the most powerful actress I'd ever seen, and also what disqualified her from celebrity. She couldn't play the game. That's what had become of Kim Stanley.

The party dwindled. It was late when the last of the group—me, our hostess, and the two great actresses—made our way to the door. As I neared the entrance, Kim blocked my path.

"People think I should apologize for what I said, and I want to," she said. "I'm sorry."

"That's all right," I said, remembering not to smile and shaking my head to deny hurt feelings.

"No, it's *not* all right," she insisted. "I really do want to *apologize*. I'm sorry."

I was pinned beneath her gaze, recalling that once, in Curt's class, I'd been able to identify, and speak, my spontaneous feelings. They were now required. I searched for some while Kim Stanley waited.

"I guess," I finally said, "that I can't think of anything to say to 'I'm sorry' except 'You're forgiven'."

She nodded, and we fell in step, heading for the exit. The maitre d' said good night. At the door, I stepped back to let Kim pass; Pearls before Swine, as Dorothy Parker had once said.

We were outside when Kim stopped me again.

"But why do you do it?" she asked.

"What?"

"Smile like that?"

Only in acting class had my smile ever been questioned. The president of Universal Television Casting had declared it the greatest smile he'd ever seen on any living human being. Such fatuous overstatement was not unfamiliar or unpleasant to me. My smile was helping me become a star.

"I guess...it's because I'm afraid."

"We're all afraid," said Kim soothingly, but also dismissing fear as an explanation. The limo driver was holding the door for her.

"Come on, Kim," called Maureen from inside.

"I guess...I don't know what else to do. If I don't smile." I was amazed at how difficult it was to access my feelings. It was as if being myself for public consumption was gradually erasing the person upon whom that self was based.

"You could watch other people," suggested Kim in a helpful tone.

Yes, I thought. I used to do that. I'd become an actress because of it. My ability to watch other people had once made me capable of melting into them, portraying anything they felt and did. Now that I was so eager to be watched, things had changed.

"I *do* watch other people," I said. "But I don't want them to *see* me watching. I smile so they won't see."

This made perfect sense to Kim Stanley, who stood on tiptoe to kiss my forehead before she got in the car.

At last, I'd received a blessing, and from the greatest of actresses. But for what? She'd planted her lips right over my third eye. As I walked home, I thought I could feel it, open and blinking in the dark.

30.

The Hit

The evening before "Three Girls Three" went on the air, Rick Hashagan took me out for a celebratory dinner. Larry was in an Off-Off Broadway show, so it was just me and my agent. Our postprandial stroll took us to the Seventy-Nineth Street newsstand near First Avenue, where we bought the next day's *Times* to check out John J. O'Connor's review. Together we opened the paper beneath a streetlight.

First I saw the ad, featuring Debbie's, Ellen's and my singing faces. "Hey!" read the copy, "Let's do a variety series about 3 unknown-but-terribly-talented-girls doing a variety series about 3 unknown-but-terribly-talented-girls!"

Had the copywriter intended comic ambiguity? The thought occurs to me now. Then, I was simply enraptured, especially by the follow-up: "And boy, if it's a hit, their lives will never be the same!"

I moved on to the review.

"The freshest, liveliest, and most exciting premier of a series that television has concocted in years!" wrote Mr. O'Connor, beneath the headline "TV: INSTANT STARDOM FOR 3 GIRLS".

There it was, in the paper of record. I was a Star. That was the moment I tasted success. Even if you can't believe everything you read.

That night, as the last credits rolled, just before the phone started to ring off the hook with congratulatory calls from my friends and family, an announcer's voice interrupted the music to say, "'Three Girls Three' will be seen later in the season on this network. Check for local listings for time and date.'"

Our debut hour had garnered a twenty-nine overnight share and a twenty-five nationally. This was not enough, in 1977, to make a show a hit. Especially when the head of Variety at NBC had said, "If we're going to have three girls on this network, let's at least have three *beautiful* girls." He began developing a show more to his taste, about show girls in Las Vegas who were also kooky moms, called "Who's Minding the Kids?" When it didn't do well, it got revamped as "Blansky's Beauties" with Nancy Walker, presumably to add comedy to legs and kids.

It was the same guy who'd declared me too dark a loaf for "Saturday Night Live"'s repertory cast. He was also the one whose idea it was, years later, to boost ratings by replacing Jane Pauley on "The Today Show" with younger, blonder

Deborah Norville. I think that was the decision that eventually took him to the sports division, where his views on feminine pulchritude could revert to the personal sphere, presumably, and do less widespread damage.

Blinded by "Three Girl's Three"'s resounding critical success, I considered the delay in airing all the shows disappointing but not fatal. The show's packaging agents had all but warned us of trouble ahead when they'd asked us to extend our option. I kept the faith.

Later, an agent trying to woo me to another agency, who therefore must be considered a purposefully nasty source, said to me: "You had incredible heat in this town, and the way they let it die was downright embarrassing!"

Evidently, I'd been the actress of choice in Hollywood's little world of pilot development during the time of the extension, but the excitement was all in California. My life was unruffled in New York, where I never heard a thing.

Waiting for news of the show's rescheduling on the network, I landed the lead in a musical at the Manhattan Theater Club, in James Wann and Bland Simpson's *Hot Grog*. I knew I was cast because I'd been on television. James Wann's wife, Cass Morgan, a beautiful singer, had originated the role in North Carolina and desperately wanted to make her New York debut as Anne Bonney, the governor's daughter who dresses as a man and stows on a pirate ship to join her lover. But she couldn't compete with the boost the tube gave my career. I'm happy to report Mrs. Wann went on to star in a later Wann-Simpson musical, *Pump Boys and Dinettes*, which was a hit in New York, unlike our pirate musical. "'Hot Grog' Warmed-Over Cider" ran the headline over our *New York Times* review. I thought that was unfair. I was praised for my "fine, clear voice" and "appealing awkwardness in her sailor's costume," but that didn't quite make up for the way I thought the beautiful music and powerful story were overlooked. But there had been trouble signs.

Some productions just don't gel. I suspected ours might be one of them when my costar, the week of opening previews, came to me and said he'd finally figured out his character. "I realized," he explained, "that I never really love you. I love my Captain. Anne Bonney is just in the way."

This somewhat deflated, for me, the love songs that made up at least half the show's score, but I hoped the audience wouldn't notice. Harder to hide were the production choices meant to highlight the show's comic elements, such as the pirates' fanciful painters' overalls, identical to those I'd worn in the Indiana Repertory Theater children's troupe when we toured the Indianapolis public school system with big smiles and guitars. One swabby had a teddy bear peeking out from his back pocket, for a character touch. In all, I felt the show's grand themes of feminism, romance, adventure, death, and rescue-from-hanging-by-pregnancy suffered, but maybe I was just trying to protect my own interests.

The night of tech rehearsal, Louis Zorich, the captain, had an accident on the New Jersey turnpike that landed him in the hospital with two broken legs. We were stunned. The wreck had been terrible; his survival was miraculous. The show went on; that is theater tradition. At first audience dress-rehearsal, the director read the role onstage. By the following night we had an actor on-book and on-stage. By the next night he'd memorized the part.

Louis recovered entirely. The next time I saw him was on the platform of the Democratic convention. He and his actress-wife Olympia Dukakis were standing behind presidential candidate Michael, who was Olympia's cousin. Louis looked fabulous, no worse for the wear than if he'd never been in the accident, ten years previous, that swept him off our pirate ship just before it sank.

I was happy in the show, despite its problems. I walked to work singing for joy—I was the *lead* in a New York musical! The Manhattan Theater Club had a subscription audience; the theater was filled despite the reviews. When I sang my final solo—"Raise a glass for a woman's romance!"—pregnant in my prison-smock, my lover and father dead, I usually hear the satisfying sound of people sniffling in the house.

Larry had gotten me roller skates for my twenty-ninth birthday. I'd asked for them because I'd had so much fun roller-skating the Venice beach path when I was in LA. I wanted to skate in New York. Why not? I'd grown up skating city sidewalks.

I hadn't noticed that California skates had thick polyurethane wheels. Ever the imagist, I'd assumed the secret to adult outdoor skating lay in the boots' ankle support. Larry'd had to search hard for the "Chicago" roller skates he'd found. Neither of us realized they were intended for indoor rinks of smooth, sanded wood, not the rubble that passed for pavement in New York. One day I donned the skates to roll downtown to *Hot Grog* rehearsal.

Negotiating York Avenue was more difficult than I'd imagined. I huffed laboriously up and rolled perilously down pitched concrete slabs and deceptively gradual inclines, hurling myself onto mailboxes and street signs to prevent myself from being killed at the intersections. People stared. I'd wanted them to look, of course, so my fun would set an example and spread the skating trend eastward. But my onlookers didn't see fun. They saw peril.

The following day I chose the East River Esplanade as a more suitable route. It was a nice roll across Eighty-Seventh to Gracie Mansion, but the downtown trek proved difficult from the beginning, because the esplanade, I'd failed to recall, was made of grouted pavers. My wheels clattered up and down the miniature hillocks, and skittered across the cracks, until my teeth shook. Around Seventy-third Street, two of my wheels fell off. I put on my rehearsal flats, shouldered my disabled skates, and walked to work. Thus ended my one-woman-crusade to bring California skating to the sidewalks of New York.

About two years later, a skate-rental concession opened in Central Park. It attracted an eager clientele. The skate wheels were polyurethane.

In early November, Larry and I got the insurance settlement for which we'd waited a year and a half. It was five thousand dollars, more money than either of us had ever had. We went to the diamond district and bought a ring that looked like a radio, with a convex roll of sapphire baguettes. I loved it. I lost it from my upper overall pocket at Yankee Stadium on a trip to the ladies' room, having forgotten I'd removed it in order to applaud without fear of shaking loose the stones. I'd stashed it in my top pocket; it fell out, unnoticed, when I unbuttoned, and was never seen again, though I went back to look. But I loved my ring while I had it, and it did the job. Larry and I got engaged, announcing the news formally to both sets of parents over Thanksgiving.

Just before the holiday, late in the day on November 15, I phoned the California ICM packaging agent in charge of "Three Girls Three." I was sure by that late business hour the network had rendered its decision. Trembling with nerves, I braced myself to hear the all-important news.

The agent got on the line. He sounded surprised, but pleased, to hear from me.

"Hey there!" he began heartily. "You in California?"

"No," I said. "New York! I'm calling about the show!"

There was a brief cross-continental silence.

"What show?"

"'Three Girls Three'!" I said. "It's mid-November!...Isn't the option expiring today? What *happened?*"

There was a long pause before my agent spoke and I learned Everything I Ever Wanted To Know About Network Television But Had Been Afraid To Ask:

"Honey, that show died a long time ago. It's been dead since last summer. Before the last three ever went on the air."

31.

L'Hotel Ideal

The wedding was set for May 27, 1978. Larry and I spent February and March in LA, because the LA agents, feeling guilty, had arranged a little role for me in a packaged TV movie for which I didn't have to audition. It was called, ironically, *Getting Married.*

We flew to California and stayed with Gail Parent. We went to Cher's roller skating parties, for which Cher rented suburban roller rinks in LA neighborhoods like Reseda, which no one knew how to get to. But assistants phoned for directions, and limousine drivers knew, so the most amazing people showed up—Joni Mitchell and Sara Dylan being the two that stunned me—to roll around for three hours to fabulous music and check each other out like a bunch of eighth-graders.

Gail gave a party of her own, with the help of some friends who were ex-Los Angeles Rams. Hugh Hefner came, because the footballers were frequent guests at his mansion, and when he arrived, a shiver of excitement swept the crowd. Gail's boyfriend leapt to the door to squire him around for introductions; as they passed me, he slowed Hef down. I was still trailing social sparkle as the star of Gail's brilliant-but-failed television show. Hef looked me up and down. "Not necessary," he said to Gail's footballer, and the two moved on.

I was hurt. I admit it. I don't know how many American women of the time wouldn't have been, deep down. This man had convinced most others that he was the ultimate hip arbiter of feminine beauty. Then I was pissed. You got that right, you desiccated old thrill-seeker, I spat at him silently. I ain't no fuckin' bunny.

Getting Married starred Richard Thomas, Bess Armstrong and Mark Harmon and is still on the air occasionally, like a lacy Hallmark card. Richard, happily married at the time, was delighted to hear of my wedding plans.

"You want kids?" he asked me from his makeup chair.

"Oh, sure," I said, though I didn't, anytime soon.

"Kids are the best," said Richard warmly. "They put your life in line like nothing else." This was even before he and his wife had triplets. When the trio arrived years later, I thought, it couldn't have happened to a better actor-father.

Kids were not, in fact, on my mind. Pregnancy would interrupt my career, and I had no time for that. I'd never been eager for motherhood as a child. My dolls were royal personages, dignified adults. They didn't ride in baby carriages or take bottles. As a teenager, I'd baby-sat real children only occasionally and reluctantly; I'd always been slightly cowed by my pesky charges.

Once, on the *Grease* tour, I'd had a pleasant dream in which I'd seen myself walking in a park with two children, holding their hands. The dream had been terribly self-serving; in it, I'd been a man seeing motherhood as something that made me, the woman, more attractive. Children as feminizing accessories.

But most of my dreams about motherhood were fraught with sorrow and inadequacy. I would dream that I'd *had* a baby but had *forgotten* about it, and when I remembered, I couldn't remember where I'd *put* it. I would realize weeks had gone by since I'd had it, but where was it? I hadn't fed it. After a frantic search I'd find the tiny homunculus in my bureau drawer. It would be no bigger than an inch, almost starved to death. With terrible remorse, and overwhelmed with love, I would pick it up, determined to learn how to feed it. When I touched it, I killed it; the baby would disintegrate between my fingers, leaving no evidence that it had ever lived.

Small wonder that I awoke on my wedding morning and thought, "It's too late now." I was looking out the window of my old dressing room, at Rochester's beautiful emerald greens, standing not far from the spot where long ago I'd caught my own eyes in the mirror and realized I was going to be an actress. I'd dreamed of being an actress. I hadn't dreamed of being a wife and mother.

I'd tried to dream of being a bride, at least. My mother brought home wedding cake throughout my childhood for this expressed purpose; I would put the napkin-wrapped slice beneath my pillow to stimulate a dream about my future husband. It never worked. In grammar school, the nuns had taught us to pray for our future spouses, somewhere out in the world struggling to remain pure as they wound their ways to our Kismets. All this had made me a raving romantic, but I'd never dreamed of my future husband, or myself as a blushing bride.

My junior year in high school we read John Keats' poem, "St. Agnes Eve." I was so entranced by it I performed the ritual Keats described, by which virgins could induce a dream of their future husbands on the night of January 21. I fasted all day, wore white to bed, and left a candle and dish of sweets on my bedside table.

To my embarrassment at the time, I dreamed of our family friend the priest, Father O'Malley. I saw his smiling face so vividly it woke me up, startled. Father O'Malley looked like Frank Sinatra to me; did I want to marry someone who looked like Frank Sinatra? Was there a Freudian message about priests and father figures to the dream?

It was Father O'Malley's face that smiled on Larry and me as we took our vows. He performed the marriage rite.

His smile turned to tears at one point. I began to cry too, and when I felt Larry's hand touch mine, I looked over and saw tears rolling down his face.

"What were you thinking of?" I asked him later. "When you cried?"

"Cisco and Molly," he told me.

That's what had happened to me. I'd thought of the two children.

Larry and I, like most couples, had fantasized about the children we'd have together. We'd named them. The names were my choices, from my girlhood devotion to Our Lady of Fatima, and the little visionaries who saw her and prayed for
world peace. The boy would be Francisco, nicknamed Cisco, and the girl would
be Mary Jacinta, called Molly. At that point in the nuptial mass I'd felt them arrive, two blobs of essence hovering to our right. Their thought was: Thank God
you've done it. Now we can come.

As if they'd been waiting.

●

Etiquette assigns the groom responsibility for the honeymoon because the
bride's family must produce the wedding. Frankly, Larry as a travel agent made me
nervous. He hated to plan. Planning, especially for travel, had been a religion with
my father. Thinking of my parents' gracious midlife tour of Europe, where they'd
stayed at wonderful hotels like the Villa D'Este and been treated like American
royalty—Kennedys!—I begged Larry to make reservations at least for Paris, where
we'd arrive at the height of the tourist season. We'd also be motoring around the
country with tourist hordes. "I don't want to be begging our way around France
on our *honeymoon* like two penniless *college* students!" I'd wailed in the grip of
bridal panic, certain my husband meant to subject me to hardships my father
would never have permitted me to endure. In the old days, of course, the major
hardship for the sheltered bride would be sex.

Larry soothed and promised: he would make reservations. Remembering his
failed promise about medical insurance made me distrust him, so I pushed things
a little by giving him the name and address of a hotel I remembered as one my sister had chosen for our fabulous sibling European vacation, courtesy of her Pan Am
free miles, in 1972. The place had been sunny, with balconies, and reasonably
priced. Larry wrote to the hotel, then called. It was inexplicably difficult to reach,
but he finally managed to book a room there for three nights, sending an interna-
tional money order at the manager's insistence.

We spent our honeymoon night at the Plaza, in the bridal suite booked by
Larry's brother, the best man. We hated to leave the Plaza, but Paris was the best
possible reason. Our plane landed at Orly in the evening. The cabby we got didn't
know our hotel, but he knew the location of the address. As we wound our way
into Paris's interior, ending in the twisted, dark streets of the little Isle de St. Louis,
my stomach dropped. There was no spacious auto-ronde here, like I recalled near
the hotel my sister had booked. The cab stopped before a heap of shabby build-
ings that seemed to be propping each other up.

"Hotel Henry Quartre," the cabby announced.

Larry leapt out, not daring to express any doubt about the wisdom of my choice. He paid the cabby and shouldered our bags. I was in shock even before we climbed the dark, spiraling stairway that reeked of urine. At its top we came upon the concierge's window, behind which sat a fat, unshaven man in a t-shirt, smoking. Larry gave his name and said he had a reservation. The man grunted, turned a big book toward Larry for signing, then handed over the key. I said nothing, holding back my tears until Larry and I were alone. Our room was up more stairs. It was dominated by a bed whose sagging mattress tilted off its frame toward the floor. A lumpy orange-red cotton spread, and the peach wallpaper above it, showed big oil stains.

Now I recognized where I'd seen the place before and how I knew its name. It was where I'd stayed on my clandestine trip to Paris with Jonathan, my college lover. Like two college students, on my honeymoon—just what I'd told Larry I didn't want to be. I began to sob.

"We can't stay here!"

"This isn't the place you thought?" Larry said.

"No!"

"I didn't think so. But you have to admit it's funny. I went through hell to get this reservation." He was laughing.

I confessed about Jonathan, which made Larry laugh even harder. Marriage had put him in a good mood. I laughed too, but it didn't stop the tears. I couldn't believe I'd dragged me and my husband back to one of the most painful and uncertain times of my life. On our goddamn honeymoon.

Larry shoved the mattress into place and pulled back the disgusting spread so I could lie down on sheets that were presumably clean. I cried myself to sleep. Making love, under these circumstances and on top of that bed, was out of the question.

I awoke in the middle of the night to see Larry silhouetted at the window. He was sitting in a chair.

"You can't sleep?"

"No. But it's all right. I'm enjoying looking out."

When I woke up again, he wasn't with me. The window showed silver-gray light. I imagined he'd gone out and envied him being on the streets of Paris. I couldn't wait until he got back so I could join him outside this hellhole. I hoped it would be soon.

The air had just turned lemony at the window when he came through the door.

"Come on," he said. "I've found a hotel. We can walk. It's beautiful outside."

I got dressed and we walked out with our bags.

After we'd taken a few turns, the sun came out fully; we'd arrived on a street where there was a sparkling white building with bright French-blue shutters and windowboxes loaded with red geraniums.

"This is it," he said. "I've already got the room."

I climbed the stairs. On a gleaming brass plaque next to the door, I read the name of the place my husband had brought me to:

"L'Hotel Ideal."

32.

Snowed In

The honeymoon continued in New York City. In those blissful days, Larry and I stayed up half the night, slept late, and pursued our art. After his post-Lampoon recuperation, Larry had acted at Washington, DC's Folger Theater in David Hare's *Teeth and Smiles*. Now, in New York, he did an adaptation of Kafka's *Josephine, the Mouse Singer*, by avant-garde poet and playwright Michael McClure. All the actors played mice, wearing big ears and squeaking. The production won an Obie and gave Larry his own memorable brush with the great actress Kim Stanley. She came to the show, thrilling the cast with her presence. But when the narrator mouse declared the show's denouement with his usual line—"And now our little tale comes to an end!"—that night there was an audible growl from Kim's location in the dark: "And not a moment too soon."

I, too, did an avant-garde piece. Mine was a production at the Public Theater. I was so happy to be working there that I would have framed my first paycheck if I hadn't needed the $125 so much. Every actor in town wanted to work at the Public. Its casting office could choose from the creme de la creme of our profession. I'd done two general auditions without ever having been asked to read for a production. After "Three Girls Three," I was. In the wonderful world of show business, the tube gave me entree to the avant-garde.

The Master and Margarita was adapted by Andrei Serban for the stage from Mikhail Bulgakov's surreal Russian novel. The story juxtaposed the persecution of a writer in Soviet Russia with that of Jesus in Roman Palestine. Working under Andrei's direction was the closest I ever got to performing under the "alienation" principles of German playwright Bertolt Brecht. Andrei's staging was overtly presentational; he disdained psychological and emotional exploration in favor of expressionist political allegory. Like Brecht, he had little patience for actors or audience wallowing in the self-dramatization of the petit bourgeoisie.

I sympathized with the politics of this stance, but its aesthetics challenged my acting technique. While I pondered an Objective and Emotional Preparation for my frenzied one-scene monologue as a terrified secretary whose boss has turned into a talking suit, Andrei's direction was: "Do it like a chicken who has the neck only! Who has—how you say it? The head…" he emphatically slashed his hand across his throat. "The head cut off?" I offered. "Yes! A chicken with the head off!"

Andrei urged excitedly. "More. More crazy!" I ran around the stage screaming, no idea why, and Andrei was satisfied; I mugged more broadly for him than ever I'd done in television sketch comedy. Meanwhile, Wallace Shawn did his part, a cigar-smoking cat Devil, with the most arrestingly flat affect I'd ever seen.

Andrei often worked separately with his leads, F. Murray Abraham and Laura Esterman, while sending chorus actors, me and Michael Jeter among them, to the Green Room, where we worked out upcoming scenes by ourselves. At first, we were shy with each other, but eventually we proposed ideas and warmed to collective improvisation; the first time Andrei sent for us, we arrayed ourselves excitedly onstage, proud to show what we'd done. It was something expressionist and Martha Grahamesque; I was kneeling. "Wrong! All wrong!" Andrei began to scream within minutes. "Why you do it like that?!" He promptly restaged us. The third time this happened, I screamed back:

"Don't *yell* at us, Andrei! It's just an *experiment!*" I'd owned my anger in Curt Dempster's class, and I can't stand being yelled at. "You said to come *up* with something and we *did!* If you don't like it, *change* it, but stop *yelling* at us for doing what you *said!*"

Andrei smiled at this comradely defense of our group's fledgling collective instincts. He appeared delighted to find himself being scolded by a rich American feminist, which is what he seemed to think I was, probably because my name was Kennedy. This may have been the reason why he was fleetingly sad to see me leave *Master and Margarita* after a week and a half's rehearsal.

I left to play Stockard Channing's sister in her TV pilot, for which I'd auditioned on videotape before being cast in Andrei's play. I'd walked into a soundproofed studio thinking I'd tape a reading to be sent to LA and never heard from again. When I'd seen Stockard by the tripod, smiling and ready to read with all comers, I'd known the audition was serious.

Stockard's unforgettable movie debut as a woebegone heiress in *The Fortune* with Warren Beatty and Jack Nicholson had won my loyal fanship. I'd often quoted her character's byword, "Oh, boo-hoo!" to amuse my friends. In person, Stockard confirmed the delightful impression I'd gleaned from the movie: she sounded a lot like the girls I'd known at summer camp and the country club. The accent involved is sometimes called "Long Island Lockjaw," but its national ubiquity defies regional description. To affect it, you simply speak as if your mouth is full of money which, if you open too far, will all fall out. One must tighten one's jaw to preserve one's capital.

I read the part of Stockard's older sister in full-blown lockjaw. "Susan!" I trilled through clenched teeth "It's me, Victoria! Over here, in the Mercedes! No, the other Mercedes! No, the *other* Mercedes!" Stockard's laugh was instant encouragement, but weeks passed before I heard I got the part.

When my agent called with the news, I went to Mary Colquhoun, the Public Theater's casting director. She knew how much I'd wanted to work at the Public, having been privy to my history of general auditions, and she also knew the potential importance of a series to an actor's career. She asked one question: Was the role a good one? I assured her it was. She accompanied me to Andrei and explained my necessary departure. We approached him at a lunch break. After Andrei listened to Mary with a regretful look on his face, he bade me a fond, distracted farewell and resumed penciling his script.

The next week, the actor playing Jesus found out that his TV pilot had sold. He was under contract; he had no choice but to leave the play. Mary's odds-on bet, when Andrei had decided to cast the actor, was that this might not happen. When it did, she agreed once again to translate the actor's good news into bad news for the director.

This time Andrei's reaction was furious and swift, the cry of a wounded man. He called together the cast and publicly shamed Jesus/Yeshua, the absent me, and all American actors for having bad values. We loved money too much! We wanted the easy life! America would never have great theater, Andrei railed, until its actors committed to art!

The wild Rumanian was absolutely right about great theater requiring commitment. But what he didn't know was how many American actors were unable to audition for productions like his until they'd risen to a level of favorable public notice. In capitalist America, even not-for-profit theaters vied for audiences, and well-known actors were, at that time, increasingly being offered stage work denied the lesser known. Plenty of American actors wanted to commit to art, but art didn't always ask us until we'd done movies or television—by which time we came burdened with agents, contracts, and prior commitments.

❖

Stockard's pilot, directed by Robert Drivas, took two weeks to tape in LA. I returned to New York afterward, but by the time CBS had ordered midseason episodes I was back in Los Angeles, standing by for Lucie Arnaz at the Ahmanson Theater in *They're Playing Our Song*.

I'd auditioned for the Neil Simon–Marvin Hamlisch–Carole Bayer Sager musical in New York. My reputation as a musical performer had been firmly established by "Three Girls Three" and I dared hope that my audition, with a Carly Simon ballad, and my reading might land me the lead. But I learned that had been all-but-promised to Ms. Arnaz. I grabbed the stand-by offer, wanting to increase my musical repertoire the way British actors learn their Shakespeare—by doing. When I arrived in LA, Lucie greeted me with "Hi, you're cute, you're never going on."

I never did. But I watched the musical take shape for Broadway under the skillful self-editing of Neil "Doc" Simon and had the pleasure of being his sole audience backstage for a sight gag he couldn't resist. He and producer Manny Azenburg were walking to a meeting, several paces ahead of me, when they passed a pile of props that included a mannequin. Neil stopped to stare at the thing while Manny, oblivious, moved on. As I drew closer, Neil threw me a deadpan backward glance to enlist my witness, then muttered "Dummy!" with exquisite reproach at the mannequin before hustling to catch up with Manny. His glee in staging this private moment made me his fan for life. Sclerotic critics who carp that Neil Simon's facility with jokes subverts other aspects of his genius fail to appreciate that facility with jokes is a huge part of his genius, and squelching it is a misguided, mean-spirited thing to do.

Marvin Hamlisch didn't seem to like my counterpart, John Getz, who stood by for Robert Klein. The composer refused to speak to John, calling him "That Guy" even in John's presence. John couldn't imagine what he'd done to offend, but my guess was that Marvin's identification with the lead male character, Vernon, who was essentially Marvin during his romance with Carole Bayer Sager, was too great to abide its being played by John's physical type —curly-headed and blonde, with a big, toothy grin. I told John not to worry, that the role didn't *have* to be played by an intense brunette. In fact, I assured him, you look *just like* another famous New York songwriter, Burt Bacharach! I knew Burt's picture from my old Bacharach-David songbook, a veritable anthology of Shirelles and Dionne Warwick hits. I thought John would be wonderfully credible, though different, as Vernon.

Carole Bayer Sager showed up during previews to write lyrics for some new songs. I privately hoped her presence would rekindle the romance I saw depicted nightly onstage. I'd grown fond of the fictional couple, and I secretly suspected Marvin of carrying a torch. But nothing happened.

When I read that Carole had married Burt Bacharach, I knew, regardless of whether or not that courtship stemmed from the Ahmanson days, why Marvin Hamlisch never liked John Getz. Love sees eternally.

I left *They're Playing Our Song* before it closed in LA and flew home to help Larry vacate our apartment; my job in an on-air series meant it was time for us to move to California. We deconstructed our modest living quarters, putting orange crates and posters on the street to be requisitioned by scavengers within the hour, and sending footlockers and stereo by a moving company, which requisitioned the stereo unbidden. We piled everything else in a car from an agency that promised vehicle delivery to its owner's destination. Our car, bound for LA, was—what else?—a Mercedes.

It had a diesel-fueled engine, of the type then being touted as salvation for the environment and the economy. Diesel cars failed to ignite the American imagination in part, I think, because they failed to ignite in cold weather. We learned this in Flagstaff, Arizona, where we found the luxury loaner dead as a doornail in the motel parking lot, one morning, beside an impressive line-up of tractor-trailers. A trucker sauntered over to inform us that our diesel fuel had turned to jelly in Flagstaff's overnight, subzero temperatures, and until the sun rose high over Little America and warmed our gas tanks, there was nothing to do but suck coffee and wait.

Outside Palm Springs, we hit a blizzard. Highway patrol diverted traffic into the city, closing the interstate until borrowed snow equipment could arrive from surrounding ski areas. Plows were not part of the Palm Springs municipal fleet. Larry and I checked into a motel, and I called the "Just Friends" producers to explain that bad weather had caused a final delay that would prevent my being at the morning's table reading. As I spoke, Larry was donning his bathing suit to head for the Little Jacuzzi That Could, which we'd seen steaming bravely through the snow covering the motel's roadside spa.

"We're snowed in, in Palm Springs," I said.

This excuse caused a laugh riot in the production office, as I heard it being relayed to the building's farthest reaches as I waited for the producer to pick up the phone. After I'd been in LA a while, I got the joke: Palm Springs is so reliably hot, dry, and sunny that Angelenos depend on it year round for sun and stupefaction when the going gets tough and chilly in LA. Snow in Palm Springs was the proverbial Cold Day in Hell.

"Snow," I also discovered in Hollywood, was a euphemism for cocaine, which was then a notorious scourge of budgets, brains, and production schedules. For a newly hired actress to excuse her absence from her first day of work by saying she was snowed in, in Palm Springs, seemed less a rare irony, to some, than a double-entendre of unmitigated gall.

"Just Friends" was wonderful. I loved playing Stockard's sister; the cast, including Garret Graham, Sydney Goldsmith, and Lou Criscuolo, was great, and guest stars like Harry Shearer dazzled me. But when the show was renewed for a second season, much of the cast was not. Sydney Goldsmith and I were kept on.

I asked for a weekly $500 more than my contractual salary raise. I'd heard that's what actors *did* on renewed series, to show professional self-esteem. "Are you sure you want to do this?" my California agent asked dubiously. I told her yes, surprised she would question it. The amount, I knew, was nominal by television standards in those days. What I didn't realize, and she didn't bother to explain, was that I was reopening contract negotiations. I'd presumed that the worst that could happen was that the producers would turn me down, and I'd go back to work at my normal raise. Had I ignored Hollywood versions of self-esteem and followed the parental lesson, "I don't care if everyone's doing it, you don't," I might have spared myself a painful lesson. But heeding parental dicta is not what Hollywood inspires in its young.

The third new producer hired over the summer to revamp the show dumped me. My fellow fired actors, whose contracts had been violated, drew salaries throughout that second season. I, who'd put myself in breach-of-contract with my fancy bargaining, got nothing, which was an interesting lesson in greed. The re-tooled show foundered a year and then died. I'm not sure how things went so awry, but I heard snow had something to do with it.

33.

TV Guides

W hy didn't you stay on that show?" a newspaper critic once asked me, of "Just Friends." "You were on your way to becoming one of the most popular characters in television!" Five hundred bucks, I told him, and ignorance.

I knew fans had liked my character. One told me at a taping that her sister had gone into labor during the episode that focused on Victoria; she'd insisted on watching all the way to the end before going to the hospital and delivering the daughter she named Victoria.

This story pleased me immensely, because I'd become obsessed with babies. I wanted one, as I'd told Stockard that first season. I dared believe I had job security; the show seemed to be a hit, and Stockard was pictured on the cover of *Time* magazine, which had praised her as an entrepreneurial television actress in the mold of Lucille Ball and Mary Tyler Moore. Victoria was married on the show. These factors combined to make me think I could sneak in a baby who wouldn't interrupt my burgeoning career. I put away my diaphragm and began to make love like an orthodox Catholic.

But I didn't get pregnant.

This surprised me. After several months, I humbly began taking my morning temperature to pinpoint ovulation. The mercury always read 97.3, which I at first assumed was an aberration, but which proved invariable. I gave up the thermometer. Larry's cousin, who had two children and believed in organic remedies, cautioned me to "stay clear" of intoxicants for a few months while learning the changes in my cervical mucous. This was more clinical than I'd wanted to get, but it was already obvious that my experience with reproduction would not be the wild, backseat affair it always seemed to be for people who'd wished that it wasn't. I became expert at identifying ovulation by the cousin's method, and Larry and I became happy slaves to its indications.

But I did not get pregnant.

My make-up woman on "Just Friends," who had a gorgeous baby boy, recommended her Santa Monica obstetrician to me as a fertility specialist. I went to Dr. Frohl while I still working on "Just Friends" and continued after I was unemployed. Once I realized a baby might be hard to come by, getting one seemed more important than getting my next acting job. I knew Larry and I could live on my television savings. I hadn't yet learned the myriad ways, or acquired the human retinue, that could spend big money as fast as I could make it. This shift away from career-building toward my personal life as a priority marked the beginning of my long education in nurture.

Dr. Frohl had pictures in his office: of the four Lennon Sisters, whom he'd ushered into this world to grow up and become singing stars on Lawrence Welk's television show, and of their extended family—children, siblings, and siblings' children. He'd delivered almost everyone in the latter photo. It was impressive testimony to his knack with reproduction.

Larry's sperm was first to go under the microscope. I was directed to sterilize a container for transport of his precious bodily fluids, which were to be collected at home. I boiled a mayonnaise jar, the widest-mouthed receptacle I could find, and left Larry alone with it in the bedroom, hoping fantasy would suffice to provoke the deposit, which had to be free of coital taint. I feared laughing if I even tried to participate from the sidelines, which would interfere with either Larry's arousal or his aim at the finish. The jar itself was enough of an obstacle to the erotic imagination.

The sperm were fine. Next I had to report to Dr. Frohl immediately after intercourse to determine whether my internal environment killed Larry's sperm. Some couples, I was horrified to learn, suffered this cruel fate—they were each other's biological poison. Why hadn't I ever heard of *that,* I wondered, when people listed reasons for Catholic marriage annulment?

While I was still in the stirrups, Dr. Frohl suctioned a second specimen. I thought he needed more to test, but he kept the stainless steel turkey baster inside me and said, "Might as well put this up where it can do some good instead of letting it go to waste!" Then he shot the basterload up my cervix.

I am romantic about conception, I must admit. I'd presumed Frohl, being Catholic, was also romantic about conception, but the turkey baster suggested otherwise. I knew some children were destined to come to earth with the help of stainless steel, petri dishes, and refrigerators. But I hadn't made that choice. And I wasn't ready to; after Dr. Frohl confirmed that Larry and I were biologically compatible, we didn't see him again.

○

A job came along before a baby; I was booked to do my own comedy material for a special called "Sunday Night," produced by the most truly Hollywood producer I've ever known, Nick Vanoff. He'd bought his own studios, Sunset-Gower, with a high-risk loan as a young man because he loved its location smack-dab beneath the Hollywood sign. That's what he told me one evening as I happened upon him, standing in his main street, admiring his view.

Being an enterprising realtor as well as producer of television variety shows, Nick wanted to put two huge soundstages to use that had been lying fallow since Donny and Marie Osmond had moved production of their variety hour to Utah. The stages housed a swimming pool and an ice-skating rink; Nick joined them under one roof, adding a proscenium stage, two hundred theater seats, and a bandstand in the same gargantuan space. He'd sold NBC on the idea of a television variety extravaganza.

My part on "Sunday Night" consisted of three minutes of material I'd written myself, which had been revised to take the form of an interview conducted by Steve Allen while I soaked in a bubble-filled hot-tub, another spectacular gimmick of Nick's soundstage plumbing. The material I'd written was about my new religion, T.N.—the religion of Total Non-Existence—and was essentially a comic meditation on Eastern religious paradoxes I'd gleaned from my haphazard hippie survey. Nick loved it. After it aired he got a letter from a minister who considered the piece fabulously profound and wanted a copy of it on which to base a sermon. I sent it.

The two-hour "Sunday Night" special sold to NBC as a series called "The Big Show." It aired a season, the weekly variety hour with elephantiasis. The cast included two guest-star hosts, rare acts from around the world, and the weekly regulars: a dozen ice-skaters, a dozen synchronized swimmers, Shabba Doo's break dance crew, a full-house band, and a comedy troupe. I was part of the comedy troupe. When Nick asked me to sign for the series, I was eager to say yes, knowing Graham Chapman of Monty Python was already aboard, but I wanted to see the special before committing five years of my life. The "Just Friends" debacle had taught me the seriousness of contracts. I asked my agent if she could get me a tape.

"A tape?!!!" she exploded. "I'm not going to ask Nick Vanoff for a tape! Who do you think you are?!! *Stars* get tapes!"

I left her office and called a manager who'd been courting me for months. I drove to see him and sat in his office while he tracked Nick down by phone in Washington, DC.

"I'll be glad to send her a tape," Nick enthused. "What else does she want?" The manager mentioned twice the proffered salary; Nick said he didn't think it would be a problem. That day I signed with the manager, Erwin Stoff.

When Nick returned to LA, I went to his office to discuss the tape and my role on the series. As he stood to shake my hand, I saw a squarc leather box tucked beneath his armpit, held on by a shoulder strap. "My purse!" Nick chuckled, patting the thing. "Don't mind me. I'm just monitoring my heart. The doctor wants me to do it from time to time. So! Let's talk. Didja like the tape?"

The contraption was legit; Nick's bum ticker caused his sadly premature death. Still, Nick, the consummate showman, surely relished the machine's value as a negotiating tool. Few people, even in Hollywood, were venal enough to upset a man on a heart monitor.

I signed and arrived for my first day at work to find the set in an uproar. The synchronized swimmers weren't being filmed as scheduled, and the back-up skating number was on hold, too, because the rink's quick-freeze chemicals had fogged the water of the glass-walled pool, and the pool's heated chlorine had gotten into the air and, in turn, interfered with the proper freezing of the rink. "Who was supposed to know about the chemical reactions?" I asked a gaffer. "Didn't anyone think of those?"

"That guy," he answered, pointing to a lonely looking fellow who stood, stoop-shouldered, in the middle of the rink, tapping the slush thoughtfully with one shoe. He seemed humbled, like any good scientist would be, by his defeat at the hands of Nature.

The chemical coexistence problem was solved, but each day brought something unforeseen. Once I arrived to find an audience waiting patiently in unseasonable heat for a morning performance of ballet stars Alexander Gudunov and Cynthia Gregory. Inside the soundstage I found the shaking heads and grim smiles that always signaled a "big show" disaster. This time, the proscenium stage floor, which had been sanded and rosined the previous night to the dancers' exact specifications, had been waxed to an impeccable shine in the wee hours by a zealous cleaning person who'd obviously wanted the surface nice and pretty for the morning's television taping. Huge sanding machines had to be ordered in to undo the deed—the slick surface would have killed the dancers. Food was ordered for the audience, which was finally admitted three hours later. They filed in to the upbeat music of the house band, whose job it was to distract them from the further tedium of setting camera shots. Not a dancer had been sighted when I heard a loud clunk! in the middle of the audience's raked seats. Word spread quickly that a man had collapsed. Paramedics bore him out within minutes past the rest of his fellows, most of whom stared fixedly ahead, as if refusing to be deterred by this final, terrible mishap. When the gurney sped by, I snuck a look, and though I was greatly relieved to see the man alive and conscious, I hoped he couldn't hear the band. Obviously, they hadn't gotten word of the crisis and were playing the guy out with a fanfare that made it sound as if he'd just completed a hilarious segment on "The Tonight Show."

Sid Caesar was our guest star one week. We hadn't met each other since that long-ago summer when we'd toured in *Last of The Red Hot Lovers*; I was nervous, but excited, at the thought of seeing him. One morning he arrived on the set shouting, "Where is she?" and when I approached him, he wrapped me in an enormous bear hug. He was aware I'd made it and was happy, he said. I never would have, I told him, if you hadn't told me to go to acting school. He replied he'd learned a few things himself in those intervening eight years —they're in his book. He asked the writers to put me in several of his sketches. I was fast. He was funny. We played. It was a thrill to share the stage again with the great comedian, when I was awake, aware, and a little bit more grown up.

"The Big Show," whose NBC liaisons were Brandon Tartikoff and Warren Littlefield, was too expensive to last; it was canceled after thirteen episodes, just before Nick, or so he credibly maintained, went broke. I believed him when the make-up man showed up at season's end in a Porsche with the license plates OTMP. "Over Time, Meal Penalty," he explained. He'd paid for the car almost entirely with union salary bonus accumulated on our crushing schedule.

Erwin Stoff wasted no time in wangling me an audition for "The Two of Us," a half-hour comedy starring Peter Cook, whom I considered a genius for writing and acting in not only *Beyond the Fringe*, but the funniest dirty comedy I'd ever heard: the "Derek and Clive" tapes with Dudley Moore. My agent had previously submitted me for "The Two of Us" but had been told I was "all wrong for the part." Erwin insisted I'd be perfect.

"Can Mimi's hair ever not look like *hay?*" the casting director worried to my agent after Erwin had talked her into reading me. The news was passed to me. For the reading, "your hair, your makeup—*everything*—has to be *perfect!*"

In later years, I got the hang of what Debbie Allen called "fluffing up." Eventually, I encountered the law of diminishing returns: the more polished I got, the worse my acting became. The fun went out of showing off when sartorial perfection was a prerequisite. The stage makeup tricks I knew—toothpick eyelashes, clown white—relied on suspension of disbelief and artful lighting. The only people who employed such obvious fakery in Hollywood were cheap hookers and female impersonators. Television actresses of the type I'd become—potential series stars—were held to a higher, subtler standard. Not that it wasn't still illusion; I accepted a ride home after the pilot test of "Roller Girls"—the closest I ever came to a tits-and-ass "jiggle" show—from a fellow actress who had cannily crafted herself as a drop-dead blonde airhead. When we got in the car, she yanked off her high heels and threw them in the back seat, where they landed on a pile of clothes and shoes which, I noted with a backward glance that caught sight of some of the labels, were mostly couture and mangled beyond recognition. What the hell. They were just costumes.

I auditioned for "The Two of Us" in a polyester linen-look suit I'd bought shopping with my mother in a Rochester department store. It was red and I wore it with utter confidence, feeling like a star. No one had ever told me, as a neighbor did later, reorganizing my wardrobe after my first pregnancy, "Mimi, I'm shocked. For an actress, these clothes are so *ugly!*"

I did my own hair in hot rollers for the audition and my own make-up, loading up on lip gloss, so that when I kissed Peter good-bye after our reading, I was embarrassed by the amount I'd left on his cheek. The reading had gone well. We liked each other already.

"All natural, are we?" Peter quipped, wiping the smear away, provoking a big laugh, and probably cinching me the job.

◦

We shot four episodes of "The Two of Us" in the spring of l981. They aired promptly to good reviews and the show went on CBS's fall schedule.

I was still trying to get pregnant, which I'd hinted to producer Charlie Hauck, who'd shrugged—que sera, sera—and said, "It happens all the time. We'd shoot around it." When he'd said the word "Diocese" at our first meeting, I'd reacted like someone hearing her native language spoken after years in exile, which had prompted Charlie to go on and divulge that he'd spent two years in Catholic seminary before leaving, marrying, and becoming the father of four. Charlie Hauck did not seem to me to be a man scared of reproduction, even in the womb of his series' female lead.

Still I did not conceive. Infertility, particularly among couples who'd delayed having children, was not yet recognized as the widespread phenomenon it turned out to be, and I felt my failure as personal. Why was I barren? That was the word that occurred to me, the biblical one, the one from Garcia Lorca's *Yerma*. It's the word most women think when they desperately want a child they can't conceive.

In high school, our "Marriage and Family" class was summoned to a special, "frank talk about sex" in the music room, whose collegiate lecture-hall setting was academic enough for our science-teacher nun to say "penis" and "vagina" and look us in the face afterward as an ordinary homeroom teacher. The sex talk fell to her because the priest who taught "Marriage and Family" couldn't say "intercourse" without blushing. But the lecture did not entirely eschew euphemism. Sister Edward told us, "Menstruation is the weeping of a disappointed womb."

When she said that, I could practically feel the girl behind me squirm. I'd recently heard the rumor that she feared she might be pregnant. Caught between her and Sister Edward I glimpsed, for the first time, the distance between the celibates' romantic view of sex and a sexually active woman's reality. Since then, how many women I would know—and I'd be one—for whom the red stain was not a disappointment but an unbelievable blessing, a merciful grace. My senior classmate did turn out to be pregnant; she was barred from graduation, being deemed too scandalous a sight for a Catholic girls' high-school commencement in 1966. I don't know what happened to her or her baby.

It was contraception, bearing responsibility for my part in procreation, that allowed me to appreciate Sister Edward's metaphor as an adult. Wanting to conceive, when my womb wept, I did too. I saw that conception depended on more than my own will; my role was cooperative, not decisive. One did not simply order up a child from the universe. Larry I and tried for two years to get pregnant before letting go of the idea, and deciding to concentrate on "The Two of Us" as the best part yet of the "long, slow ride" to the top that Larry had wished me on my Broadway debut.

Peter and I were booked to be photographed for the cover of *TV Guide.* I was happy to feel the fame I'd pined for on "Saturday Night Live" and "Three Girls Three" coming round again; the day of the shoot, Peter and I were given full star treatment, with limousines and fawning ministrations. We both enjoyed it, which seemed to embarrass him as much as it did me; it was as if we'd both been caught revealing a vulgar, mutual, character flaw. Peter's cover-up was to monologize and compose at random, which he did brilliantly. That day his theme was Birthing.

"Birthing, birthing, birthing, oh, joyfully we birth!" he sang, darting in and out of his curtained dressing area as if midwifing parturition within. He laughed with a maniacal glint in his eyes that seemed descended from a long line of court jesters.

"Birthing," he said as an aside, "Isn't that the most disgusting word? Oh, birthing, birthing…" he resumed.

I knew upper-class British men were historically squeamish about female reproductive physiology, which is why mistresses were a Victorian family accessory. We Irish are fastidious enough that I associated Peter's old-fashioned, newly trendy word with orthopedic sandals and no makeup and found his song funny. But I was privately astonished to hear him riffing on the topic of my greatest anxiety. Metaphorically, we were birthing our show, and that, plus the sexual tension between us and Peter's brilliance at comic improvisations below the belt, might have explained his choice of subject. I couldn't recall discussing babies with him. Laughing about the whole thing felt good. I warmed to the day—being the center of attention, playing with this comic genius, and thinking I'd soon be on the cover of *TV Guide,* an honor I'd share, though not simultaneously, with Bob Dylan, who'd granted the magazine a cover interview during one of his reclusive periods because, he'd explained, *TV Guide* was a magazine his mother read.

The photographer set up a white background shot to take advantage of Peter's dark butler outfit and bowler hat. I donned a white blouse and black skirt whose waistband annoyed the photographer when I sat; he directed his assistant to pin a towel around it. I was secretly pleased to be party to the kind of cheap, hastily improvised illusion I'd thought verboten in television iconography.

Larry and I went to Maui during a week's break in "The Two of Us" because we'd heard a Hawaiian vacation often led to pregnancy. Ours didn't; afterward, my womb wept. In September, on my birthday, we dined at Michael's, a fabulous and incredibly expensive restaurant newly opened in Santa Monica. We ordered red wine and forgot, for the first time in ages, about staying clear for conception.

The *TV Guide* cover came out November 7, 1981. The towel was visible if you looked closely. That same week, I found out I was pregnant, having conceived in late September.

34.

Why Was I Acting?

The Two of Us" was canceled after a season. By then I was used to television death, and I'd perceived a vital loss of clout when our parent company, Marble Arch, went bankrupt due to Sir Lew Grade's sinking of his money into *Raise the Titanic,* a movie that stayed right on the box-office floor. The last flicker of hope I had for our show guttered the morning I arrived at work to see Peter, roaring drunk and wrapped in the British flag, ranting about the day's upcoming lunch with executives anxious to gauge his commitment to a second season. It didn't matter that John J. O'Connor of the *New York Times* had called us the best sitcom couple since Lucy and Desi. It didn't matter that Norman Lear told Charlie Hauck later that, "If it'd been my show, it'd never have gone off the air." These things happen for a reason, as Maureen Stapleton once reminded me. And all that crap.

I was four months pregnant at cancellation. At home I grew quietly huge, remembering the words of two actresses on the set. One, who'd played my mother, was a mother in real life. She told me, in response to my saying I wanted a baby soon, "Just know that having a child will affect your career. You don't think it will but it does. Don't fool yourself."

I'd wanted to tell her, You don't understand. I'm not like you. I'd never settle for guest-star roles. I have ambition and ego.

She understood. It's why she'd bothered to say anything.

The other actress read my palm. It was the last week of the show and I was obviously pregnant but didn't know the sex of the fetus. "You are going to have a son!" she said delightedly, looking at me with deep, dark eyes. "He is going to make you so proud! This will be the most exciting summer of your whole life!"

After the show wrapped, I was shopping one day at the Santa Monica market that offered the best gourmet foods and top-quality produce when I was suddenly overcome by despair. "I'm a me-first person," I thought with surprising bitterness, "and always will be. What am I doing having a baby?"

I'd gone after pregnancy the same way I'd gone after everything else in life, singlemindedly lobbying heaven until I had my way. I saw that being a mother would be my comeuppance; I wasn't fit and didn't want to be one.

I fled the market in tears, abandoning my cart in its suffocating aisle of food and nurture. Inside my car, I bawled.

I wrote to my mother, the only person I trusted to reassure me that I was capable of mothering even though I was a selfish bitch. She wrote back that when she'd been pregnant with my brother, and my father was newly home from the war, she'd hostessed a dinner party. During cocktails, she'd started to cry uncontrollably. A woman guest had taken her upstairs while the others excused themselves awkwardly, leaving my father mystified. My letter brought the moment back to her, she wrote, in all its terror of change and the responsibility of bringing someone utterly dependent on her into the world. These things, she assured me, happen in pregnancy.

I knew this from the media's onslaught of pregnancy information. The phrase "raging hormones" was popular; I hated it as jokey and dismissive. But I was gratified to be photographed and interviewed for *Time* magazine's cover story on the baby boomlet, though I was only slightly pregnant at the time and the photographer had to stuff a pillow beneath my dress. Jacqueline Smith was featured on *Time*'s cover; it was no Demi Moore shot. Ours was the hippie generation. Jackie wore a denim dress and a wide smile that seemed to say, sue me, I'm fat. Birthing, birthing, birthing, so joyfully we birth. In *Time*'s text I was listed as "American royalty" having my baby right alongside Princess Di's heir to the British throne. Johnny Carson invited me on "The Tonight Show" three times while I was pregnant. I'd always wanted to be famous, I told him, and now I was, for doing something most women did: having a baby. Pretty ironic, I quipped to my charming host. Don't you think?

❊

Cisco was born sixteen days after his due date, despite the fact that Larry and I observed every labor-inducing ritual recommended in our LaMaze class, from extra-garlic pizza to orgasmic sex. We even walked thirty blocks under a lunar eclipse. Nothing hastened Cisco's own sweet timetable, except, perhaps, the man I saw in a dream the night before labor, whom I saw again before Molly was born. He's African-American, dressed like a train conductor of the nineteen-thirties, and he conducted my children to me. In the first dream, he came upon a little boy crouched in a ditch during his patrol of the switching yards. He called out loudly, "YOU GET UP BOY, AN' CALL YO' MAMA!' as if malingering in the dark when light beckoned tried his otherworldly patience.

It was the most exciting summer of my life. And it did affect my career.

❊

It also affected Larry's. That summer, he decided to give up acting and become a teacher.

He'd been doing "Equity-waver" plays in Hollywood. These were the equivalent of New York's Off-Off Broadway plays, in which actors don't get paid. He'd taken class with Viola Spolin. He'd done some interesting work, the most memorable of which, to me, was an AFI student project opposite a brilliant teenager named Jennifer Jason Leigh. But he was restless and getting too old to play the callow-youth parts for which he was still being called to audition.

When we'd gone on the Lampoon tour, sometimes the company had burst into song to pass the time, running through the American musical repertoire most actors know from high school and college productions, or cast albums memorized for love. I sang along enthusiastically, and at one point during "I Don't Know How to Love Him," I'd looked over at Larry's face and seen him looking like he was about to vomit. I'd asked him:

"How come you won't sing?"

"I can't stand this stuff," he'd replied.

In that moment I'd doubted that Larry burned to be an actor quite as fiercely as the rest of us did.

When I was pregnant, we had bitter fights about who would support the family. He resented me saying he ought to get a regular job; I told him he had to. I couldn't work full time and care for the baby, and my acting career was the only one making money. Finally, he applied to UCLA and took some teaching courses. What decided him, he said, was the image of his son watching him "at work." "Daddy sits around all day and waits for the phone to ring for a living," were words he didn't want to hear or say.

He student-taught and studied during Cisco's infancy. He got his first teaching job, as a third- and fourth-grade reading teacher, right after he completed his last acting job, as the Con-Ed hardhat worker in *Ghostbusters* who releases all the ghost energy and says "Shi-i-i-it." This moment memorialized his acting career on film and gave him lasting cachet as a high-school English teacher, which is where he's found his calling and his bliss.

I nursed Cisco for two-and-a-half years, during which I did short TV projects, a play at the Mark Taper Forum, and a television series that looked like a meal ticket until its star, Chad Lowe, quit, fearing the hysterical teenage screams at our tapings augured a career like his brother Rob's, which foundered painfully in the aftermath of teen idolatry. Chad's walk-out got him mercilessly banned from television for five years. But when he returned, he won an Emmy as a dramatic actor.

In order to work occasionally and continue auditioning, I hired a woman to help me with child-care and domestic tasks. I kept her on, whether I was working or not. Faced with the choice between house and housekeeper, I chose housekeeper and stayed in our apartment. Gladys preserved my sanity, was a wonderful companion, and helped maintain my lifeline to my acting dream. We lived off my television savings, and watched the bank account drain slowly, hoping it would last until there was more to replenish it.

As if I myself were a child again, my world shrank. And the me-first attitude that had made me fear for my sanity as a mother instead helped me adjust, because I fell so deeply in love with my son, I wanted to be with him all the time. I wanted to be his teacher. So I went ahead and did it.

Babies, I found, weren't just empty vessels needing to be filled with earthly information. They come into the world as full vessels, bearing information we desperately need about the origins and purpose of human existence, the workings of consciousness. As I walked with Cisco around our apartment, around our neighborhood, listening, touching, naming things at every time of day and season, his reactions stirred my soul. He became my teacher. His learning process fascinated me. One day, as we shared a project of mine, under guise of mother-child play at the kitchen table, Cisco was on his turn as I watched with increasingly evident frustration at the time the task was consuming. My eye was on the finish, but as Cisco worked his baby hands in the materials, he counseled aloud, "See Mommy? You take *time*. It's better when you take time."

I was stunned to hear him identify what I'd long since discovered as my lifetime learning disability: impatience. My junior year abroad in London, I'd gone with some friends on a lark to a man everyone called "The Queen Mother's psychic." He'd warned me my trouble card was impatience, from a spread that otherwise, he beamed, was "almost too good to be true." I'd laughed it off, but looking back, it was inarguable. Every time I tried a cosmic shortcut, I was busted for trespassing, and had to begin again.

I finally took time to accompany my child.

It wasn't easy for me, a lifelong glamour-and-attention addict, to live in a world that lacked adult collegiality, where spills and smells and goo abounded. The few small spaces I'd preserved for Zen-like aesthetics in our apartment filled up with ugly plastic objects in primary colors that I found jarring. It wasn't easy to get through days when I felt totally spent by nine in the morning. One afternoon I woke up in the hall, on the hardwood floor, across from one-year-old Cisco. The pile of blocks I'd put down when he'd resisted taking a nap were still between us, and he was still playing with them, but I, who'd needed a nap desperately, had gone from sitting, to supine, to sleeping without even knowing it.

When I insisted on watching awards shows, which Larry derided as masochistic, I would end up crying over my moribund career, aborted celebrity, and unattainable glory. But with my child at my breast, I began to view the rituals of show business as if from the afterlife—they were part of a world in which I no longer lived, though seeing it stimulated my craving for the old sensations. I lived in a new world, where I'd been led, by my heart, to be with someone I could no longer do without.

One night Larry and I were watching Ingmar Bergman's *Fanny and Alexander* on cable because, like most new parents, we relied heavily on home entertainment. Those were the years that made video stores into franchise giants.

The movie begins with a little company of actors rehearsing *Hamlet*. The elderly paterfamilias is rehearsing his part as Hamlet's ghost when he suddenly keels over. His actress-wife runs to take him in her arms as the company gathers anxiously above. The old man opens his eyes and asks:

"What happened?"

You collapsed, they tell him.

He looks puzzled. "What was I doing?"

"You were acting," says his wife, as if this were the most reassuring answer in the world.

The man does not look reassured.

"Why…was I acting?" he says. Then he dies.

My blood froze. I recognized the question as one I'd been asking for some time, subliminally, not wanting to grant it conscious attention. Now I knew I'd have to; it looked like a lousy deathbed question. The actor in the movie clearly conveyed that, by eternal light, acting seemed a foolish and redundant task on which to have lavished a lifetime. Of course, Bergman's actor was *acting*.

Bergman redeems actors in the movie, several times over, by celebrating their fearless generosity of spirit in contrast to a punitive bishop's joyless repression. But from that night, *Fanny and Alexander* prompted my first serious questioning of my vocation since I'd received it, in a moment of stunning clairvoyance, before my childhood mirror.

Why was I acting? I couldn't avoid the question any longer. I didn't want to ask it with eternity staring me in the face. I had a child to teach. To do that well, I'd need an answer.

Part Six

KINGDOM COME
1982–1996

"It's this business of *desiring,* if you want to know the
goddamn truth, that makes an actor in the first place.
Why're you making me tell you things you already know?
Somewhere along the line—in one damn incarnation or
another, if you like—you not only had a hankering to be
an actor or actress but to be a *good* one. You're stuck with
it now. You can't just *walk out* on the results of your own
hankerings. Cause and effect, buddy, cause and effect."

J.D. Salinger, Franny and Zooey

35.

Taking Time

I stand outside the bedroom door with a fake fur bunny mask on my face. Inside, my daughter composes herself in pretend sleep for a game called "Characters," which evolved from my brother Jimmy's Christmas gift of animal masks into the ritual we're poised to enact. It's eight forty-five in the morning, and I'm exhausted.

The kitchen is dirty, the beds are unmade and I'm feeling overwhelmed. I don't want to play Characters. I want to do a million other things with my life that I can't do because I've been stuck in this cluttered apartment rearing my children for six years, playing with blocks and masks.

I open the door. If I cannot have what I want right now, at least I can provide it for someone else. This game is Molly's heart's desire. And tired as I am, I never forget that she's here partly because of my desire. I helped create her, and while she's little, I satisfy her desirous heart in large measure just by keeping her company, because I'm her mother. And when I relinquish impatience, that's what satisfies me, too.

Molly's eyelids flutter with anticipation. She won't open her eyes until I speak. Characters began as a silent game, but Molly saw *La Bamba* on cable TV during a family vacation, by mistake, and fixated on Lou Diamond Phillips as Ritchie Valens. During the bunny's next visit she asked "Are you Ritchie?" with such trembling hope that I couldn't help saying "Yes"—in a fifties' Chicano accent. Now I'm stuck. I'm a big white bunny from Pacoima.

"Mollee…eet's me, Reetchie!"

She opens her eyes and arms. We hug. Then she gets up to show me around her room; she gives me various possessions, and I try to say something nonjudgmental and affirming about each. Then we play with her current favorite toy, a purse my mother sent her that opens up to become a miniature doll house. After about fifteen minutes I say I must leave. At first Molly coaxes me to stay and I do, but the mask makes breathing and seeing difficult. My neck aches from holding it at an angle by which I can see to play on the floor, and my face is hot and wet with exhalations. Soon I do leave, and Molly gets back on her bed.

I close the door behind me, take off the mask, and toss it in the hall linen cupboard. After a few deep breaths I knock on Molly's door and reenter as Mom; she gives me the exciting news that once again, Ritchie has been and gone! And once again I have missed him!

After Characters, Molly plays contentedly, and I can do chores and phone calls. Our mutual pacification is a great benefit of the game, but I play it because she desires it, and because it teaches what I know about truth from acting: that we are all sacred beings, attending each other from behind a mask.

◦

After I gave birth to my son, my interest in acting waxed and waned. When I had good parts like the repressed sister in Jules Feiffer's play, *Grown Ups,* or the romantic lead opposite Jeff Goldblum in Aubrey Wertheim's literate comedy, *Popular Neurotics,* my work was better than before. In projects that shall go unnamed it was decidedly worse. I suffered the pains of Nina in *The Seagull:* "You can't imagine what it's like to feel you are acting abominably."

My agents were unhappy with my postpartum ambivalence. The scrutiny to which I subjected mom roles made them especially nervous because it smacked of moral zealotry. Moral zealotry is hard on agents. Careers need all the gung-ho enthusiasm they can get, and when an agent procures an audition only to have the client turn it down, that client is understandably seen as obstreperous and ungrateful.

But I couldn't help seeing mother roles in a new light. A Dennis-the-Menace strain of comedy resurfaced during the baby boomlet, as if my generation, like senile kings, feared the young's usurpation of our cultural domain and therefore imputed to them evil motives. I found the trend dishonest and paranoid; my real-life mothering experience confirmed the old saw that "As the twig is bent, so grows the tree." Evil children did not spring from nowhere. The difficult ones I knew in real life were defending themselves against mixed signals, emotional chaos, and deep social or neurological problems. These situations weren't funny.

So I declined to audition for a television series whose adolescent character lied, cheated, and stole, and whose Mom thought him perfect because he fooled her with his good manners. In the pilot script Mom occupied herself mostly with dating because she was single and had a cute boyfriend. My agents were convinced it would be a great comeback role for me—nurturing *and* sexy!

"I don't like her," I complained to them. "Where was she when her son's character was being formed?"

"It's *funny,*" came the reply. "Eddie Haskell did this shtick on "Leave It to Beaver" for years, and he was the funniest thing on that show."

As a child I'd refused to watch "Leave it to Beaver." For some reason, I'd hated the look and sound of the show.

"That was thirty years ago," I persisted. "Do you still think people will find ignorant parents funny?"

"Get on the show and change it!" came the reply. This sort of talk, meant to be supportive, was slightly disingenuous coming from the very people whose job it would be to shut me up at the first signs of annoyance from the producers.

I didn't audition. When I caught the pilot on TV, I saw actors doing their best, but the premise defeated them, and the show tanked.

My agents sent another script that they hoped would thrill me. So did I; I was beginning to worry about our family's finances. On series I'd made the equivalent of my husband's annual teaching salary every two weeks.

The script was the pilot for a series starring a nineteen-year-old Australian bombshell. The role for me was that of a working, nursing mother—a potential perfect fit!

I opened the script. The first scene showed Mom waiting nervously in her living room for the new babysitter to show. It's Mom's first day back to work, and the au-pair hasn't arrived! The doorbell rings: enter bombshell, so apologetic, reassuring, and nurturing that Mom forgets she'd asked for a mature woman. She hands baby over and drives away.

Bad infant-mother separation process, I thought, and then silenced that portion of my brain. Falling short of the ideal was, I knew, what put the "sit" in sitcom!

The teenage boy comes home from school that afternoon, sees the au-pair for the first time, and goes hormonally ga-ga. He hears her planning to take a shower! He stashes sleeping baby in a distant room, so shower will proceed uninterrupted. He kneels to watch through the bathroom keyhole. Baby wakes as bombshell disrobes. She, with ears as keen as a dog's, hears it. Teenager must scramble to restore baby to crib before ruse is discovered. Power laughs ensue.

Nudity, lecherous teen, baby treated like a football—the plot choices seemed smarmy to me. But I realized the show hadn't been written to delight thirty-something mothers; it was pitched to teenage boys' lower chakras. I read on.

Mom gets home and flops on the couch because she's so exhausted from working and shopping all lunch hour that her feet hurt. She wants a foot massage and doesn't want to see the baby right away.

I stopped reading. A nursing, working mother would be screaming for her baby to suckle the minute she walked in the door. She would not have shopped during lunch hour; she would have spent it hunkering in some locked cubicle pumping milk from her engorged breasts. Not to do so would risk mastitis, an infection that once landed me in the hospital when I worked sudden long hours in the middle of a breastfeeding schedule. Mom would be in such breast pain coming home she wouldn't even know she *had* feet.

Doubting the makers of a sitcom starring nubile teenage breasts would care to explore the humor of accurate maternal mammary function, I called my agents and passed on the project.

The producers of *The Mouse and the Motorcycle,* an ABC children's special in which I appeared, did once purge a script of dangerous misinformation. Beverly Cleary had written her delightful novel long before the film was made, and the plot involved a mother and a mouse searching for aspirin to give her son, who spikes a fever while the family is stranded at a remote hotel. By the time I was offered the project I knew, from the newspaper and my pediatrician, that I must never, ever give my child aspirin for fever. It led to Reyes' syndrome in some children, resulting in seizures, brain damage, and death.

"Could we change 'aspirin' to 'Tylenol'?" I asked after reading the script. No, came the answer—"Tylenol" is a brand name. "How about aceta...acetanimo ...acetomenaphin?" I ventured, illustrating the potential number of takes I'd blow every time I'd have to say the word. Producers and director regretfully explained that expensive footage had already been shot of mechanical mice saying "aspirin" to the mouse soundtrack, also already in the can.

But Churchill Films was a proud producer of quality children's television; someone in the office called local pediatricians to get their views, and the response was overwhelming. To present aspirin as the cure for child fever, they unanimously agreed, would be dangerously irresponsible in light of current research and would undermine the AMA's urgent information campaign. The fictional brand-name "Tempquit" was coined, inserted into the script, and dubbed on the soundtrack. The movie won a Peabody Award and enjoyed wide distribution in video, where the wrong information would have lived forever, with untold damage, had the producers not done the right thing.

The head of my agency's television department phoned me after I rejected the au-pair series script.

"This is reality calling," he stated grimly. "You're not getting any younger and you can't afford to turn down seventeen thousand dollars a week."

I was hurt, but I held my ground.

Secretly I did worry that motherhood would pauperize me because I'd turned into a humorless prig. Then I read the script for "Married with Children." I knew that was funny. I was glad to see satire, after the pastel-decor family fare whose benign look cloaked inexplicably ugly views about women, children, and sex.

I auditioned for Peg initially as a sort of San Fernando Valley vulgarian, wearing a denim miniskirt, cowgirl boots, a rhinestone-studded T-shirt, and a push-up bra. But even this get-up didn't make the fart jokes come out of my mouth any easier; when I was invited to test for the role at the network, I declined. My manager was apoplectic. Where was my old *vanity,* he worried, that once made me believe I was the best choice for *everything?*

It was tempered by self-knowledge, I knew—the gift of my children to me. The first time I saw Katy Sagal wiggle across my TV set as Peg, I thought: *That's* how to do it. And knew I'd never even have come close.

o

I did play some comedy moms I liked. One was featured in the Disney TV movies, *Mr. Boogedy* and *Bride of Boogedy,* the sequel representing the only title role of my career. Both projects were directed by Oz Scott, with whom I'd worked at the Eugene O'Neill Theater Festival, and featured great casts, including Richard Masur as my husband, Eugene Levy, Kristy Swanson, Tammy Lauren, and Leonard Frey. The scripts were witty and the work was good.

When *Mr. Boogedy* aired on a Sunday night, Disney, ABC, and their affiliate stations got irate calls from parents whose kids had been terrified by Boogedy's face, a putrefying Puritan countenance glowering beneath a magic phosphorescent hood. Some of my preschool mother friends had turned it off; others reported that it gave their kids a good shiver without ungluing them. Older children loved it because they got the jokes.

My son's neighborhood playmates were allowed to watch, fascinated that I was *in* the scary story on television *and* Cisco's Mom. We talked a lot about how this could be. When they grasped the notion that acting was my job and the filming of the movie had been an event in the past, they wanted to know, "Were you scared in the movie?"

"It was all pretend for us actors," I explained. "Sometimes the actor playing Boogedy wasn't even *there* when we filmed our scenes, so we had to *pretend* to see him *and* pretend to be scared!"

Cisco had visited the set and seen Boogedy's mask in repose on a towel in the make-up trailer. Years later he told me he wasn't as impressed by movies as his friends because he knew "all the tricks that make them seem real." Whether this refusal to suspend disbelief for films was an asset or liability, I've since noticed it's a common stage of development for the children of movie professionals.

Bride of Boogedy, more elaborate than its predecessor, had a climactic town Halloween celebration at which Boogedy levitates me to the top of the town bandstand in order to be his bride, because in my Puritan costume, I remind him of his old flame. (At last I played in a Puritan costume to my heart's content!) I rise into the air, entranced, and a reverse shot shows my three screaming children crying, "Mommy! Mommy! Come back!"

While watching this being filmed, Richard Masur said, "You know…if we got calls on the last one…maybe it wouldn't be a bad idea to have a psychologist discussing the themes of altered and vanishing parents the night this airs."

Everyone nodded and no one did a thing.

On *Bride of Boogedy*'s air date, I was watching with my family in our living room, Cisco in the emotional safety of my lap, when the phone rang. The crying children scene had just ended. I handed Cisco to Larry and picked up the phone; it was my neighbor Steve calling, the single father of Cisco's four-year-old playmate, Jack. I'd warned Steve before the movie that the mother gets kidnapped, because his wife had left him two years earlier, the day she weaned Jack. Her guru said her spiritual path didn't include her husband or son, and everyone would be better off if she split.

"Jack's really scared by the movie and he wanted me to call you," Steve said. "I thought maybe you could tell him some things about making the movie. I've tried to tell him, but he really wants to talk to you."

Sheila's desertion of Jack—it was hard to think of it as anything else—rocked our neighborhood, but no one spoke of it in front of Jack, who'd only been two at the time. The silence had solidified around him.

I moved into the bedroom to concentrate in quiet, and after a bit more preparatory chat from Steve, Jack came on the line.

"Wh-wh-why did you l-leave, Mimi?" He was whimpering. Jack was a big boy. I'd never seen him show fear. He sounded devastated. "Are you coming back?"

"Yes, Jack, I'm coming back in the movie. And in real life, I haven't gone anywhere. I'm watching in the living room with Cisco and Larry, just like you and your Dad are watching at your house. But you know what? I was thinking about you, Jack."

"Y-You were?"

"Yes. I knew you'd be scared."

"So-o-o scared!" he affirmed.

Anyone who denies the impact of screen stories on young children should have heard Jack that night; talking him down from the movie was exactly like talking my best friend in college down from a near-psychotic acid episode.

We talked about real and pretend. I told him Mr. Boogedy's face was a mask.

"Underneath is an actor named Howard. He's a nice man. He looks sort of like Frank, in our building. But you know what? Whenever Howard was playing Mr. Boogedy he couldn't eat! The mouth-hole in the mask was so small he could only fit a straw through it, and he had to have soda all day, even for lunch! He was so hungry watching us other actors eat! Poor Howard. He was good at being scary, but he hated wearing that mask!"

"Oh," said Jack. Almost seeing, almost believing.

I said that Howard was probably in his living room, too, watching the movie.

"Wh-what about your children in the movie? A-are they a-actors or...?"

"They're actors, too," I said. "They live with their real families in the valley. They're probably watching in their living rooms right now. I haven't seen them since we did the movie last summer. Remember when you were going to the pool with Cisco and the baby-sitter? That's when I was working on the movie. It was over a long time ago. Now it's just on TV. The costumes and the mask are all put away in a building."

"But it's scary, though."

"Yeah. And I knew you'd especially be scared"—I took the leap—"because the mom goes away in the movie. And your mom went away. And didn't come back."

"Yeah."

"I know that was sad for you, Jack. And so scary."

Jack was silent. I went on to let him know that other people had noticed the bad thing that had happened to him and didn't think it was his fault. Or his Dad's. Or his Mom's, for that matter. It was the guru I'd never forgive, and his name didn't come up.

After that night, Jack and I talked freely about his mother and retrieved good parts of our shared past. I gave him a picture of the two of them together at Cisco's first birthday party, lined up with the other neighborhood mothers and sons. He's thirteen as I write and has just returned from a week's visit with her. She's still with the guru, but has obviously found there's no such thing as a spiritual path that excludes one's children.

"These things happen for a reason. And all that crap," said Maureen Stapleton to me once, when I'd lost a coveted role. After I became a mother, I began to suspect that the parts I did get happened for reasons, too.

36.

Cause and Effect

Baby Girl Scott, a TV movie that starred my friend John Lithgow, was a project in which I was thrilled to participate. My role was small, but I was grateful for small roles in those days, being too depleted at home to handle more than two or three days' consecutive shooting.

My character appeared in a support group for mothers of premature babies. This was during the time when TV movies were often cruelly dismissed as "Disease of the Week" projects. During the meeting, I tell the story of my son's birth and its aftermath to Mary Beth Hurt's character, whose newborn is on a respirator. I tell her that my child seemed tortured by the technological invasion of his body after birth and I wanted it to stop, but didn't feel I could intervene. At age eight, he has the mental capacity of a two-year-old. He cries whenever we go to the hospital, because, though he's blind, he seems to know where we're going, and the nurses who used to think he was cute don't think he's so cute anymore. They treat him like he's a pain in the ass. What will happen to him when he's twenty? Or forty—if I'm not around?

I cried helplessly saying these things at the audition. After hearing I'd gotten the role, I made visits to the local public school for special needs children, where Phys.Ed. consisted of teachers jumping on inflated playgrounds to bounce the children who couldn't control their own limbs, and St. John's Center for developmentally slow children, where I saw adults seated behind preschool chairs, pinning the little occupants into them with big, adamant hugs.

"What are they doing?" I asked my guide.

"They're volunteers," she replied. "Some of the children just need to be held all day, so we have people come in and do that."

Anyone whose arms ache for vanished little ones, take note! Some volunteer jobs require, pure and simple, the holding of children!

I talked to Helen Harrison, the woman upon whom my part was based. The producers gave me her number; when I called, she was cooking dinner, but she talked generously, lovingly, about her son. He was eighteen, and the center of her life. "That's him you hear," she said, referring to thumping and vocalizing in the background. "I still ache to see how difficult everything is for him. His life is so hard."

By the time I'd arrived on set, my grief had been tempered by the courage I'd seen and heard. Torn between what I felt and what I knew, I gave a performance that never quite satisfied me, though it had the virtue of being unfussy and direct. Still, it grieved me not to be brilliant in the first acting job I'd had in months.

I suspect I never recovered from the director's phone call. The day after I'd been cast, he phoned to discuss my scene; he did ask if it were a good time for us to talk.

I hadn't had many serious role-preparation discussions in my largely comedy career, and I'd wanted to have this one; it made me feel very film-star. So, though it was my fussy baby's and wound-up toddler's dinner hour, and I was the only adult at home, on-duty, I said it was a fine time, fearing there'd be no other.

Plugging my outer ear against Cisco's loud chanting, I'd walked into the kitchen to concentrate. While the director talked, the water steaming the broccoli burned down, and I had to unplug my ear, dump the stinking vegetables, and douse the pan, all the while hiding my divided attention from the director. I irrationally feared being fired if he sensed the chaos in my home.

Then the line went dead. I saw Cisco, who'd stopped running around the table, looking quizzically at his foot, which had caught the phone wire and ripped it out of the phone jack. Frantically, I retrieved the plastic end and started trying to stuff it back in. This took forever; by the time the jack connected, Cisco was asking me something in a very loud voice and Molly was banging on her high-chair tray. I exploded in frustration, sure I'd lost the director.

"SHUT UP!!!" There was a shocked silence. The children froze to hear those words; Mother had broken a taboo.

In the quiet, I heard nothing at my ear, too. I realized, with a sinking feeling, that if the director had really been disconnected I should have been hearing a dial tone. There was only dead air.

"John?"

"Yes."

There was no disguising what he'd heard.

"Real nice. Oh dear. I can't believe you just heard that. I'm sorry. It's just that...oh well."

"I think you know what the part is," he said coolly, as if suddenly eager to wrap things up. I never knew if he'd heard; he completely ignored my confusion. If he had heard, I knew he fervently wished that he hadn't.

"We saw that rich compassion that you brought to the audition."

Ah yes. That rich compassion. Fooled you.

In that moment I was ambushed by the situation I'd foreseen long ago, as a child, but had avoided thinking about as an adult: Mother and Actress would not easily combine, even after the physical changes of childbearing had disappeared. I was faced with a choice: I could showboat maternity, in public and in private, or I could try to be the kind of mother my heart urged me to be.

The temptation to withdraw was great. In turning over my children to others, I could carry them with me as sentimentalized projections and draw solace from those without having to give myself in return, as real children demanded. And I could project a better, more special image of myself as Mother than the cranky, oppressive, tired woman they often saw.

I thought this choice would shortchange my children and break my heart. Why would I make it? For money, glory, esteem? We lived in a rent-controlled apartment. Our physical survival was not at stake. But my mental health was. How could I convince my head, the me-first person, the actress who wasn't yet satisfied by her achievements, to follow my heart?

In Curt Dempster's class, where I'd finally learned to act, the key had been prying my focus off myself and giving it to my fellow actors, those onstage with me. This opened up a fascination with finding out what would happen next between us and had given me a deep emotional connection to each moment. It had saved my career. Now it saved my sanity, because it also proved to be the secret of hands-on mothering for me. This, however, was no finite improvisation. This was real-life development, part of a journey that began and ended in eternity. I focused on my children, and once again was rewarded with the opening of the path of mutual exchange, which brought freedom, creativity and joy.

Months after *Baby Girl Scott* aired, my cousin Tim called me. I hadn't heard from him in years, but his hesitant response to my gushing hello told me he was calling with bad news. His wife and he were in a Rochester hospital where their newborn daughter was on a respirator, her prognosis so grim that even its best version didn't include sight, hearing, voluntary muscle activity, or involuntary muscle activities like swallowing. Her brain waves were minimal; only technology kept her alive.

The couple had gone from the heaven of a normal delivery to this hell in a few short days. Their original obstetrician had gone into emergency ulcer surgery the day after Connie gave birth and the couple's case had been transferred to another doctor. When they discussed their fears with him, he shamed Connie for rejecting her child "just because she's not a Gerber baby."

Still trying, years later, to understand the insensitivity of someone who'd say this to a grieving mother whose newborn's brain failed to perform minimum survival tasks, Connie sighed to me, "He collected sports cars."

They'd opted for transfer to a teaching hospital, holding out hope for a better prognosis. Instead, they were delivered the bleakest possible news: Elinore would probably never survive on her own and would certainly have died without the hook-up of hospital machinery. Tim and Connie decided to petition the bio-ethics committee with their request that the medical intervention be stopped, a decision they'd made in grief and prayer. A neurologist opposed them; he'd never seen brain waves like Elinore's and wanted to track their development. "At what point," Tim and Connie asked him, "would you stop the experiment? If you saw the pain to the child outweighed the benefits to science, or to her?" "Never," the doctor had said.

"Connie remembered you were in a TV movie last spring that was about a situation like this," Tim concluded. "She thought maybe you would know some people we could talk to, who could help us think. We're so isolated here. We don't know what to do."

I gave him Helen Harrison's number. Tim called her; her empathy alone helped him, but her advice that he gather local emotional and spiritual support before going to the bio-ethics committee was crucial. He contacted the priest who'd married the couple. Our cousin, a nun, came to their side. Quietly, Elinore's existence was allowed to take its natural course without technology while Tim and Connie kept vigil. Tim was in the room when Elinore breathed her last, her brief time on earth having introduced her to her parents for eternity, and having profoundly affected several lives before her quick departure. Tim had baptized his daughter as she lay covered with tubes and wires in the neonatal unit shortly after her birth, when it was increasingly clear something was terribly wrong. Ever since he's been haunted and consoled by water imagery; much of his subsequent architectural work has been designing fountains for public spaces. Each one is his daughter's memorial.

Before motherhood, I'd made career choices for myself alone. My criteria had been: Will this role enhance my image and my name? Can it attract a nomination? Will my TV-Q go up? Choosing badly meant diminishing my fragile prestige and laboring in anonymity, both of which I dreaded.

After motherhood, I knew I had to make career choices with others in mind. There was my family to think of; that was obvious. To stay close to my husband and children, I had to choose accordingly. But the evidence of my child-neighbor and previously distant cousin being profoundly affected by roles I'd thought professionally insignificant gave me courage to consider carefully the potential effect of anything I did in the mass media.

Bilocation, I'd learned as a child, was an attribute of the saints. Reports of appearances and interventions by physically distant persons was strong testimony, in the church, for canonization. All of us have this potential now, because of mass media. We can travel through the world in word and picture, and we haven't had to develop one iota of spiritual discipline beforehand. If our appearances, messages, and interventions lack saintly wisdom or beneficence, they nonetheless proceed apace. Actors have been in the vanguard of this proliferation; friends have reported seeing me on their hotel television sets in Cairo and Beijing, in years-old episodes of "Family" and "Dance Fever." Each project took a day of my life. They were fine entertainments, but I'd never pictured them circling the globe for decades, reaching people in distant, hard-to-access places. Knowing they do, regardless of the quality of attention they're given, has inspired in me a sobering respect for even my smallest and silliest involvements in the mass media. People are ultimately responsible for the images they cast into the world; actors' go further and last longer than some of us might have imagined. But the facts are incontrovertible; the images persist and have effects. We ought to at least try to imagine them before creating the cause.

37.

Homefront

Molly began to ask, "Are you Ritchie?" I smiled, not wanting to lie. But neither did I want to rob her of the belief that gave her so much pleasure. I thought my smile was a gentle hint: Yes, my darling, I'm Ritchie. She did not assume that. She thought my smile meant that even *I* didn't know if I were Ritchie or not. I'd unwittingly deepened the mystery; seeing that, I resolved to let her discover the truth on her own.

It came with age, like object-constancy and toilet training. When she found out—shyly hinting at first that she knew, then proudly declaring it—she still craved the game. Her joy at being with Ritchie evolved into the joy of transforming everyday reality by the power of imagination and desire, which could change even her mighty mother, for a moment, into the being she'd once believed in with all her heart.

That time didn't last forever. The September morning Molly went to kindergarten, departing with brother and father, I turned and walked back to the apartment kitchen, knowing there was some opportunity, now, to do one or two of those other million things.

By then, my acting career had foundered so badly that friends I'd made as fellow school-parents, Lynn Latham and Bernard Lechowick, offered me a temporary writing job on "Knots Landing," which they produced with David Jacobs. I substituted for Dianne Messina as story editor because her husband was diagnosed, suddenly, with cancer; she was keeping vigil at his bedside and tending their two children. Later, still in mourning, she returned to work for structure and solace, and we became friends. Lynn and Bernard asked me to stay on. Dianne and Jim Stanley taught me the ropes of developing story lines for one-hour drama; a year later, when they wed, I realized their courtship had blossomed under my nose, but I'd been too intent on my writing lessons to suspect a thing.

In November, Lynn and Bernard gave us the script of their new pilot to read and respond to with staff notes. It was called "The View From Kurtland Hill." Viewers would later see it as "Homefront."

I read it without making a single writer's note. I was reading helplessly as an actor, salivating over the parts.

"We want you to audition when the time comes," Lynn assured me. I thought she was just being nice. My agency no longer sent me out on anything but commercials, which I routinely failed to get.

In early spring, Jim Stanley wrote a scene on "Knots" that required an encounter between the show's nasty blonde and her mother.

Jim and Dianne insisted I play the mother.

Terrified to perform with actors for whom I'd been writing all year and knowing I'd be scrutinized in dailies by my writing colleagues, I spent money I could ill afford to have my hair dyed blonde by the nasty-blonde actress's colorist so I could believe myself as her onscreen mother. The external support worked; I loved doing the scene.

But it meant going in to read for the role of Anne Metcalf in "Kurtland Hill" as a blonde. Anne was described as auburn-haired, and a factory worker. I knew I didn't look or sound like the perfect Rosie-the-Riveter, but Lynn and Bernard complimented my reading, saying only one other actress was competition: Wendy Phillips.

"Would you consider coming back and reading Mrs. Sloan?" Lynn asked me. "It's a small part, but…would you mind?"

Ruth Sloan was the part to which I'd been attracted when I'd read the script. She'd been featured at the Sloan dining-room table, and I'd envisioned her instantly, lit by the glow of candles on good silver. This is home, I thought to myself; these are people I understand. I auditioned for Lynn and Bernard as Ruth, wearing a crisp navy-blue suit and my mother's hand-me-down accessories: white gloves and spectator pumps. It was effortless; I was approved to test at the network.

Network auditions are scary. Everyone's in a nervous state and actors greet each other with twitching smiles and breathless hello's. I wanted to banish anxiety by reading my scene privately with a partner, so I scouted the men I presumed to be reading for Mr. Sloan and one stood out immediately. He simply was Mr. Sloan. I approached him.

"Would you mind reading the Sloan scene with me over in the corridor?" I asked him.

"No. Wouldn't mind at all!" he said, affably, and withdrew from the knot of actors to whom he'd been speaking.

He was fabulous. We clicked. He was Ken Jenkins, who became Mr. Sloan.

We auditioned separately. My reading went well. I never had trouble with anything Lynn and Bernard wrote. Their words were always a delight.

Later Lynn reported what happened when I left the room.

"I like Mimi," declared one executive. "But she's too young for the role."

Lynn had no intention of casting anyone else as Ruth.

"Oh, I know Mimi really well!" she countered. "I've been writing with her in a little room every day now for a year and I know how old she really is. Trust me —she's *old!*"

"But not enough for the role," said someone else.

Lynn panicked. She repeated something she'd once heard me say in despair, something which would have been automatic disqualification from most female film roles in Hollywood:

"And have you seen the way Mimi photographs lately? She can really look like shit!" This won me the best role of my career.

"Homefront" chronicled the lives of people in a small Ohio town after World War II. Ruth, the rich wife of the factory owner, was so like some women of my own past, though more thoroughly blinded by prejudice, that playing her was comparatively effortless. I stayed blonde, and further physical transformation was effected by the Emmy-winning team who produced an eerie combination in me of my mother and grandmothers. To prepare for a scene, I had only to memorize my lines, be coiffed and made up, and dress before a mirror. I became Ruth.

The show lasted two years. I rarely worked more than four days of an eight-day shoot. I was still very much involved at home, a wonderful situation for a working mother.

After the first season, I was nominated for an American Television Award. These awards bore the slight stigma of being newly coined and Not-The-Emmys, but the voters were the nation's television critics, so I considered the nomination a high honor. It couldn't be bought. I hadn't been nominated for an acting award since high school and was disappointed not to have been invited to the ceremony, but the category winners were announced with the nominations, and I hadn't won. I assumed also-rans weren't asked to attend. The night of the television show, I sat at home, watching my own picture being projected on a giant screen as the presenters announced my name to resounding applause.

Lucky her, I caught myself thinking. Must be nice. Twenty-five years in show business had given me an envy reflex so chronic it riled at my own success.

Weeks later I came across the nomination announcement on my desk. There was a number to RSVP for the ceremony; I'd been invited, but I'd been too thrilled with the nomination to notice. I was glad; envying myself was an enlightening moment I wouldn't have missed for the world.

"Homefront"'s future after our second season was still uncertain the night I filmed my final scene. Afterward, walking to my dressing room, I heard a crew member call through the dark: "Good-bye, Ruth!" The Sloans had been favorites of the crew; they'd admired our performances and appreciated the easy days we'd given them.

I knew the experience was over. I went in my trailer, took off the Ruth mask, and cried.

38.
Masks

As I contemplated ending this book, I dreamed one night of a gated city with a statue of St. Francis, the saint who loved the earth, in its central square. Francis' arm was lifted and his finger pointed at the open gate, toward which a bird flew. I took it to mean I was beginning the last chapter and soon would be done.

"All the saint knows," said the dream, "is that the kingdom of heaven is within."

What I know as an actress is that the world is a stage, as Shakespeare said, and all of us take to it to discover who we are. Here in the light we are celebrated, "lessened" and "lessoned." Some of us bring new members into the company before we take off our costumes and say good night. My orthodox religion gave me a script for how to behave here; I followed it, until I began to improvise. This was dangerous, but it was the only way to "be myself."

Fourteen years ago I'd thought, in response to an actress who warned me that having a child would affect my career: "I'm not like you. I'd never settle for guest star roles. I have ego. And ambition."

Doing one of my many recent guest-star jobs, I was sitting in the hairstylist's chair studying my part when the excitement around me began to depress me. It was a high-profile pilot, and the cast and crew were intoxicated with the attention that comes when powers-that-be smell a hit. I remembered how it felt to be at the center of these events. I was now barely on the periphery. I felt like crying, but doing so would have been a disaster; I was already in full make-up. I lifted my eyes to the hair guy for diversion. His name was Gus, and he was amusing to look at; he wore a racetrack fedora, thick-framed, yellow-tinted glasses, and a graying goatee. I watched him tease my hair and before long noticed that his skin was luminous. It was more beautiful than most women's. I decided to ask him about it, in order to maintain my distraction and get a couple of beauty tips. What else are you going to talk about with a hair guy?

I complimented his complexion.

"Yeah," he chuckled, meeting my eyes briefly in the mirror. "Isn't that something? Comes from eating right and not worrying. I used to be in terrible health. You know how old I am? Seventy-five."

I was truly stunned. He looked fifty-something.

"Yeah. Seventy-five," he continued. "and never thought I'd live to this age. I almost died when I was twenty-nine. Aneurysm—boom! Took me two years to recover. I couldn't move. They thought I'd never walk again. I amazed them. But I knew I would. Know how I knew?" He caught my eyes in the mirror. "Cause I went somewhere while I was out."

"Where?" I asked, guessing. Wanting to hear.

"Oh, you know…" he held my gaze. "Out. I can't describe it, but…it was *so big*. It was…you can't believe how *big* what we are is. I was me, but I wasn't me. It was…I didn't know how I was going to fit back into my body again but…that's just it—you see—'m not just *me*. I'm also—It—is *you*. It's the *same thing*. We're both *it*. So when I love you, I'm loving me as well, you see? And it's…so beautiful!" He exhaled and put down his comb. Then, returning his eyes to mine in the mirror, he put his hands on my shoulders. "And I *came back*…and it's *all happening*…because out there you can't"—he brought his hands down on my shoulders twice, boom! boom! "—*do this! I'm Here!*"

Tears rolled down his beautiful cheeks. "And what's amazing is that…after I knew…I understood why everyone's always said the experience is impossible to describe. You can't describe it because everyone has to experience it for themselves! If we could describe it—that would rob us of the joy! And we're all supposed to have it! No one will be robbed of it—No one!"

Thus Gus the Hair Stylist, dressed as Jimmy the Greek, confirms to Mimi the Actress, whom he is transforming into the role of the Realtor from Hell, her first catechism lesson of great existential hope: God made us to show forth His goodness and share with us His everlasting happiness in heaven.

Gus picked up his comb and went back to teasing my hair. I stared, transfixed, until he nodded at me in the mirror again, smiling encouragement. Then I bent to my script and studied my part, because somewhere along the line I'd had the hankering to be an actress, and to be a good one, and we can't just walk out on the results of our own hankerings.

o

Religions rely on appearance because people want to see God, any way they can. The orthodoxy in which I was raised taught me that God was hidden in bread and wine; He arrived when the priest said, "This is My Body, This is My Blood," during the miracle of Transubstantiation. Every Catholic child I knew waited, as I did, for the day when the priest would return the chalice to the altar, after raising it to heaven accompanied by ringing bells, and freeze, his face gone white. Then we'd know the miracle had been completed, and the cup would be filled with viscous human blood.

The sacred was vivid to me; I imagined the saints dwelled within their life-sized statues, attending my fervent prayers with their stone ears, a smile almost playing on their stone lips. So much in my religious upbringing stimulated my ardent imagination! Is it any wonder I longed for heaven, the world of light, and resolved to remain untainted by this mortal passage?

And is it any wonder that, when I sat in a darkened theater for the first time, watching actors bathed in light, I wanted to join them?

Or that, when I saw beings of flickering light on my television, I was drawn to the world of those friendly faces?

Or that, when Tammy Grimes emerged from her white-hot dressing room to greet me after a performance, I felt I was meeting a heavenly being?

Or that, when my first lover introduced me to the ecstasy of physical love, I grieved even in my joy, because I knew accepting it meant giving up heaven for earth?

When I studied my son in his first weeks here, my sense that his eyes had looked upon God before closing in the darkness of the womb, to reopen in the light of this world, was acute. He used to lie on our bed at night staring out our bedroom window at a carriage lamp. His gaze toward that light was so fixed that he seemed to enter it, even as his baby body lay helpless on its back. This stirred my lifelong meditations on heaven and eternity, and I began to think that adults who have no image or hope of such things have been deprived of their own earliest memories.

Heaven, or the afterlife—whatever form it takes—is increasingly populated with many of my closest loved ones. My parents are there; so are Aunt Fran, Uncle George, and William Roerick. So many actors have died of AIDS that sometimes, in a group of actors, I feel as if we are separated from our departed friends by only the thinnest of veils, and our colleagues, adept at communication and illusion in their lifetimes, approach it easily to whisper instruction and inspiration.

I was raised to get to heaven; heaven was an end, life was the means. But I've begun to take seriously those words in the Lord's Prayer "Thy kingdom come." I'm no longer in a hurry to leave this world, as I was in fifth grade, when Father Whelan conjured the angel at our classroom door who was asking for voluntary departures. Now I'd keep my hand down. It's not just because I'm the sin-sullied adult I feared, as a child, that I'd become, but because I'm bound here now, by love and duty.

This world, in all its suffering imperfection, is the place where I've glimpsed God and met the ones I love. This world's chemicals and minerals make the sacred visible. And I am, admittedly, attached.

When I saw my own newborn children, I realized, keenly, that all human work must contribute to preserving this meeting-place for those who have yet to come. It is so uniquely suited to the mysterious work of love and justice, because it follows the laws of "cause and effect, buddy, cause and effect."

When people love something, they will sacrifice to preserve it; actors are geniuses at seduction. We can make people fall in love with this place, and see its value. We can make them love their own lives, and the idea of life, even though it includes great tragedy. We can inspire planetary repair work and put our own hands to it as well.

My bout with infertility taught me that entry into this world is not assured, any more than is conditions of entry or length of stay. But increasingly I've come to suspect that a human lifetime is a hard-won goal, an opportunity whose squandering causes the deepest of sorrows, an opportunity that is accepted, even under the worst of conditions, because here in the light we can see each other, settle necessary debts, and experience love, behind the mask.

Perhaps—as in acting—when we discover what is the same behind all masks, we can work more directly. Until then, most sages warn, the face of God, straight on, is an almost unbearable sight.

So we take up the mask, on earth. Let us nurture this place with all the grace and enthusiasm we can muster, because whoever we are, and for whatever particular reason we've come, there is joy meant for us, and no one will be robbed of it. That's why we've taken to the stage.